The Cantata of Love

BLAISE ARMINJON, S.J.

The Cantata of Love

A Verse-by-Verse Reading
of the Song of Songs

Prefaced by a Letter from
HENRI CARDINAL DE LUBAC

Translated by Nelly Marans

IGNATIUS PRESS   SAN FRANCISCO

Title of the French original:
La Cantate de l'Amour:
Lecture suivie du Cantiques des Cantiques
© 1983 Desclée de Brower

Excerpts from the Jerusalem Bible
© 1966 by Darton, Longman, and Todd, Ltd., and Doubleday,
a division of Bantam, Doubleday, Dell Publishing Group, Inc.
Reprinted by permission of the publisher.

Cover design by Roxanne Mei Lum

Published with ecclesiastical approval
Second printing 2005
© 1988 by Ignatius Press, San Francisco

ISBN 978-0-89870-188-3 (PB)
ISBN 978-1-68149-467-8 (eBook)
Library of Congress control number 87-83533

Printed in the United States of America ∞

While the exhausted intellect
remains without,
love states:
"I shall go in!"

Jan van Ruysbroeck
The Adornment of the Spiritual Marriage

Contents

Preface

A letter from Cardinal Henri de Lubac

Paris — March 7, 1983

Very dear Father,

You won me over. I started to read your book in a somewhat sceptical vein. But the more I read, the more it seemed to me that the principle of interpretation was plausible — highly plausible; indeed, it was almost forcing itself upon me. Moreover, it was strengthened by a proof *a contrario*: a sustained "naturalistic" reading of the text would obviously be very difficult.

Chouraqui and others have greatly helped you. The vast quantity of texts culled from Scripture in both the Old and New Testaments that you quote so pertinently upholds through its abundance and weight this magnificent flowering of Christian Tradition rooted in Jewish tradition and elucidated by many from Origen to Claudel: a long chain in which the main links are geniuses or saints (among whom your dear Saint Francis de Sales did not fail to leave his brilliant mark).

I like the fact that you constantly intersect the three planes of this unique love story — Israel, the Church, the soul, i.e., each personal destiny — and that you show their unity in Christ. What I also like is that you discern in the five successive poems, as you differentiate them (whatever the original source might be), the phases of one single adventure, thereby offering us — without the slightest abstraction — a whole treatise on the unfolding of spiritual life. To be sure, none of this was made up by you, thanks be to God!, but I do not think that anyone has ever "wrapped it up" so well before. Again, you followed your predecessors in availing yourself of the great freedom that the Church has always granted to those who read the Scriptures under the guidance of the principle of "analogy of faith"; it may be that each individual detail is not convincing, but at least the whole holds together by itself.

The five poems whose links you bring to light do not describe in their symbols the stages of a continuous ascent, as would be the case in a new *Itinerarium mentis ad Deum*: one could, rather, compare them with the five acts of a drama. Your exegesis, being more realistic than others, clearly suggests this, though you were able to avoid the self-confidence of an excessively didactic tone, giving the key as you do from the outset to the reader himself. Thus his feeling of discovery is not spoiled as he progresses step by step and watches the contrasting scenes of this wonderful story.

This is a work that was brought slowly to maturity, lovingly polished and solidly built. It was nourished by your apostolic experience and your meditations. The dramatic realism I mentioned will be a help to those great but weak souls who might be tempted to give up somewhere along the way. You took great pains when editing the text with an art that is as restrained as it is sensitive. May it be published soon!

HENRI DE LUBAC, S.J.

Introduction

This is not a scholarly book. The exegetes will not discover anything new in it, save probably much room for improvement. It was written for all the men and women who, in a world of aridity and violence, are becoming more and more vocal in expressing their thirst for the Word of love and life.

To all these, God is still writing the wonderful letter he once sent to Israel, his betrothed, the Song of Songs. It is a love letter in which God gives free rein to his sovereign inspiration as artist, poet, painter and musician; in which he engages the whole of his creation — flowers and fruits, the seasons of the year, birds and precious minerals — and in which, above all, he pours out without restraint the ardent love of a Bridegroom for an entire people as well as for the humblest among us.

Slowly, patiently, lovingly also, we will welcome one after the other, in the very depths of our soul, each and every word of the eternally new Letter, whispered to us by Love so confidentially and yet so openly before the whole world.

In order to better hear this language, which is clear and veiled at the same time, we will frequently turn for help to the people — be they Fathers of the Church, mystical authors or plain folk — who, throughout the centuries, were given by the Holy Spirit an ear especially attuned to his Song.

This book thus aims to be at the same time an initiation of sorts into love's ways — so rarefied yet so accessible to all — and a genuine little treatise on spiritual theology, in the spirit of those masters of the science of love that the Lord has never failed to send among us.

As a matter of fact, they were the ones who wrote most of this book. I simply had to let them talk, though I was not always able to specify who was talking nor even to realize what I was borrowing from them.

And what of it? Montaigne used to say that the substance of his book was made up of all the books he had read and that each author could find himself in it. Let it be so in this book, and through the outpouring of all the themes let us hear the only composer, beyond Mozart himself, who ever conceived a symphony of Love — the Spirit, the composer of the universe.

Marseilles 1973–Annecy 1983

Abbreviations

2. BIBLE

The reference text is the Jerusalem Bible.

3. QUOTATIONS

The translations of the various texts quoted by Fr. Arminjon were all made by the translator herself.

The Song of Songs, Which Is Solomon's

PROLOGUE

THE BRIDE

Let him kiss me with the kisses of his mouth.
Your love is more delightful than wine;
delicate is the fragrance of your perfume,
your name is an oil poured out,
and that is why the maidens love you.
Draw me in your footsteps, let us run.
The King has brought me into his rooms;
you will be our joy and our gladness.
We shall praise your love above wine;
how right it is to love you.

FIRST POEM

THE BRIDE

I am black but lovely, daughters of Jerusalem,
like the tents of Kedar,
like the pavilions of Salmah.
Take no notice of my swarthiness,
it is the sun that has burned me.
My mother's sons turned their anger on me,
they made me look after their vineyards.
Had I only looked after my own!

15

Tell me then, you whom my heart loves:
Where will you lead your flock to graze,
where will you rest it at noon?
That I may not wander like a vagabond
beside the flocks of your companions.

THE CHORUS

If you do not know this, O loveliest of women,
follow the tracks of the flock,
and take your kids to graze
close by the shepherds' tents.

THE BRIDEGROOM

To my mare harnessed to Pharaoh's chariot
I compare you, my love.
Your cheeks show fair between their pendants
and your neck within its necklaces.
We shall make you golden earrings
and beads of silver.

DIALOGUE OF THE BRIDE AND BRIDEGROOM

—While the King rests in his own room
my nard yields its perfume.
My Beloved is a sachet of myrrh
lying between my breasts.
My Beloved is a cluster of henna flowers
among the vines of Engedi.

—How beautiful you are, my love,
how beautiful you are!
Your eyes are doves.

—How beautiful you are, my Beloved,
and how delightful!
All green is our bed.

— The beams of our house are of cedar,
the paneling of cypress.

—*I am the rose of Sharon,*
the lily of the valleys.
—*As a lily among the thistles,*
so is my love among the maidens.
—*As an apple tree among the trees of the orchard,*
so is my Beloved among the young men.
In his longed-for shade I am seated
and his fruit is sweet to my taste.
He has taken me to his banquet hall,
and the banner he raises over me is love.
Feed me with raisin cakes,
restore me with apples,
for I am sick with love.

His left arm is under my head,
his right embraces me.

—*I charge you,*
daughters of Jerusalem,
by the gazelles, by the hinds of the field,
not to stir my love, nor rouse it,
until it please to awake.

SECOND POEM

THE BRIDE

I hear my Beloved.
See how he comes
leaping on the mountains,
bounding over the hills.
My Beloved is like a gazelle,
like a young stag.

See where he stands
behind our wall.

He looks in at the window,
he peers through the lattice.

My Beloved lifts up his voice,
he says to me,
"Come then, my love,
my lovely one, come.
For see, winter is past,
the rains are over and gone.
The flowers appear on the earth.
The season of glad songs has come,
the cooing of the turtledove is heard
in our land.
The fig tree is forming its first figs
and the blossoming vines give out their fragrance.
Come then, my love,
my lovely one, come.
My dove, hiding in the clefts of the rock,
in the coverts of the cliff,
show me your face,
let me hear your voice;
for your voice is sweet
and your face is beautiful."

THE BRIDEGROOM

Catch the foxes for us,
the little foxes
that made havoc of the vineyards,
for our vineyards are in flower.

THE BRIDE

My Beloved is mine and I am his.
He pastures his flock among the lilies.

Before the dawn wind rises,
before the shadows flee,
return! Be, my Beloved,
like a gazelle,

a young stag,
on the mountains of the covenant.

On my bed, at night, I sought him
whom my heart loves.
I sought him but did not find him.
So I will rise and go through the City;
in the streets and the squares
I will seek him whom my heart loves.
. . . I sought but did not find him.

The watchmen came upon me
on their rounds in the City:
"Have you seen him whom my heart loves?"

Scarcely had I passed them
than I found him whom my heart loves.
I held him fast, nor would I let him go
till I had brought him
into my mother's house,
into the room of her who conceived me.

THE BRIDEGROOM

I charge you,
daughters of Jerusalem,
by the gazelles, by the hinds of the field,
not to stir my love, nor rouse it,
until it please to awake.

THIRD POEM

THE CHORUS

What is this coming up from the desert
like a column of smoke,

breathing of myrrh and frankincense
and every perfume the merchant knows?

See, it is the litter of Solomon.
Around it are sixty champions,
the flower of the warriors of Israel;
all of them skilled swordsmen,
veterans of battle.
Each man has his sword at his side,
against alarms by night.

King Solomon
has made himself a throne
of wood from Lebanon.
The posts he has made of silver,
the canopy of gold,
the seat of purple;
the back is inlaid with ebony.

Daughters of Zion,
come and see
King Solomon,
wearing the diadem with which his mother crowned him
on his wedding day,
on the day of his heart's joy.

THE BRIDEGROOM

How beautiful you are, my love,
how beautiful you are!
Your eyes, behind your veil,
are doves;
your hair is like a flock of goats
frisking down the slopes of Gilead.
Your teeth are like a flock of shorn ewes
as they come up from the washing.
Each one has its twin,
not one unpaired with another.
her lips are a scarlet thread

and your words enchanting.
Your cheeks, behind your veil,
are halves of pomegranate.
Your neck is the tower of David
built as a fortress,
hung around with a thousand bucklers,
and each the shield of a hero.
Your two breasts are two fawns,
twins of a gazelle,
that feed among the lilies.

Before the dawn wind rises,
before the shadows flee,
I will go to the mountain of myrrh,
to the hill of frankincense.

You are wholly beautiful, my love,
and without a blemish.

Come from Lebanon, my promised bride,
come from Lebanon, come on your way.
Lower your gaze, from the heights of Amana,
from the crests of Senir and Hermon,
the haunts of lions,
the mountains of leopards.

You ravish my heart,
my sister, my promised bride,
you ravish my heart
with a single one of your glances,
with one single pearl of your necklace.
What spells lie in your love,
my sister, my promised bride!
How delicious is your love, more delicious than wine!
How fragrant your perfumes,
more fragrant than all other spices!
Your lips, my promised one,
distill wild honey.

Honey and milk
are under your tongue;
and the scent of your garments
is like the scent of Lebanon.

She is a garden enclosed,
my sister, my promised bride;
a garden enclosed,
a sealed fountain.
Your shoots form an orchard of pomegranate trees,
the rarest essences are yours:
nard and saffron,
calamus and cinnamon,
with all the incense-bearing trees;
myrrh and aloes,
with the subtlest odors.
Fountain that makes the garden fertile,
well of living water,
streams flowing down from Lebanon.

THE BRIDE

Awake, north wind,
come, wind of the south!
Breathe over my garden,
to spread its sweet smell around.
Let my Beloved come into his garden,
let him taste its rarest fruits.

THE BRIDEGROOM

I come into my garden,
my sister, my promised bride,
I gather my myrrh and balsam,
I eat my honey and my honeycomb,
I drink my wine and my milk.
Eat, friends, and drink,
drink deep, my dearest friends.

Fourth Poem

The Bride

> I sleep, but my heart is awake.
> I hear my Beloved knocking.
> "Open to me, my sister, my love,
> my dove, my perfect one,
> for my head is covered with dew,
> my locks with the drops of night."
> "—I have taken off my tunic,
> am I to put it on again?
> I have washed my feet,
> am I to dirty them again?"
> My Beloved thrust his hand
> through the hole in the door;
> I trembled to the core of my being.
> Then I rose
> to open to my Beloved,
> myrrh ran off my hands,
> pure myrrh off my fingers,
> on to the handle of the bolt.
>
> I opened to my Beloved,
> but he had turned his back and gone!
> My soul failed at his flight.
> I sought him but I did not find him,
> I called to him but he did not answer.
> The watchmen came upon me
> as they made their rounds in the City.
> They beat me, they wounded me,
> they took away my cloak,
> they who guard the ramparts.
>
> I charge you,
> daughters of Jerusalem,
> if you should find my Beloved,

what must you tell him . . . ?
That I am sick with love.

The Chorus

What makes your Beloved better than other lovers,
O loveliest of women?
What makes your Beloved better than other lovers,
to give us a charge like this?

The Bride

My Beloved is fresh and ruddy,
to be known among ten thousand.
His head is golden, purest gold,
his locks are palm fronds
and black as the raven.
His eyes are doves
at a pool of water,
bathed in milk,
at rest on a pool.
His cheeks are beds of spices,
banks sweetly scented.
His lips are lilies,
distilling pure myrrh.
His hands are golden, rounded,
set with jewels of Tarshish.
His belly a block of ivory
covered with sapphires.
His legs are alabaster columns
set in sockets of pure gold.
His appearance is that of Lebanon,
unrivaled as the cedars.
His conversation is sweetness itself,
he is altogether lovable.
Such is my Beloved, such is my friend,
O daughters of Jerusalem!

THE CHORUS

Where did your Beloved go,
O loveliest of women?
Which way did your Beloved turn
so that we can help you look for him?

THE BRIDE

My Beloved went down to his garden,
to the beds of spices,
to pasture his flock in the gardens
and gather lilies.
I am my Beloved's, and my Beloved is mine.
He pastures his flock among the lilies.

FIFTH POEM

THE BRIDEGROOM

You are beautiful as Tirzah, my love,
fair as Jerusalem,
terrible as an army with banners.
Turn your eyes away,
for they hold me captive.
Your hair is like a flock of goats
frisking down the slopes of Gilead.
Your teeth are like a flock of sheep
as they come up from the washing.
Each one has its twin,
not one unpaired with another.
Your cheeks, behind your veil,
are halves of pomegranate.

There are sixty queens
and eighty concubines

(and countless maidens).
But my dove is unique,
mine, unique and perfect.
She is the darling of her mother,
the favorite of the one who bore her.
The maidens saw her, and proclaimed her blessed,
queens and concubines sang her praises:

THE CHORUS

"Who is this arising like the dawn,
fair as the moon,
resplendent as the sun,
terrible as an army with banners?"

THE BRIDEGROOM

I went down to the nut orchard
to see what was sprouting in the valley,
to see if the vines were budding
and the pomegranate trees in flower.
Before I knew . . . my desire had hurled me
on the chariots of my people, as their prince.

THE CHORUS

Return, return, O maid of Shulam,
return, return, that we may gaze on you!

THE BRIDEGROOM

Why do you gaze on the maid of Shulam
dancing as though between two rows of dancers?

THE CHORUS

How beautiful are your feet in their sandals,
O prince's daughter!
The curve of your thighs is like the curve of a necklace,

work of a master hand.
Your navel is a bowl well rounded
with no lack of wine,
your belly a heap of wheat
surrounded with lilies.
Your two breasts are two fawns,
twins of a gazelle.
Your neck is an ivory tower.
Your eyes, the pools of Heshbon,
by the gate of Bath-rabbim.
Your nose, the Tower of Lebanon,
sentinel facing Damascus.
Your head is held high like Carmel,
and its plaits are as dark as purple;
a king is held captive in your tresses.

THE BRIDEGROOM

How beautiful you are, how charming,
my love, my delight!
In stature like the palm tree,
its fruit clusters your breasts.
"I will climb the palm tree," I resolved,
"I will seize its clusters of dates."
May your breasts be clusters of grapes,
your breath sweet-scented as apples,
your speaking, superlative wine.

THE BRIDE

Wine flowing straight to my Beloved,
as it runs on the lips of those who sleep.
I am my Beloved's,
and his desire is for me.
Come, my Beloved,
let us go to the fields.
We will spend the night in the villages,

and in the morning we will go to the vineyards.
We will see if the vines are budding,
if their blossoms are opening,
if the pomegranate trees are in flower.
Then I shall give you
the gift of my love.
The mandrakes yield their fragrance,
the rarest fruits are at our doors;
the new as well as the old,
I have stored them for you, my Beloved.

Ah, why are you not my brother,
nursed at my mother's breast!
Then if I met you out of doors, I could kiss you
without people thinking ill of me.
I should lead you, I should take you
into my mother's house, and you would teach me!
I should give you spiced wine to drink,
juice of my pomegranates.

His left arm is under my head
and his right embraces me.

THE BRIDEGROOM

I charge you,
daughters of Jerusalem,
not to stir my love, nor rouse it,
until it please to awake.

Conclusion

The Chorus

Who is this coming up from the desert
leaning on her Beloved?

The Bridegroom

I awakened you under the apple tree,
there where your mother conceived you,
there where she who gave birth to you conceived you.

The Bride

Set me like a seal on your heart,
like a seal on your arm.
For love is strong as Death,
jealousy relentless as Sheol.
The flash of it is a flash of fire,
a flame of Yahweh himself.
Love no flood can quench,
no torrents drown.

Introduction to the Song of Songs

Title and Date of the Poem

The Song of Songs — *Shir HaShirim* in Hebrew — is the poem of poems, the song above all other songs, as one says "wonder of wonders", "king of kings", or — to describe the feast of Easter — the "solemnity of solemnities", as Israel used to call "Holy of Holies" what was actually the holiest part of the Temple in Jerusalem. Moreover, Origen himself, who, together with Hippolytus, was the first among the Fathers of the Church to comment on the Song, stresses the comparison with the Holy of Holies: "Happy", he writes, "is he who enters the Holy of Holies. . . . Likewise, happy is he who understands the songs [of the Bible] and sings them . . . , but happier yet is he who sings the Song of Songs."

When was the Poem written? The style and vocabulary would suggest the fifth or fourth century B.C. It is possible to suggest with some likelihood the date — which remains, of course, indicative only but easy to memorize — of 444, i.e., the time of Nehemiah, who, together with Ezra, rebuilt Jerusalem and the Temple after the exile. The Song would thus have been written shortly after the Book of Job, almost at the same time as the final writing of the Book of Proverbs and of many psalms. It would therefore belong to the great poetic epoch of the Bible. Sophocles was composing *Antigone* and *Oedipus Rex* in Greece at about the same time.

In spite of its title — *The Song of Songs, Which Is Solomon's* — the book could obviously not have been written by the son of David, who lived during the tenth century, i.e., at least five centuries earlier. Naming Solomon as the author, a practice that was common until the nineteenth century, can be explained by the fact that nothing could have been more fitting

31

than to credit the wisest and most glorious among the kings of Israel, a poet himself (1 K 5:12), with the authorship of a poem seen as the most beautiful of the whole Bible.

Moreover, it is not beyond imagination that, at a certain stage of its composition or in one or another of its parts, the Song of Songs might have originated with Solomon or even before his time. One could think that before it even reached the polished and perfect form in which we know it, the poem had started to evolve slowly and to mature in the hidden heart of Israel. Such a hypothesis is, of course, beyond proof; but don't we already have, for instance, a foreshadowing of the Song in the first verses of Isaiah's famous eighth-century song of the vineyard?

> "Let me sing to my friend
> the song of his love for his vineyard.
> My friend had a vineyard . . ." (Is 5:1).

Interpretations of the Song

However, the date of the Song is far from provoking as many discussions as do its interpretations. This very short text, one of the shortest in the Bible (117 verses, 1,251 words, 5,148 letters), probably has been not only the most commented on of all Holy Scripture but also the most passionately disputed. The exegetes follow three main schools:

The Lay and Naturalistic Interpretation

Some of the so-called naturalistic school see the Song as a mere poem, or better yet as a collection of poems, not inspired by religion at all but purely secular if not indeed erotic. "The free sheaf of songs celebrates only one thing: the splendid, radiant and terrifying glory of eros between man and woman. . . . Eros itself vibrates without any other purpose than natural love. . . . Eros is sufficient unto itself. The eros of the Song is not the agape of God."[1] Especially in the celebration of the betrothal and wedding, these verses sing the love between man and woman in terms that though veiled by poetry are nonetheless extremely realistic and quite frequently even very graphic. This thesis of a purely secular Song, held almost only by Theodore of Mopsuestia in all of Christian antiquity, was condemned by the Fifth Council of Constantinople in 553.

The Literal Interpretation

Other authors have a quite different bent: for them the Song has no other purpose at the beginning but love between man and woman, without however its being a secular love. The Song does indeed celebrate human love as the most beautiful gift of the Creator to the heart of man. As the New Jerusalem Bible puts it, in its introduction to the Song of Songs: "[It] is a collection of songs celebrating the loyal and mutual love that leads to marriage. [It] proclaims the lawfulness and exalts the value of human love; and the subject is not only profane, since God has blessed marriage." Extrapolating from the second chapter of Genesis, the Song exalts human love such as God has willed it to be since the beginning, a state of fervor and innocence at the same time, which a couple who is faithful to God should strive to achieve. Thus this book is quite appropriately part of the Bible, and its divine origin is not disputed. There is no difficulty either then in extending to the love of God and man, as many mystical authors did, what can be applied literally only to human love. "The many ecclesial commentators on the Song are at last right again when they interpret [it] in terms of Christ and his bride 'without wrinkle or stain'."[2]

---

[1] Hans Urs von Balthasar, *La gloire et la croix,* vol. 3 (Paris: Aubier, 1974), 115–116, 124; quoting the viewpoint of Gerleman.

[2] Ibid., 120.

We have a rather spirited expression of the literal interpretation in Canon Osty's Bible: "The Song", he writes, "celebrates love, human love, and only human love. . . . The tons of comments poured over this booklet did not succeed in hiding the truth which is so clear to the eyes of the unprepared reader: in its literal, first and direct meaning, the Song deals with human love uniting man and woman in marriage."[3]

It must be admitted that such a stance, quite common today among the exegetes, does not seem at first sight to lack impressive arguments. Here is a book that has a feature unique in the entire Bible: God never intervenes in it. There is not even the slightest reference to him. God is not even named except once in passing and in a quite ambiguous way.

Moreover, properly speaking, there is not a single expression of religious feeling in the whole Song. There is apparently no concern for theology, apologetics, teaching or morality, contrary to all the other books of the Bible and especially the Wisdom books, among which it is ordinarily included. Moreover, the tone of the Song is so passionate, even so daring here and there, and it makes such an appeal to the senses (to all the senses), that it is difficult to see how it could be suitable to the expression of God's love. The love of the Bridegroom and his Bride is that of beings made of flesh and blood.

Lastly, is it not strange that there is not a single quotation from the Song, not even a reference to one verse or another, in all of the New Testament? Neither Jesus nor Paul seems to know it. As to the parallels that people thought might be drawn with passages in the Old Testament, they can also be found in the same ingenious way in the universal literature of love. Interesting studies have been made for a long time that show, in particular, strong similarities between the Song and poems of that era from the Near and Middle East, especially from Egypt.

---

[3] Émile Osty, "Introduction au Cantique des Cantiques", *La Bible* (Paris: Seuil, 1973), 1356. (See also the New Jerusalem Bible, 1028.)

The Allegorical Interpretation

However, the arguments that have just been presented in favor of a purely literal interpretation are quite far from being generally accepted. Traditional Judaism and the Christian churches were quasi-unanimous almost until the nineteenth century in giving a very different fundamental explanation of the Song. Rather than making a celebration of human love, which would then be permitted to extend to the love of God, the first and literal meaning, this third school of interpretation on the contrary sees the love of God as the first and direct object of the sacred author of the Song, making it then legitimately applicable to love between man and woman because, as Paul explains to the Ephesians, marriage's vocation is to signify the union between Christ and the Church.[4]

We are naturally always more inclined to think that human love comes first. "Therefore, when one reproaches mysticism", writes Bergson in an admirable passage of *Deux sources,* "for expressing itself in the manner of a loving passion, one forgets that it was love that plagiarized mysticism and borrowed from it all its fervor, drive and ecstasy."[5]

In any event, it is striking that even though love expresses itself in the freest way, nothing ever made Israel change her view of the Song as the holiest of her books. "If all the Scriptures are indeed holy," the celebrated Rabbi Aqiba said in the second century, "the Song, for its part, is very holy to the extent that the whole world is not worth the day when the Song was given to Israel." Would Rabbi Aqiba have spoken in such

---

[4] Ep 5:31–32. Note f in TOB: In a very compact sentence, Jean-Paul Audet expresses this very clearly: "The apparent theme of the Song is the love between the Bridegroom and the Bride; but its real theme is the prophetic theme of the love of Yahweh for his people." Jean-Paul Audet, *Revue Biblique,* no. 62 (1955): p. 207.

[5] Henri Bergson, *Les deux sources de la morale et de la religion,* Oeuvres (Paris: Presses Universitaires de France, 1970), 1010.

a way had he not had the conviction, shared by all the pious men of Israel, that the Poem of Poems celebrated not human love — no matter how wonderful and holy it may be — but the very love of God for his people and for mankind; if he had not recognized, in the Song, the same language of tenderness already spoken by God to his bride, Israel: "Your time had come, the time for love. . . . I bound myself by oath, I made a covenant with you — it is the Lord Yahweh who speaks — and you became mine" (Ezk 16:8)?

A son of the chosen people, André Chouraqui, says that today he reads the Song like Rabbi Aqiba and all the long line of his ancestors as well as like his own contemporaries: "I was born in a Jewish family faithful to the traditions of Israel. Since early childhood, I heard the Song of Songs chanted on the ancient rhythms that inspired the Gregorian. While I was a child, I was imbued, every Friday night, with the fervor that filled our beautiful synagogue of Ain-Temounchent during the evening office as it started with the recitation of the Poem introducing the liturgies of the Sabbath. Men, women, children were singing this text or listening to it as if in ecstasy. It was indeed a sacred text, a transcendent song. Nobody ever imagined that there could be in it anything obscene, trivial or even carnal. . . . All sang lovingly this Poem of love, and it never occurred to anybody to censure or expurgate it. . . . In all my life, I have never heard from the mouth of those who live in the intimacy of the Poem a single complaisant innuendo about its content. Being transparent, it was welcomed in the transparency of pure hearts. It was understood in reference to the Bible, to the love of *Adonai* for creation, for his people, for each one of his creatures. We were too carried away by the great and powerful current of Hebrew thought to see in the poem anything but the song of absolute love, on the heights of the loftiest revelations. Strange as it is, it remains true that for over two thousand years, the Jews never saw in the Shulamite anything but a symbol, that of Israel; in the King, anything but a reference to God; in the love uniting them, anything but the revelation of the mystery of divine love."[6]

The Witnessing of the Fathers of the Church and the Mystics

For centuries, the vast majority of the Christians did not read the Song otherwise. Very early, the Fathers of the Church developed what will be called the allegorical interpretation or spiritual significance of the Song. "This little book is understood from beginning to end as expressing the heart of the revelation diffused in all of Scripture: it celebrates symbolically the great mystery of love, the union of God and man, foreshadowed in Israel and achieved through the Incarnation of the Word."[7]

Origen, in the third century, Gregory of Nyssa, Basil, Ambrose in the fourth century, as well as Saint Augustine at a later date and Gregory the Great in the seventh century, can be described as unanimous in perceiving in the Song the poem of the marriage of God with his people, of God with the Church, of God with any soul intent on loving him. " 'The mystical preaching' of this 'divine book' is understood by all [the Fathers] in the same way when it comes to its essentials."[8] They will not be quoted here because the book is replete with their commentaries. We can only mention one name, as we did earlier: Theodore of Mopsuestia, who deviated from their opinion in the fifth century.

How can we also not admire the fact that, in the wake of the Fathers of the Church, mystics of all times were always attracted and fascinated, as it were, by the Song, discovering in these burning verses the most personal expression of their

---

[6] André Chouraqui, "Introduction au Poème des Poèmes", *La Bible* (Paris: Desclée de Brouwer, 1975), 27.

[7] Henri de Lubac, *Exégèse médiévale*, pt. 1, vol. 2 (Paris: Aubier, 1959), 560.

[8] Ibid., 560.

love? There is no inhibition, not the slightest reticence, among the purest and most transparent of them when they address God with the images and words — apparently overloaded with human passion — of the Song. This can be seen in Ruysbroeck, Tauler, Catherine of Siena, Teresa of Avila, John of the Cross — but we would have to quote almost all of them. Francis de Sales was only seventeen years old in 1584, when he took a course in Paris with Génébrard on the Song of Songs. He was dazzled. "The Song of Songs", says Henri Bremond, "became his favorite book. No one perhaps has 'lived' it as he did."[9] His *Traité de l'amour de Dieu* bears witness to this in almost all its pages.

Such a love for the Song of Songs is characteristic not only of the contemplatives who have left the world. Marie de l'Incarnation, an Ursuline sister from Tours, who can be seen as one of the greatest figures of the missionary epic and whom John Paul II, in his beatification speech, was to call "the mother of the Canadian Church", had no dearer book for her private prayers. "In the words of the Song which she read in its entirety in 1631 or 1632 [i.e., during her novitiate], she recognized, as is pointed out by Dom Oury, her excellent biographer, a description of her personal experience. . . . And from then on, the book of the Song was to be the most often quoted by her when writing about her inner life. . . . Dom Claude Martin [her son] even states that in her conversations 'the words of Scripture that were heard the most frequently in her mouth came from the Song of Songs.' Submistress of the novices, she suggested to them topics that came generally from Holy Scripture and especially from the Song of Songs."[10]

It was very daring; and we find this again in Thérèse of the Child Jesus, proclaimed patron saint of all the missions by Pius XI. She too was submistress of the novitiate when she was about twenty years old, and we know from the testimony of

[9] Henri Bremond, *Sainte Chantal*, coll: "Les saints" (Paris: Victor Lecoffre, 1912), 56.

[10] Guy-Marie Oury, *Marie de l'Incarnation*, vol. 1 (Québec/Abbaye de Saint-Pierre, Solesmes: Presses de l'Université Laval, 1973), 234.

Mary of the Trinity at the beatification trial that she had wished — at her age, to novices, and in those days! — to explain the Song of Songs. "If I had the time," she confides, "I would like to comment on the Song of Songs. I have discovered in this book such profound things about the union of the soul with her beloved." Father Hans Urs von Balthasar was able to say from the pulpit of Notre Dame that "the Song of Songs, which for thousands of years has been, as it were, a secret sanctuary for the Church, stands at the center of Thérèse's spirituality."

And so it was already at the core of the spirituality of her father, John of the Cross, of whom it is said that at the point of death "he interrupted the prior of the Carmelites who had started to read the prayers of recommendation for the soul. 'Tell me about the Song of Songs *(los Cantares!)*; this other thing is of no use to me', he gently implored. And when the verses of the Song were read to him, he commented as if in a dream: 'Oh, what precious pearls!' "[11]

Would it be possible that the Holy Spirit had thus let entire generations of mystics err in good faith, by permitting them to take as a word of his love what was in fact a wholly human passion? That he could have allowed to such a degree in their hearts, aflame with the sole love of God, a song that would have been born of nothing but love between man and woman and would have no other object? That he communicated interiorly to his friends, in order to draw them to himself, such a spontaneous and deep taste for stanzas composed for the intentions of newlyweds at their marriage feast? Was it then through such a detour that the beloved of God were going to him, without being aware of it? But how could the mystics themselves, these beings who are so sensitized to what comes from God and so instinctively aware of what is not from him, not have discerned that they were being duped when they spoke so lovingly to God in the language of the Song?

[11] Crisogono de Jésus, *Jean de la Croix, sa vie* (Paris: Cerf, 1982), 383.

Let us suppose now that they did not already have this strong instinct: their familiarity with God's Word would have been enough to strengthen them in their conviction that by reading the Song they were reading the love letter of God to his people. The countless links between the Poem and the other books of the Bible do indeed testify all the time that, under the rich apparel of the symbols and the fantastic poetical incantation, it is the very Word of God that is heard. The Song is not an isolated poem in Scripture. From this viewpoint, the parallels that were quite suggestively drawn between the Song and the love songs of the Near and Middle East, especially those of ancient Egypt, are not by far as compelling as those that definitely tie it with prophetic literature.

First, with the Book of Hosea, Henri Cazelles points this out quite objectively: "The Song", he writes, "belongs in fact to the theological thinking of the prophet Hosea, who was the first to compare the relationships between Yahweh and his people to those that obtain between a man and his wife."[12] "It

---

[12] Quoted by Raymond Tournay in "Les affinités du Ps XLV avec le Cantique des Cantiques et leur interprétation messionique", *Supplements to Vetus Testamentum IX,* Congress Volume (Bonn, 1962), 168–212. While maintaining very firmly the essentially messianic perspective of the Song, Tournay questions however certain "very important points" that he had once held in common with André Robert. He explains this quite clearly in the preface of his recent work: "It was during the Persian era that an inspired poet selected old love songs of Egyptian origin and incorporated them with many other texts of diverse origins into his original poetic work meant for believing Jews of his time. Being perfectly initiated in the history and traditions of their people, the faithful of Yahweh needed them to be stimulated and strengthened in their messianic waiting, which was running the risk of getting weaker and even of disappearing because of the apparently indefinite delay in the advent of a new Solomon, son of David. We can then understand why certain parts of the Song, which undoubtedly had a purely erotic significance, acquired a new and genuinely biblical meaning through their insertion in a booklet expressing the requited love of the new Solomon, the longed-for messiah, and of his betrothed, the daughter of Zion." *Quand Dieu parle aux hommes le langage de amour* (Paris: Gabalda, 1982), 45.

is also now my personal conviction", writes Father Tournay, "that it is impossible to account for the complete text [of the Song] if one does not see it as a lyrical transposition, full of fantasy to be sure, of the traditional prophetical theme of the wedding between Yahweh and Israel. And only the nuptial allegory as it appears in Hosea, Jeremiah, Ezekiel and the second and third parts of Isaiah can give a normal and homogeneous meaning to all the parts of the Song." Which enables André Robert to say for his part and without the slightest exaggeration: "The Song is superlatively biblical." In the same vein, did not Origen already point out that "located in the middle of the Bible, the Song lifts to its height the great fundamental image, going from the first chapters of Genesis to the last chapter of Revelation: mankind has become the bride of God"? And it is indeed because he reads the Song with the eyes of all the Fathers of the Church and her mystics that Pope John Paul II, while talking to French women Religious on May 30, 1980, was able to tell them so clearly: "Your personal journey must be like an original new edition of the famous poem in the Song of Songs."

Flesh and Spirit

However, even though they were convinced that the Song, in its first and literal meaning, is the poem above all others of the wedding of God and man, the Fathers of the Church and mystics throughout the centuries were always conscious of the serious problem posed by the Song for the unprepared reader. "Such passages," writes Saint John of the Cross, "if they are not read in the simplicity of the spirit of love and of intelligence that fills them, might seem to be rather extravagant and not a sensible discourse; as can be seen in the Songs of Solomon and other treatises of Holy Scripture in which the Holy Spirit, not being able to express a deep meaning in common and vulgar words, uses veiled terms with images and strange similitudes."[13]

The risk is in fact so great that if the eyes are not sufficiently purified, one can be trapped by the sensual aspect of the images and words.

It is after all possible to read the Song at a very human and even gross level. It is unavoidable for those who still live under the sway of the senses. Teresa of Avila deemed it necessary to warn her Carmelites: "It will seem to you that in these Songs certain things might have another style. Our stupidity is such that this would not surprise me. I heard certain people say that they would rather avoid listening to them. Merciful God, how great is our stupidity!"[14]

Among "certain people", there was probably a place of honor for Father Diego de Yanguas, who was so shocked by Teresa's "thoughts" about the Song that he wrote immediately to her: "Throw this into the fire! It is not decent for a woman to write about the Song."[15]

God is the one who, in his desire to touch the heart of man, does not hesitate to use the language that is the most accessible to his sensibilities. "He stooped", Saint Gregory of Nyssa says, "to the language of our weakness."[16] Just as the Word had one day to empty itself in our flesh and to take on the lowliness of our condition, he did from the start of his revelation empty himself in his written word, committing himself to our words and carnal images. "In order to inflame our hearts to his sacred love," as Saint Gregory the Great states in his magnificent style, "he goes as far as using the language of our crude love, and, stooping thus in his words, he raises up our under-

---

[13] Saint John of the Cross, *Cantique spirituel*, Prologue, *Oeuvres complètes*, Bibliothèque européenne (Paris: Desclée de Brouwer, 1958), 525.

[14] Saint Teresa of Avila, *Pensées sur l' amour de Dieu*, *Oeuvres complètes*, Bibliothèque européenne (Paris: Desclée de Brouwer, 1964), 1:3, 562.

[15] Ibid., 1146nn.

[16] Saint Gregory the Great, *Moralium*, XX, XXXII; PL 76, 175A.

standing; indeed, it is through the language of this love that we learn how strongly we must burn with divine love."[17] If God had not dared to speak the most human and ardent language of love, would we have had the audacity to believe in the passion his Heart contains for us? This is also why, far from being reserved to certain privileged souls, "the Song is a book for all people, a book that makes us rediscover and walk the way of love's journey."[18]

We must however be warned about this pedagogy; we must not at the beginning of the score of divine music change the key indecently; we must not come to the wedding without wearing "a wedding garment" (Mt 22:12). If, consequently, as Gregory of Nyssa puts it, "the soul of certain people is not ready to listen [to the Song], let them listen to Moses admonishing us not to dare start the climb on the spiritual mountain. . . . We must," Gregory adds, "when we want to devote ourselves to contemplation [of the Song], forget thoughts related to marriage . . . so that, having extinguished all carnal appetites, it will be only through the spirit that our intelligence will simmer lovingly, warmed by the fire that the Lord has come to bring on earth."[19] Then, as Origen had already affirmed, "one will not run the risk of being scandalized by images depicting and representing the love of the Bride for the heavenly Bridegroom."[20]

After these serious warnings about the Song, we are quite startled, not to say discouraged, when we read Saint Bernard reiterating them while addressing his monks. Here is how he opens his preaching on the Song before his brothers at Clairvaux: "Saint Paul says: 'We preach wisdom to the perfect'; I

---

[17] Saint Gregory the Great, *Expositio in Canticum Canticorum* 3; CCL 144, 4.

[18] André Robert, "Le Cantique des Cantiques", *La Bible de Jérusalem* (Paris: Cerf, 1958), 25.

[19] Saint Gregory of Nyssa, *In Canticum Canticorum*, Homily 1, PG 44, 763ff.

[20] Origen, *In Canticum Canticorum*, PG 13, 75–76.

would like to believe that you are perfect! . . . One cannot
start reading this book [the Song] unless he has reached a certain degree of purity. Any other reading would be unworthy if
the flesh had not been tamed, if it had not yet been submitted
to the spirit by an exacting discipline. . . . Light is useless to
the eyes of a blind man, and the animal in man does not perceive what comes from the Spirit of God."[21] How could such
words not affect us? If monks might not be pure enough to receive the Song worthily, how could we be ready to approach
it?

It seems to us, though, that in the back of one of the last stalls
of the abbey choir, while Bernard is speaking, a small Cistercian novice, still callow and poorly initiated in the Word of
Wisdom, quite new to the science of love, is however listening
to the words of his abbot with delight. He does not bother to
ask himself whether he has reached the necessary degree of purity and maturity. Quite simply: he is happy. And when he
hears Brother Bernard exclaim at the end, "Who will break the
bread of the Word? Here is the father of the family! Recognize
him who is breaking the bread; it is the Lord!", the little monk
has no hesitation: it is for him, above all for the smallest among
them, that the father of the family has broken the wonderful
bread.

With the same daring trust and the same avidity, we in turn
would like to receive even a few crumbs of this bread since we
are still very imperfect children, but also loving ones.

*
* *

Note: This introduction did not touch upon the composition
of the Song of Songs. Does it make any sense in this case to talk
about composition? Many exegetes believe that there is no order to be sought. Rather than one Poem, the Song would be

[21] Saint Bernard, *Sermons sur le Cantique des Cantiques, Oeuvres mystiques,*
Sermon 1 (Paris: Seuil, 1953), 85–86.

only a collection of poems of various origins, an "anthology of songs" (Dhorme), grouped together only because of their common inspiration and beauty. Still, we will attempt to show in the following pages that the division into five poems, preceded by a Prologue and followed by a Conclusion — as adopted by André Robert — is fully justified.

Overture to the Four Seasons of Love

The Song of Songs, Which Is Solomon's

PROLOGUE

Chapter 1:2–4

THE BRIDE

Let him kiss me with the kisses of his mouth.
Your love is more delightful than wine;
delicate is the fragrance of your perfume,
your name is an oil poured out,
and that is why the maidens love you.
Draw me in your footsteps, let us run.
The King has brought me into his rooms;
you will be our joy and our gladness.
We shall praise your love above wine;
how right it is to love you.

Overture to the Four Seasons of Love

1:2–4 THE BRIDE

> *Let him kiss me with the kisses of his mouth.*
> *Your love is more delightful than wine;*
> *delicate is the fragrance of your perfume,*
> *your name is an oil poured out,*
> *and that is why the maidens love you.*
> *Draw me in your footsteps, let us run.*
> *The King has brought me into his rooms;*
> *you will be our joy and our gladness.*
> *We shall praise your love above wine;*
> *how right it is to love you.*

The first three verses of the Song of Songs form a portico of sorts — better yet, a prelude — to the whole poem. The tone is set, the various themes announced, and we can already see the stages and the whole unfolding of the drama, which will be that of love's triumph.

First, the Bride expresses the most ardent desire: "Let him kiss me with the kisses of his mouth."

Then, she entreats him whom she loves not to let her languish any longer in waiting but to run to her and draw her with him: "Draw me in your footsteps, let us run."

The Bridegroom hastens indeed without delay, takes her with him and leads her to his home: "The King has brought me into his rooms".

And then comes the mutual and blessed possession that seems to have no end: "you will be our joy and our gladness."

1:2 *Let him kiss me with the kisses of his mouth.*

As Paul Claudel points out: "The Song of Songs starts with a kiss."[1] "Such is indeed the start of the symphony", as Chouraqui puts it. "Pleasant discourse", Saint Bernard had already said, "that starts with a kiss."[2]

However, we are somewhat surprised: Who is talking? And who is addressed? And of whom does one speak? We must admit that this beginning of the Song is as mysterious as it is abrupt and sudden. No preparation, no introduction of the characters, as is the rule in a well-structured play, not a single presentation. "Tell us, I entreat you," Saint Bernard says, "by whom, for whom, why, it is said: 'Let him kiss me with the kisses of his mouth'? Why such a sudden start? It is as if one were beginning in the middle of a speech! One might think that the author of the book gave the floor to a first character and that we hear only the response of the second one, who has arrived suddenly, whose name is not given, and who demands a kiss."[3] And Saint Bernard refers then to a kind of *"exordium* without *exordium".*[4]

Also strange and bound to surprise us is the sudden shift in the first two verses from "him" to "you": "Let him kiss. . . your love". It is understandable that many exegetes did, for this reason, seek to correct the text out of concern for a logical coherence.[5]

But the grammar of passion does not mind such difficulties! For, obviously, the Bride is speaking here and from the start of

---

[1] Paul Claudel, *Paul Claudel interroge le Cantique des Cantiques* (Paris: NRF–Gallimard, 1948), 32.

[2] Saint Bernard, *Sermons sur le Cantique des Cantiques, Oeuvres mystiques,* Sermon 1 (Paris: Seuil, 1953), 87.

[3] Ibid., 87.

[4] Ibid., 88.

[5] Thus Denis Buzy translates: "Kiss me with the kisses of your mouth." "Le Cantique des Cantiques", in Louis Pirot and Albert Clamer, *La Sainte Bible,* vol. 6 (Paris: Letouzey, 1943), 281ff.

the first verse; she invokes the Bridegroom, of whom her heart is full, even in his absence. How can she speak about him without wanting to talk to him? Thus she addresses the beloved as if he were present; and in fact he is present since he is in her heart. As Graetz subtly points out: "The Bride, in the intensity of her feelings, jumps from the third to the second person and talks about the one who is absent as if he were present."[6] And she really does not need to name him since it is so obvious that he is the only one in the whole world! Let us remember Mary Magdalen in the garden on the morning of the Resurrection: "Sir, if you have taken him away, tell me where you have put him" (Jn 20:15). Taken away whom? Of whom are you talking? And to whom are you talking? Thus, in her exile, in her remoteness, the Bride can think only about the one who, in her heart, is the only living being.

It is noteworthy that only this first verse, the verse that introduced the poem, is phrased in the third person, as if it were a long cry, a long call in the night: "Let him kiss me with the kisses of his mouth."

All the other verses, except the opening one in the second stanza of the Prologue — "The King has brought me into his rooms" — are written in direct style, the second person: "your love", "your perfume", "your name", "you will be", as if the omnipotence of the call had made the absent Bridegroom suddenly present.

Saint John of the Cross gives a beautiful commentary on the first verse of the Song: "Let him kiss me with the kisses of his mouth." He explains that the Bride, in her exile, does not want anymore to be told about her Bridegroom, no matter how beautifully. Now she wants to talk directly to him, without any intermediary, and to be with him at last. The messages of those who had been sent, i.e., the prophets and wise men of the Old Testament, cannot content her any longer. She needs Jesus

---

[6] H. Graetz, *Shir HaShirim oder des Salmonische Hohelied* (Vienna, 1871).

Christ now and immediately. The first verse therefore contains all the waiting, all the desire, of the Old Testament ardently expecting the messiah.

In the same way, the great Origen already understands this initial verse of the Song: "Until when will my beloved send me his kisses through Moses? Will he send me his kisses through the prophets? I want to be sealed by the very lips of my beloved. Let him come himself. Ah, let him come down himself."[7] The time of the prophets is over, let the messiah come at last! The time of the messengers, the ones who are sent, is over; let the Bridegroom himself come! For, Origen goes on, the prophets, "in order to fire me with love and desire, promise me that he will come in their prophetic messages; and, under the sway of the Holy Spirit, they do not cease telling me about his countless virtues and his prodigious feats. They also praise his beauty, his lovable mien and his tenderness: so much so that they ignite in me an unbearable desire. But now, as I see it very well, the end of time is near, and his presence has not yet been given to me. Only his servants are going up and coming down (Gn 28:13). Therefore I turn to you, Father of the one who has been promised to me: have mercy on our love at last and send him to me! No, let him not speak to me through his servants, angels or prophets! Let him come himself and kiss me with the kisses of his mouth!"[8]

Saint Bernard, obviously inspired by Origen, follows the same line: "Of what use to me now are the obscure sentences of the prophets? I am awaiting the fairest among the children of men: let him kiss me with the kisses of his mouth! The tongue of Moses is slow (Ex 4:11); the lips of Isaiah are unclean (Is 6:5); Jeremiah is a child who does not know how to talk (Jr 1:6). All the prophets are deprived of the gift of tongues. He himself, the one of whom they speak, must talk to me now, and kiss me

---

[7] Origen, *Homélies sur le Cantique des Cantiques* (cf. SC 37 bis), Homily I:2 (Paris: Cerf, 1966), 73.

[8] Origen, *In Canticum Canticorum*, PG 13, 84–85.

with the kisses of his mouth. . . . I will not be content anymore with visions and dreams; I will refuse figures and enigmas; I am tired of the angelic apparitions . . . . I want neither
the kisses of the angels nor the kisses of a man, but he is the one
I entreat to grant me the kisses of his mouth."[9] Divine kiss that
is also, we might be tempted to add, the kiss of creation, the
kiss of forgiveness and reconciliation, the kiss of divinization
and of union.

One, though, cannot help but be struck by the extraordinary
insistence, the passionate amplification stressed by the triple
repetition of the same words within this first verse of the Song:
"Let him kiss me with the kisses of his mouth." As Saint Teresa of Avila points out with her customary spontaneity: "The
Bride could easily say only: let him kiss me. Her request would
thus have been put in fewer words. Why this stress: the kisses
of his mouth? . . . It is quite certain though that not a single
word is superfluous. But why? I don't understand, yet I will
say something about it."[10] Saint Bernard was already struck by
this repetition: "As if those who kiss", he said, "were doing it
in another way and not with the mouth and their own mouth!
Better yet, we are not simply reading, let him kiss me with his
mouth, but these rather uncommon words: let him kiss me
with the kisses of his mouth."[11] Hence the temptation to sim-
plify this text, with the serious error of taste that this might
create.[12]

Passion in itself is enough to explain this redundancy, which
is not simply a mere repetition. There is, in fact, from one of
these words to the other, a progression in the experience of
love: here he is; here is a kiss from him; here is a kiss from his
very mouth. When we formulate the verse in such a way, it

[9] Saint Bernard, *Sermons,* Sermon 2, 93.
[10] Saint Teresa of Avila, *Pensées sur l'amour de Dieu, Oeuvres complètes,* Bibliothèque européenne (Paris: Desclée de Brouwer, 1964), 573.
[11] Saint Bernard, *Sermons,* Sermon 1, 87.
[12] Thus in the TOB: "Let him kiss me with a full mouth."

somehow brings what it is calling for. It is as if it were going from wish to reality.

Saint Bernard makes a profound commentary about the stage of spiritual life corresponding to the kiss of the Bridegroom. The soul, at the time of its conversion, is granted the privilege of merely kissing the feet of the Lord, as, for instance, in the case of the sinful woman in Luke 7. Then the soul rises, at a second stage, and kisses the hand, a mark of its friendship, familiarity and intimacy with the Lord, its friend. But only at the end of the ascent will it be granted the kiss of the mouth, which is that of union with the Bridegroom — kiss that the soul could not presume to give of its own volition, but that it can expect and receive only from its Bridegroom: "Let him kiss me with the kisses of his mouth", thus follows the wise advice given by Saint Bernard: "Remain, O holy soul, in your reserve, for he is your Lord, and, instead of kissing him, you might have to worship him together with the Father and the Holy Spirit."[13]

In the overture to the Song, the bride does not yearn for anything else than these supreme kisses. As Saint Bernard stresses with sensitivity, the Bride does not request from her all-powerful friend freedom (though she is in exile), or some reward or gift, or at the least an appeasing word of compassion. She demands only kisses. From the one she loves, she expects nothing but love. "Love is sufficient in itself. . . . I love because I love. I love in order to love."[14]

However, the Fathers of the Church, from Origen to Saint Bernard, do not see in the triple repetition of the words in the first verse of the Song merely the exalted expression of loving passion and the ultimate stage of progression in belonging to God. They read this first verse in the light of and, as it were, from within the trinitarian mystery. They seem to have per-

[13] Saint Bernard, *Sermons*, Sermon 8, 140.
[14] Ibid., Sermon 83, 849.

ceived the presence of the three divine persons in the first
words of the Song — the presence of the Father, the Son and the
Spirit, evoked prophetically together as early as the first burst
of the most beautiful love song of the Bible — as they have already sensed it in the first verse of the Bible itself: "In the beginning God created the heavens and the earth. . . . God's
spirit [*Ruah* = the Spirit] hovered over the water. . . . God
said [the Word of God]" (Gn 1:1–2).

In the same way, in the first verse of the Song — *Let him kiss
me!* the Father is thus implored. For all initiative is his. "He is
the origin", as Saint Paul says. He is the principle of tenderness, the source of love. All excellent gifts come from him and
originate in him.

The mouth is his only Son, the Word revealing the Father, his
Word, his mouth. "Then he began to speak" (Mt 5:2), the
evangelist says at the start of the Sermon on the Mount. All that
we know about God was received from the mouth of his only
Son. "The mouth of the Bridegroom", says Saint Gregory of
Nyssa, "is the source from which spring the words of eternal
life (Jn 6:68): if anyone is thirsty, let him come to me and drink!
For this reason the thirsty soul wants to offer its mouth to the
mouth from which life springs by saying, 'Let him kiss me
with the kisses of his mouth.' "[15]

The kiss. The Holy Spirit is the kiss that the mouth of the beloved Son imprints forever on our hearts (Rm 5:5). The same
kiss eternally uniting the Father and the Son within the Trinity
is now uniting us to them: "so that the love with which you
loved me may be in them", Jesus says at the conclusion of the
priestly prayer (Jn 17:26). The same kiss, the same love, the
same Holy Spirit. "The superadorable Word", writes Marie de
l'Incarnation while meditating on this first word of the Song,
"fills the soul with his spirit and life through the kisses of his

---

[15] Saint Gregory of Nyssa, *In Canticum Canticorum*, Homily 1, PG 44,
763ff.

divine mouth."[16] Thus are we introduced, secretly as it were, from the very start of the Song, to the trinitarian intimacy.

Going farther yet in this proposed outlook, some Fathers of the fourth century such as Cyril of Jerusalem and Ambrose show in their Easter catechesis that the ardent wish of the bride—"Let him kiss me with the kisses of his mouth"—is essentially fulfilled in the Eucharist: "When the body of Christ will touch your lips," Cyril says to the catechumens, "then the wish of the Bride will be fulfilled for you: let him kiss me with the kisses of his mouth! The unity of love in the Spirit is then consummated."

We must note, however, that in the rest of the Song, we shall never encounter anymore this ardent desire of the Bride for the kisses of the Bridegroom, which was her very first cry. Does this not mean that the definitive union achieved in these kisses, even though it was the first wish of the soul, is not meant for this life, but will be fully attained only in the Kingdom?

1:2 *Your love*—she says now—*is more delightful than wine;*

What is remarkable is that when the Bride first evokes the Bridegroom, she does not bring up his face, his gestures, his look or even the words he whispers to her. In fact, she says nothing that could make him seen or heard, that could show him to the eyes of others as to her own eyes. It seems that she herself does not discern him except through the countless proofs of love he showers on her: "Your love", she says, "is more delightful than wine".

The word *love*[17] translates the Hebrew *dodim,* plural form of *dod,* or Bridegroom: these are manifestations of the Bride-

---

[16] Guy-Marie Oury, *Marie de l'Incarnation,* vol. 1 (Québec/Abbaye de Saint-Pierre, Solesmes: Presses de l'Université Laval, 1973), 124.

[17] Paul Joüon, *Le Cantique des Cantiques* (Paris: Beauchesne, 1909). Émile Osty, "Introduction au Cantique des Cantiques", *La Bible* (Paris: Seuil, 1973). JB.

groom's tenderness, his caresses (Dhorme, Osty),[18] his kisses, his embraces. And then the bride adds immediately: your perfume and your name. Your love, your perfume, your name are, as it were, the triple mode of the presence of the only One in the heart of the Bride. She first perceives her beloved through the proofs of his tenderness, more intoxicating than wine, and even simply through the perfume that is always with him, and even, at last, through his name as she utters it in her heart, as she alone indeed is capable of uttering it!

We would like to pause here and consider these three modes of the presence of the Bridegroom in the soul — still steeped in the night — of his love, and to reflect on the link between the three symbols of wine, perfume and oil.

1. *Your love is more delightful than wine;*

The Bride will use this analogy with wine again at the end of the Prologue: "We shall praise your love above wine", and also, for a third time, at the very end of the poem: "I should give you spiced wine to drink" (8:2). The Bridegroom himself will tell her: "How delicious is your love, more delicious than wine" (4:10), and at the wedding banquet: "I drink my wine" (5:1); finally in the fifth and last poem: "Your navel is a bowl well rounded with no lack of wine" (7:3); "your speaking, superlative wine" (7:10). Thus the theme of wine is repeated seven times in the Song on the lips of the Bride and the Bridegroom to express what is at the same time sweet, strong, festive and joyful — in other words, intoxicating — in the love that possesses them both.

Wine is indeed the very symbol of joy in Holy Scripture. Old Ecclesiastes, meaning to say that he never gave up any pleasure during his life, confesses, "I resolved to have my body

---

[18] Édouard Dhorme, *La Bible,* Bibliothèque de la Pléiade (Paris: NRF-Gallimard, 1959).

cheered with wine" (Qo 2:3). In a more subtle vein, the psalmist talks about "wine to make them cheerful" (Ps 104:15). And
Isaiah shows us God himself, preparing for his chosen ones
"on this mountain . . . a banquet of fine wines" (Is 25:6).

But it is in the Gospel that wine, in relation to love as it is in
the Song, sees its symbolism magnified. The very first of Jesus'
signs in the Gospel of John will be very significantly enacted
during a wedding feast at Cana in Galilee, where a wine such as
man had never tasted before ("you have kept the best wine till
now") is served in abundance to the guests (Jn 2:7–10). The
very first public testimony given of himself by the living Love
is that of wine poured at a wedding feast. Thus, for the first
time, he will manifest his glory, and from then on his disciples
will believe in him (Jn 2:11–12). The feast at Cana, during
which the only ones who share, indeed the only ones to be
named (while nothing is said about the bridal couple, who are
not even seen!), are the true Bridegroom and his Bride, foreshadows that other solemn feast on the last evening of Jesus'
life when the cup of "the new covenant" (Lk 22:20) will seal
the final wedding of the Bride with the Bridegroom.

It is noteworthy, in connection with our text of the Song,
that in the Hebrew language, in which letters are also numbers,
the words *wine (ya'in)* and *mystery (sod)* have the same numer-
ical value of seventy. Thus there is already a prefigurative link
between these three words — love, wine and mystery — as it
will exist one day in the Eucharist.

For the Bride of the Song, the proofs of tenderness of the
Bridegroom are thus filled with all the joys of the world, all
the intoxications, and — as she senses it — even more in fact,
since she says, "Your love is more delightful than wine." In the
past, Isaiah had sung, "My friend had a vineyard" (Is 5:1); the
Bride of the Song, using the same theme, says that the Bridegroom is himself the intoxicating wine of that vineyard, a
thousand times more intoxicating than the wine of the vineyard! Yes, above all joys, all madness, all intoxication: "Your

love is more delightful than wine!" When the apostles, on the morning of Pentecost, were filled with the Holy Spirit, the Spirit of Love, did not the people say that they were drunk with wine?

2. *delicate is the fragrance of your perfume,*

Perfume plays an important role in the Song; with the exception of the second poem, it is mentioned in all the parts of the Song, taking up fifteen verses. And ten kinds of perfumes are named: nard, myrrh, henna flowers, frankincense, saffron, calamus, cinnamon, aloes, apple fragrance and mandrake scent (1:3, 12, 13, 14; 3:6; 4:6, 10, 11, 14, 16; 5:5, 13; 7:9, 14; 8:2).

The reason is that perfume suggests very strongly the all-powerful attraction of the Bridegroom. Indeed, as perfume penetrates all things, enters everywhere, becomes an irresistible part of all there is, so the love of the Bridegroom enfolds, invades, penetrates, impregnates all of life, all the fibers of life and even the least moments in the life of the one who loves him, abiding with her day and night, everywhere. Thus the caresses of the Bridegroom, though they be more intoxicating than wine, are not alone in captivating the bride: independently from these proofs that he showers on her in his regal way, what enchants her is his perfume, this perfume that follows him everywhere and radiates from him; this perfume that announces his arrival and also lingers for a long time after him; this perfume that is uniquely his, absolutely unique in the world, that is immaterially his very presence, and that causes his Bride, when she inhales it, to say immediately and without hesitation: there he is, this is he!

Origen was naturally struck by this verse of the Song: "delicate is the fragrance of your perfume". "The bride realized", as he puts it, "that all the scents she has been using until now were far from having the sweetness of this new perfume. . . . To be sure, the queen from the south brought perfumes to Sol-

omon. And many others had scents. But one could have as
many as he wants, and never could they be compared with the
perfume of Christ, of which the Bride says here: 'delicate is the
fragrance of your perfume'. "[19]

3. *your name is an oil poured out,*

"The name of the lover is known after his perfume,"
Chouraqui points out, "and, as the perfume, it penetrates the
beloved, obsesses her, haunts her."[20] Moreover, in Hebrew,
there is a connection between the word for perfume *(shemen)*
and the word *shem* (name): there is an assonance, a call from
one word to the other. However, the name of the Bridegroom
that the Bride whispers here is not revealed. It remains secret,
unknown, mysterious. The Bridegroom of the Song does not
have any particular identity. No particular name can be given
to him. All that can be said about him is that he is identified
with Love itself. Thus he is not named, and yet he is named!
For Love is truly his name, as the entire poem, from the very
first verses, clearly suggests. "Love is my name," Jesus tells
Marie de l' Incarnation, "and it is thus that I want to be called.
Men give me many names but none pleases me more or expresses better what I am for them than this one."[21]

Now in a way that is more intimate than through his caresses themselves ("your love is more delightful than wine"),
more subtle than through his perfume itself ("delicate is the
fragrance of your perfume"), the Bridegroom surrenders himself through his name. As Chouraqui notes quite aptly: "The
name is the living person of the lover in the beloved, identical
to his perfume but more real and more personal than a
perfume."[22]

[19] Origen, *In Canticum Canticorum,* 91.
[20] André Chouraqui, *Le Cantique des Cantiques* (Paris: Presses Universitaires
de France, 1970), 38.
[21] Oury, *Marie de l' Incarnation,* 83.
[22] Chouraqui, *Le Cantique des Cantiques,* 38.

Yes, if the caresses of the Bridegroom intoxicate the Bride more than wine, and if the perfume of the Bridegroom obsesses her memory and her heart, the power of his name over her, in her, is — as she admits herself — even more intimate and penetrating: it is an oil poured out, she says, an oil reaching little by little the very core of life, piercing all the covers of the soul, all its defenses, invading all, going down to the very roots of the being with the strength, the sweetness, the gentleness and the penetration that are proper to oil. Thus, William of Saint-Thierry, Saint Bernard's friend, grasps very well the feeling of the Bride when he has her say: "From you pours out to be poured into me the oil of your name, softening all that is hard in me, soothing all that is rough in me, healing all my infirmities. . . . The echo of your name — whether it be 'Lord' or 'Jesus' or 'Christ' — brings a sudden joy and cheerfulness to my ear. For as soon as your name rings in my ear, the mystery of your name shines in my heart."[23]

1:3 *your name is an oil poured out,*

The association between name and oil, a penetrating oil, cannot fail to evoke the anointed of the Lord (*messiah* in Hebrew, *Christ* in Greek): the one who receives the anointing of oil as a sign of the penetration of the Spirit of God investing him for a mission. The name of the beloved thus appears, as early as these first verses of the Song, as that of the anointed of the Lord, the messiah, the Christ. The one to whom it is said in Psalm 45: "God, your God, has anointed you with the oil of gladness, above all your rivals" (Ps 45:8).[24] One can therefore think that, like the psalmist, the Bride of the Song, when she says "your name is an oil poured out", is prophetically speaking about him in the words of Isaiah: "The Spirit of the Lord Yahweh has been given to me, for Yahweh has anointed me"

[23] William of Saint-Thierry, *Exposé sur le Cantique des Cantiques* (cf. SC 82) (Paris: Cerf, 1966), 125–127.
[24] Cf. TOB, *Isaiah*, 45:1, 677n (Paris: Le Livre de Poche).

(Is 61:1). And the Bride, for her part, is in a way sacralized by
this oil of anointing, which is the name of her Bridegroom in
her. "If the Bridegroom comes indeed to touch me"—Origen
thinks—"I too will have a sweet smell and will be anointed
with perfumes; his perfumes will be mine also so that I will be
able to say with the apostles: we are the good odor of Christ
everywhere."[25]

Among the Fathers, no one was undoubtedly more attracted
by this verse of the Song than the last of their line. It is not surprising in fact that Saint Bernard, "the honey-mouthed doc-
tor" as tradition calls him, loved to hear about the name of
Jesus what the Bride says about the name of her beloved: "your
name is an oil poured out". Bernard points out that "oil enlightens, strengthens the body and calms pain. The same thing
can be said about the name of the Bridegroom. He enlightens
when we preach him, nourishes when we meditate about him,
and is a calming balm when we invoke him."[26] There is thus a
quasi-sacramental value to the very name of Jesus when it is uttered. Indeed, what a happy prayer that which simply whispers endlessly the name of Jesus. His name is a prayer in itself.
"O Love!" Saint Teresa of Avila exclaims, "I would like to repeat your name ceaselessly."[27] It is enough in fact to say it and
to repeat it slowly; it suffices to let it go down little by little to
the depths of the soul, as a penetrating oil, for it to work by
itself every conversion, every renewal, every divinization.
For, as Claudel points out: "He rests at the bottom of our
memory, invested with a continuous power of exhalation,
suggestion and call. Sacred name whose unceasing vibration at
the bottom of our thought puts out any vulgar intrusion."[28]
Did not Isaiah already note: "Lord, the object of our desire is to
repeat Your name. . . . We have had other masters, but Your

[25] Origen, *Homélies,* Homily 1:3, 79.
[26] Saint Bernard, *Sermons,* Sermon 15, 199–201.
[27] Saint Teresa of Avila, *Pensées,* 591.
[28] Claudel, *Paul Claudel,* 33–34.

name is the only one we repeat."[29] It is true that the soul does not always know how to pronounce this name at the beginning. But as Saint Francis de Sales writes in his New Year letter of January 1, 1608: "Let us utter it often, first as we are capable of doing it! If, for the time being, we can only stammer, at the end we will for all that say it well!"

From wine to perfume, and from perfume to the oil of the name, do we not perceive now a certain progression in the approach and experience of the beloved? First, an intoxication of all the senses and of the spirit under the effect of the caresses, of immediate consolation; then, a second time, in a calmer but more obsessive and also more persistent way, a perfume invading the memory and staying long after the visit that brought the consolation of the beloved. Lastly, there is a third level, a very deep action, achieved insensibly, softly, of the oil of presence down to the deepest levels of the soul. There are thus, on the one hand, features that are common to these three symbols of wine, perfume and oil: something that attracts man, invades him, invests him — "you anoint my head with oil, my cup brims over", as the psalmist himself says (Ps 23:5) — but with a real progression, we can say, from one symbol to the other, in interiorization.

This confirms very clearly the experience of contemplative prayer: intense joy and wild intoxication when the soul has been visited. Such a joy persists a long time after the visit, but in a calmer way, like a perfume haunting and penetrating the memory all day long, as William of Saint-Thierry notes so delicately: "The smell of the perfumes going with him is a certain feeling, which perdures in the memory, of the suavity that went away, and among the remaining thoughts, a festive memory of the experienced consolation."[30] However, an even more hidden, more silent action is going on silently in the depths: the slow and very discreet invasion of the soul by the

---

[29] Isaiah, 26:8–13 (TOB).
[30] William of Saint-Thierry, *Exposé*, 131.

peace surrounding the name of the beloved, like an oil poured out and going down to the very roots of the being, intoxication of your living caresses, persistent perfume of your memory, unutterable peace of your secret presence bound to your name only in the unfathomable depths of the soul!

1:3 *and that is why the maidens love you.*

Truth to tell, we did not expect to be led to such a conclusion! Passion, when it is so violent, is naturally exclusive, and it is even easily hurt! Now we see, on the contrary, that the Bride expresses her joy that other maidens (*almoth:* young girls ready for marriage) are also falling in love with the one she loves. It would even seem that she is happy not to be the only one to love him! Though totally entranced by the spell of her love, not only does she feel the need to talk about her Bridegroom to these other maidens and to boast about the tenderness she feels for him, but one might even think that the most important result of her love is to bring new hearts to her Bridegroom: "and that is why", she says, "the maidens love you."

Could it be that the love of the other maidens for the beloved enhances, in the eyes of the Bride, the value of her own choice? It is true that all of them love the beloved; but she is his only love. All of them would like to choose him; but she is the only chosen one. So the admiration and the love of the other maidens for her beloved are in fact helping her to gain a better awareness of the extraordinary favor and privilege granted to her.

The true reason though for the other maidens' evocation is infinitely more worthy of the generous Bride. The other maidens are here not only for the purpose of increasing her happiness with the song of admiration they sing together with her. The Bride of the Song is such that she cannot love the Bridegroom without wanting all the other women — i.e., all the other nations of the world — to share her love for him and for them to also be loved by him. "In the gates of the daughter of Zion, I may recite your praises one by one", says the psalmist

(Ps 9:14–15). For the Bride, as for the psalmist, the desire, the necessity are the same. Let the beloved draw all hearts to himself, like a perfume spreading and invading the universe; this is her joy, the one who is beloved of God!

It has been, in any event, one of the noblest and most beautiful features of Israel, the bride with whom God had wanted since the origin of her history to have a covenant. If Israel is indeed aware, and very intensely so, of being the chosen people, she never considers such a choice as exclusive. God is her God, but also the God of the whole universe. If Israel is the chosen one of God, it is as a witness, a people of priests bound to attract all the nations to Yahweh. The other nations are, as it were, her younger sisters, as God puts it in the Book of Ezekiel. Even the most pagan among them, the most sinful ones, are *almoth,* called also to be one day the brides of Yahweh, as is the elder sister: "Your younger sister is Samaria, who lives on your left with her daughters" (Ezk 16:46). Israel is therefore duty bound to draw them to herself so as to draw them to God. "I take your elder and younger sisters", the Lord has told her (Ezk 16:61). Jerusalem thus had to understand that it was not only the capital of Israel but, in keeping with the magnificent prospect of Psalm 87, the metropolis of the whole world: "But all call Zion 'Mother', since all were born in her" (Ps 87:5).

Thus the beloved of the Song, in the most passionate expression of her love, could not forget mankind forever surrounding her. "The bride of Christ", Claudel says, "never ceases to be aware of this mankind whose destiny she carries in her womb. And those she here calls so tenderly 'the other maidens', without any particularism or discrimination, are seen by her at the same time as younger sisters and daughters, adolescent girls who do not yet have her experience and maturity, and she rejoices — the bride with a universal heart, the bride who has the heart of the Church — to see them associated with her own choice."[31]

---

[31] Claudel, *Paul Claudel,* 63.

Not only associated, for her great and everlasting happiness is that through her, the one beloved with a unique love, her Bridegroom will gain and draw to himself all the peoples of the earth. Such is the beautiful meaning of this "that is why", which Saint Bernard sees and comments on so well: "The maidens, she says, gave you their love for the very reason that your love brought me its perfume. This is what awakened their love. . . . My beloved, says the Bride, here is the fruit of your name poured out on me; it is the love of these maidens. Unable to seize your fullness on their own, they are sensitive to your radiance through me."[32]

This thought enchants Saint Francis de Sales, who draws on the inexhaustible treasury of his images to enrich it even more: "He", Francis writes, "who is attracted by the sweetness of your perfume enters the shop of a perfume merchant, and receiving the pleasure of the aromas he smells, goes out and shares his pleasure with others, spreading among them the fragrance of the perfumes he has taken with him."[33]

As for the Bride herself, she is not so advanced in perfection. On the contrary, she is aware of her weakness and inability to go to the one she loves! How could she do so on her own, without his help, if he himself does not come to her and draw her after him?

1:4 *Draw me in your footsteps, let us run.*

For no matter how close a friend she is, she is still miles and miles away from her beloved! Her situation is that of Israel in exile, far from Zion, the home of Yahweh and her home with him; it is the situation of the Church, the bride of Christ, walking painfully in this world on her way to her Lord; the situation of every soul loving Jesus Christ and suffering at the awareness of the distance between them. Israel, the Church and the soul

[32] Saint Bernard, *Sermons*, Sermon 19, 232–233.

[33] Saint Francis de Sales, *Traité de l'amour de Dieu, Oeuvres*, Bibliothèque de la Pléiade (Paris: NRF–Gallimard, 1969), 714.

in love with God are thus sighing for the coming of the Bridegroom. Let him hasten! Let him not tarry in coming himself to fetch his beloved from the faraway land where she is detained. Let him go on the road with her toward their home. And let him not hesitate to draw her in his footsteps if she is not going forward. Yes, "draw me, pull me behind you *(trahe me)*".[34] Again, how could she manage on her own? As Saint Gregory the Great points out, "He who says 'draw me' is at the same time willing and unable. . . . He wants to walk behind God, but, vanquished by his own weakness, he is incapable of following him as he should."[35] "Draw us then," he says together with Saint Ambrose, "for we do have the desire to follow you, desire inspired by the attraction of your perfumes. But since we are not equals in the race, pull us, so that, lifted by your help, we might be able to put our feet in your footsteps. For if you draw us, we too can run."[36]

Saint Bernard, here too, has expressed admirably the intense desire of the Bride to join him whom she loves and her inability to do so by herself. "The Bride", he writes, "must be drawn only by the one who said, 'Apart from me you can do nothing.' For well I know, she confesses, that I can join you only by following you step by step, that I could not follow you without your help. . . . Your beloved, having left everything for your sake, desires therefore to put her feet in your footsteps, to follow you always and everywhere. She knows that your ways are beautiful, that your paths are those of peace and that, in following you, one does not walk in the dark. But she asks to be drawn, pulled, because your holiness is like the mountains of God and her own strength is insufficient to climb them. She is therefore quite right in wanting to be drawn since

[34] *Biblia Sacra juxta Vulgata Versionem*, vol. 2 (Stuttgart: Würtembergische Bibelanstalt, 1969).

[35] Saint Gregory the Great, *Expositio in Canticum Canticorum* 24; CCL 144, 25.

[36] Saint Gregory the Great, *Expositio in Canticum Canticorum* 25, CCL 144, 26–27.

no one can come to the Father unless he is drawn by your Father. And those who are drawn by your Father you too draw. . . . Thus she says: 'Draw me in your footsteps, let us run.'. . . How indeed could we be surprised when she asks to be drawn, she who walks behind a giant and claims to join him who leaps over the mountains and jumps over the hills? . . . Her strength could not accomplish this. Thus she asks to be drawn. For I am tired, she says, I am faint; do not abandon me, but rather draw me in your footsteps to prevent me from following other lovers haphazardly. Draw me in your footsteps, for it is better for me to be drawn, even violently so, even threateningly so, even in punishment, rather than for you to be soft with me and leave me insecure, a prey to my own torpor. Draw me thus against my will, get my consent forcefully, tear me away from my inertia and throw me into this race. The time will come when I will not need to be pulled since we will run together, with all our heart, and effortlessly."[37]

Saint Bernard speaks as a true monk, thirsty for God, who would want to be forced by God not to oppose his will; who would want God, once and forever, to conquer him, pull him forcefully, without any possible resistance on his part. He is so well aware of his inconsistency! So often, in the past, did the Bride run after other adventures, as the Bridegroom reminds her in Jeremiah: "You said, 'I love strangers and I want to run after them'."[38]

However, we feel that when he is reading that page of Saint Bernard, Saint Francis de Sales is somehow saddened by the thought the Bride is, as it were, drawn forcefully by the Bridegroom in order to be able to run with him. Indeed, this is not very flattering! Therefore, Saint Francis de Sales, always a kindly soul, remembers perhaps a famous page in which Saint Augustine wrote about the same verse of the Song: "Do not believe that you are drawn against your will, for the spirit is

---

[37] Saint Bernard, *Sermons,* Sermon 21, 249–252, 256–257.
[38] Jeremiah, 2:25 (TOB).

also drawn by love."[39] More likely though, Francis de Sales, giving in to his natural inclination "to excuse everything, to trust, to hope" (1 Co 13:7), thinks that he can interpret, very much to the advantage of the Bride, the humiliating "pull me" of Saint Bernard. In fact, he explains, the Bride is not so much pulled as attracted: "Draw me, the sacred Bride tells the one she loves — that is to say, be the first to start. For I could not awaken by myself; I could not be moved if you did not move me. But after you will have moved me, O dear Bridegroom of my soul, we will run together, you in front and I behind you, you pulling forward and I accepting your attraction. But let no one think that you are pulling me forward as if I were a slave in bond or an inert carriage! Oh no, you are drawing me with the fragrance of your perfumes. If I am following you, it is not because you are pulling me but because you attract me. Your attraction is powerful but not violent because its strength is its very sweetness. Perfumes have no other power than their sweetness to draw one after them, and how could sweetness pull if not sweetly and pleasantly?"[40]

When Saint Ambrose, Saint Bernard, Saint Augustine or Saint Francis de Sales comment in such a vein on verse 4 of the Prologue of the Song, they are very faithful witnesses to the experience undergone by every disciple of Christ, whose desire to love and follow Jesus is surely very great, and greater yet his inability to follow him on his own.

The word we use, *draw* or *pull*, is very expressive in itself. In Hebrew, it is *mashakh*, a term belonging to a specifically prophetic vocabulary. For the prophets, it is one of the essential words of conversion. Thus we read in Jeremiah: "Yahweh has appeared to him from afar: I have loved you with an everlasting love, and this is why I draw you with kindness" (Jr 31:3). In Hosea, God, talking about the young and weak Israel, said: "I led them with reins of kindness, with leading strings of

---

[39] Saint Augustine, *In Joannem*, 26, 3; PL 35, 26, 4, c. 1608.
[40] Saint Francis de Sales, *Traité*, 450.

love" (Ho 11:4). And it can very well be surmised that Saint
John is translating the same verb, *mashakh,* when Jesus says,
"When I am lifted up from the earth, I shall draw all men to
myself [*elkuso*]" (Jn 12:32).

What matters is to let oneself be drawn! The question is not
so much to want to grasp God as to let oneself be grasped by
him. The question is not to climb up to the cross, but to want
to get up there somehow; how could we make it by ourselves?
Voluntarism leads nowhere. It is only because God, in his love,
attracts us that we find the strength in our turn to join him.
"No one can come to me unless he is drawn by the Father" (Jn
6:44).

Now how can we understand the plural "let us run" in the
verse we are reading? André Robert answers, and this is the
most obvious interpretation and also the simplest: the plural
"let us run" evokes the race to Jerusalem in which Yahweh and
his bride run together. And the antithesis itself is beautiful between the first and the second part of the verse — i.e., between
the difficulty the Bride has in taking the first steps, the need she
has of her beloved's help ("draw me"), and then her vivacity,
her drive, as soon as her friend joins her ("let us run"). She,
who had asked to be drawn, is not satisfied anymore with
walking; she wants to run, and she does!

We must, however, elaborate on this interpretation. The
"we" of "let us run" is not only that of the Bride and the Bridegroom; it is also the "we" of the Bride and her maiden companions, the maidens she just mentioned and who are
inseparable from her, the nations of the world. Saint Bernard
understands this well: "We run," he writes, "i.e., the maidens
join me in the race; we run together, I following the fragrance
of your perfume, and they following my example and my en-
couragement. The Bride indeed is imitated just as she herself is
imitating Christ. Therefore she does not use a singular form, 'I
shall run,' but 'let us run.' "[41]

[41] Saint Bernard, *Sermons,* Sermon 21, 257–258.

The same interpretation is to be found in the words of Thérèse of Lisieux, who frequently quoted this verse of the Song, in which her whole missionary spirituality seems to be condensed. "One day, after Holy Communion, Jesus let me understand this sentence of the Song: 'Draw me; we run after the fragrance of your perfumes.' O Jesus, it is therefore not necessary to say: in drawing me, also draw the souls I love. This simple phrase, 'draw me', is enough. Yes, when a soul lets itself be captured by the intoxicating smell of your perfumes, it cannot run alone. All the souls it loves are drawn together with it; this is a natural consequence of its being drawn to you. . . . I feel that the greater the fire of love ignited in my heart, the more I will say, 'draw me', and the more the souls that will come close to me will swiftly run toward the fragrance of the beloved's perfume. Yes, they will run; we will run together . . . for a soul that is afire with love cannot remain inactive."[42] Is it also necessary to remember here that when she saw herself buried, so to speak, in the depths of the Heart of Christ, Saint Margaret-Mary heard the sentence: "I want to make of you an instrument to draw [*mashakh!*] hearts to my love." Whoever is drawn to love must draw and attract others in his turn: "Ravish those you can, . . . ravish them to love" *(rapite quos potestis . . . rapite ad amorem)*. These words of Augustine become the law of her heart.[43]

Yet one should not be frustrated if, following the beloved, one does not immediately start running! Saint Francis de Sales, also on this point, comes happily to encourage us, the slow-pokes! Here is how he talks in his first Conversation with his Daughters of the Visitation: "Draw me, the Bride of the Song says, and I will run after you. . . . One must not get upset if at first one does not run immediately after the Savior, as long as one repeats 'draw me'. . . . For this congregation, like the oth-

---

[42] Saint Thérèse of the Child Jesus, *Histoire d'une âme* (Paris: Cerf/Desclée de Brouwer, 1972), 291–292, 295.

[43] Saint Augustine, *Enarrationes in Psalmos,* 33:6–7; PL 36, 311; CCL 38, 286.

ers, is not an assembly of perfect people but of people who claim that they are on the way to perfection; our assemblies are not made of running people but of people who desire to run and who, for this purpose, must first have to walk slowly, then hasten, then go on at half-trot, then at last run."[44]

Quite obviously, the bride of the Song is not going to walk slowly or even go at half-trot. This is not her temperament. However, no matter how fast she wants to go, we did not expect her to say it so early.

1:4 *The King has brought me into his rooms;*

In her imagination aflame with love, the Bride dreams she has already run so far with her beloved that she is already with him at the goal of her desires. Or, better yet, she knows quite well that, with such a Bridegroom, desire and reality are quite frequently confused! Saint John of the Cross said: "with God one gets as much as one hopes for." "The good God", as Saint Thérèse of Lisieux comments, "could not inspire desires that would be impossible to fulfill."[45] For the wildest desires, if they are in conformity with the Spirit of God, if they are desires for his love and his service, are surely begotten in us by the only one who can ensure, of necessity, their fulfillment. "He who desires God with a whole soul", says Saint Gregory the Great, "is certain to possess the one he loves."[46]

"The King", the beloved says in her certainty of being immediately fulfilled, "has brought me into his rooms." The King, whose name appears here for the first time, is Yahweh himself. King and Bridegroom, at the same time, of his people, as attested to by many prophetical texts especially after the exile and also in so many psalms: "Your creator will be your husband", Isaiah writes (Is 54:5). "My God, my King, I shall

---

[44] Saint Francis de Sales, *Recueil des entretiens spirituels*, Oeuvres (Paris: NRF-Gallimard, 1969), 1006–1007.

[45] Saint Thérèse of the Child Jesus, *Correspondance générale*, vol. 2, Letter 197 (Paris: Cerf/Desclée de Brouwer, 1973) (cf. also Letter 129).

[46] Saint Gregory the Great, *Homeliae in Evangelia*, 30, 1; PL 76, 1220C.

exalt you", says the psalmist, and he says it many times. Again, we notice that Yahweh is not named and yet his name is given. Jesus, like the Bridegroom of the Song, also received the two titles of Bridegroom and King: "Surely the bridegroom's attendants would never think of fasting while the bridegroom is still with them" (Mk 2:19), and when questioned by Pilate, "So you are a king then?", Jesus answers: "It is you who say it" (Jn 18:37).

The Bride simply says "the King". There is no qualification or specification of this title. The beloved is not a king among other kings. He is not the king of one country or another. He is King, absolutely so. However, the Bride will never be called "queen" in all the Song in which she has so many names. No matter how intimately she is united with her Bridegroom, she is not his equal.

The sixth chapter of Isaiah projects a strong light on this passage of the Song. Yahweh appears to his prophet in all his majesty, sitting on a throne, the train of his robe covering the sanctuary. Overcome with emotion, Isaiah then exclaims: "My eyes have looked at the King." The parallel with our verse of the Song is all the more impressive in that the revelation to Isaiah of Yahweh as King occurs in the Temple, in fact in the most secluded part of the Temple, the Holy of Holies. Now when the beloved of the Song says, "The King has brought me into his rooms", she is talking about the same place: "Holy of Holies" and "rooms" refer in fact to the same reality of the Lord's presence in the heart of his people.

However, *rooms* is a rather weak and impoverished rendition of the Hebrew word *heder*. Saint Jerome uses three Latin words, very suggestively, to translate this word, and we ought to retain all three: *cubiculum* (room, lodging, as the Jerusalem Bible uses it); *conclavia* (kept in the Latin version of Cardinal Bea); *cellaria* (the wine cellar, the basement), a translation that Saint Ambrose of Milan himself deems to be more precise.[47]

---

[47] Saint Ambrose, *Des sacrements, des mystères* (cf. SC 25 bis), Book V (Paris: Cerf, 1961), V, II, no. 11.

Thus the room *(cubiculum)* into which the beloved is brought is on the one hand the most secluded part of the house, the one that is usually under lock and key *(conclavia,* from *clavis:* key). We see the King of the Song not attempting at all to dazzle the one he loves by showing her his power but rather locking himself up silently with her in the most exclusive intimacy, showering her with a thousand favors. "She has good reason, indeed, to rejoice," Origen notes, "for before her eyes are the secrets of the King, his hidden wonders. . . . This is a royal chamber filled with countless and immense riches."[48] What are these riches? asks Gregory of Nyssa. "Introduced to the secrets of heaven like the great Saint Paul, the Bride", he replies, "sees invisible things and hears unutterable words."[49]

However, the locus of the wonderful intimacy and of the priceless treasures is also that of intoxication, the cellar, the basement *(cellaria)* in which wine is kept under lock and key! In the room where he retires with the one he loves, the King, who is fulfilling her, also intoxicates her with his love. This is the meaning of "wine cellar", which is preferred by Saint Bernard, a native of Burgundy. He thinks that if the beloved is in such haste to run, it is mostly because she is attracted by the intoxicating pleasures to be drunk in the cellar of her Bridegroom, "in these rooms", as he puts it, "filled with exquisite fragrances . . . toward which all the maidens run together; but the one who loves the most ardently is also the fastest and arrives there first."[50]

With a beautiful impetuosity, Teresa of Avila adopts the interpretation of Saint Bernard: "The King seems to refuse nothing to the Bride!" she exclaims. "Well, then, let her drink as much as she desires and get drunk on all these wines in the cellar of God! Let her enjoy these joys, wonder at these great things, and not fear to lose her life through drinking much

---

[48] Origen, *In Canticum Canticorum,* 99.

[49] Cf. 2 Co 12:4; Saint Gregory of Nyssa, *In Canticum Canticorum,* Homily 1, 785B.

[50] Saint Bernard, *Sermons,* Sermon 23, 271.

more than her weak nature enables her to do. Let her die, at last, in this paradise of delights; blessed death that makes one live in such a way!"[51]

Again, it must be remembered that the Bride was not able to enter by herself into the secret domain and drink from the cellar of her beloved. "The King brought me", she says quite rightly, for all the initiative came from him. However, the Bride does not say either, "The King has brought us", i.e., "myself and my maiden companions who were running with me", as one could have expected after the "let us run" of the preceding verse. For the Bride of the Song, as Origen points out, enters at first alone with the Bridegroom. The maidens remain outside. But the Bride, beautiful and perfect, without stain or wrinkle, after having entered the room of the Bridegroom in the royal house, returns later for the maidens and tells them what she alone has seen: "The King", she tells them, "has brought me into his rooms".[52] And all of them enter then after her, in the palace of the King, as is written in Psalm 45 (Ps 45:14–15).

We thus see the very same link in the Song between contemplative intimacy and evangelization. One leads to the other: the most personal and secret intimacy necessarily leads to the need of announcing to all peoples that love has been found. Father Beauchamp points out that such is the case in the psalms: "Praise leads to witnessing. . . . Being alone with God is not a frequent situation in the psalms. . . . Whether there be praise or supplication, other people are always present."[53]

After the passionate expression of desire ("Let him kiss me with the kisses of his mouth"), after the call for help ("Draw me"), after the introduction to the secret cellar of the King ("The King has brought me into his rooms"), there is now a celebration of the endless feast of mutual possession.

---

[51] Saint Teresa of Avila, *Pensées,* 596.
[52] Origen, *Homélies,* Homily 1:5, 85.
[53] Paul Beauchamp, *Psaumes nuit et jour* (Paris: Seuil, 1981), 100–101, 110.

1:4 *you will be our joy and our gladness.*

The two words that are used together here are also found very
frequently in the prophets and the psalms: "I will change their
mourning into gladness, comfort them, give them joy after
their troubles," says Jeremiah (Jr 31:13). And in the last chapter
of Isaiah, within the same context of return as that of the Song,
Yahweh proclaims: "Rejoice, Jerusalem, be glad for her, all
you who love her! Rejoice, rejoice for her" (Is 66:10). And the
psalmist echoes: "Let Israel rejoice in his maker, and Zion's
children exult in their King" (Ps 149:2); and more directly as
the Bride expresses it here: "joy and gladness for all who seek
you!" (Ps 70:4).

We must not think that there is a mere redundancy when one
talks thus about joy and gladness, no more in the Song than in
the prophets and the psalms. The two words are in fact often
used without any perceptible nuance and at times interchange-
ably. One can say, though, that the first one, which we translate as "joy", is to be linked as here to the Hebrew *gil*, rendered
generally in Latin by *exsultare* (from *ex-saltare*): to exult,
jump, dance. It is the exterior aspect of joy, the joy felt in the
entire body, the joy that makes it leap as did the child John the
Baptist in the womb of his mother. The second word, which
we translate as "gladness", corresponds to the Hebrew *simha*.
It describes the more interior aspect of joy, the deep and sustained joy penetrating the soul, jubilation (the latter word being very significantly derived from the Latin *laetitia* and *laetus*,
the first meaning of which is "fat"), a very interior joy, the secret joy of John the Baptist, who had become a friend of the
Bridegroom: "This same joy I feel," he says, "and now it is
complete" (Jn 3:29). We could thus translate our verse of the
Song almost as faithfully: "You will be our dance and our jubilation."

After the reappearance of the third person ("The King has
brought me"), we then go back to the second person: "you
will be". There is, by this fact, a very precise symmetry be-

tween the two stanzas making up the Prologue, each one opening with a verse in the third person ("Let him kiss me with the
kisses of his mouth"; "The King has brought me into his
rooms") followed by all the other verses in the second person.
It seems indeed that the beloved is not capable of talking about
the one she loves without immediately addressing him.

And just as we had noted in the first part of the Prologue, the
contrast between the singular ("let him kiss", "draw me") and
the plural ("let us run") is found again in the second part of the
stanza in a symmetrical singular ("the King has brought me")
and plural ("our joy", "our gladness", "we shall praise").
Such an alternation of singular and plural can easily be explained. The beloved is at the same time a very personal being,
a bride, Israel-the-bride, but also a whole people, the wedded
nation. In fact this alternation is a constant in the Bible. Thus in
the following passage of Deuteronomy (chosen from among
many others): "Take care therefore not to forget the covenant
which Yahweh your God has made with you, . . . for Yahweh
your God is a consuming fire" (Dt 4:23–24).

But, on the other hand, we have to reiterate that the Bride,
even in moments of greatest intimacy with the King, her
Bridegroom, is never separated from her companions, "who",
as Origen says, "run behind her, each according to her
strength: one faster, another slower, yet another one at the
very end, while that other is at the head."[54] But all are in the
footsteps of the Bride, waiting to be able one day to sit with her
at the same table and to partake of the same happiness. Then,
together:

1:4 *We shall praise your love above wine;*

That is to say, above all joy and all intoxication! The prophet
Zechariah says, "Their hearts will be full of joy, as though by
wine. Their sons will look on this in gladness, their hearts will

---

[54] Origen, *In Canticum Canticorum*, 99.

exult in Yahweh" (Zc 10:7, with the same group of words: *wine, joy* and *gladness*). The Bride of the Song goes even further in her intoxication: "We shall praise your love above wine."

This intoxication leads the Bride to praise. Is it not beautiful to observe that this word *praise,* which is constantly used in the psalms to exalt the mighty deeds of God in creation and in history, is applied here to the most typical action of God and the most manifest of all, his love? "We shall praise your love above wine"; yes, above all madness and all intoxication.

Now the bride can conclude:

1:4 *how right it is to love you.*

Yet, as Father Joüon[55] points out, how cold does this word *right* sound, especially in the last verse of the Prologue, after the warm lyricism of the preceding sentences! However, this is the word or its equivalent. Father Bea translates quite literally: "It is quite right to love you." And Dhorme: "We are right in loving you."

We must not forget, as the Jerusalem Bible notes, that for a pious Jew to love God did not mean only to follow the inclination of his heart but also to obey a commandment, the first of all that are inscribed in the Torah, the law of Israel: "You shall love Yahweh your God" (Dt 6:5). To love God, for a true child of Israel, is at the same time a passion of the heart and the first of all his duties.

Moreover, it must be added that from the very viewpoint of passion itself, this word *right* as a conclusion to the Prologue does have some strength in its humility as an understatement.

After such fervent emotions, is it not touching to hear the Bride say in an impersonal and anonymous way: it is right, yes, quite right, to love you? Passion and reason are linked. Nothing is more passionate indeed, but nothing is wiser and more sensible also than the love of the beloved. Nothing is

[55] Joüon, *Le Cantique des Cantiques,* 132.

more passionate: "We shall praise your love above wine;" all the intoxication of love leading one to laugh and to clap one's hands. But nothing is wiser and more sensible too: "how right it is to love you." Here is all the wisdom of love, which is the source of such a profound peace. Ruysbroeck puts it wonderfully: "In its ascent, love, without losing order, loses measure and finds intoxication."[56] Such intoxication and such measure at the same time are the stamp of the beloved.

[56] Jan van Ruysbroeck the Admirable, *Oeuvres choisies* (Paris: Perrin, 1947), 157.

The Winter of Exile

First Poem

Chapters 1:5–2:7

The Bride

I am black but lovely, daughters of Jerusalem,
like the tents of Kedar,
like the pavilions of Salmah.
Take no notice of my swarthiness,
it is the sun that has burned me.
My mother's sons turned their anger on me,
they made me look after the vineyards.
Had I only looked after my own!

Tell me then, you whom my heart loves:
Where will you lead your flock to graze,
where will you rest it at noon?
That I may not wander like a vagabond
beside the flocks of your companions.

The Chorus

If you do not know this, O loveliest of women,
follow the tracks of the flock,
and take your kids to graze
close by the shepherds' tents.

The Bridegroom

To my mare harnessed to Pharaoh's chariot
I compare you, my love.
Your cheeks show fair between their pendants
and your neck within its necklaces.

We shall make you golden earrings
and beads of silver.

DIALOGUE OF THE BRIDE AND BRIDEGROOM

—While the King rests in his own room
my nard yields its perfume.
My Beloved is a sachet of myrrh
lying between my breasts.
My Beloved is a cluster of henna flowers
among the vines of Engedi.

—How beautiful you are, my love,
how beautiful you are!
Your eyes are doves.

—How beautiful you are, my Beloved,
and how delightful!
All green is our bed.

—The beams of our house are of cedar,
the paneling of cypress.

—I am the rose of Sharon,
the lily of the valleys.
—As a lily among the thistles,
so is my love among the maidens.
—As an apple tree among the trees of the orchard,
so is my Beloved among the young men.
In his longed-for shade I am seated
and his fruit is sweet to my taste.
He has taken me to his banquet hall,
and the banner he raises over me is love.
Feed me with raisin cakes,
restore me with apples,
for I am sick with love.

His left arm is under my head,
his right embraces me.

—I charge you,
daughters of Jerusalem,
by the gazelles, by the hinds of the field,
not to stir my love, nor rouse it,
until it please to awake.

The Winter of Exile

After the Prologue, the first theme is heard: it is the complaint
of the exiled Bride, longing for the one she loves:

1:5 *I am black*—she sighs—*but lovely, daughters of Jerusalem,*

"I am black": this is the effect of pain that dries up, pinches and
darkens her face. The beloved is black, which is the color of the
night, the color of trial, the color of her exile. Her soul is in the
dark, and this shows in her complexion. Job, at about the same
time, is moaning in sorrow in the same way: "My skin", he
says, "blackened on me!"[1]

Inner distress is not the only cause of this darkening of the
skin. It is a fact that the Bride of the Song is not a girl who
stayed in her father's house, taking care of her delicate complexion. She had to leave her country, go the way of servitude,
and the sun of exile has burned her face. How could we not
compare the words she utters here to the lamentations of Jeremiah over the deportees of Israel: "rosier than coral their bodies, their hue as radiant as sapphire. Now with faces darker
than blackness itself, they move unrecognizable through the
streets" (Lm 4:7–8).

However, if the hard time of exile marred the face of the
Bride, it did not ruin her beauty. It would not do at all for the
daughters of Jerusalem, her companions, to take her at her
word, to misunderstand and to think that she did become
homely and ugly. The immediate retraction of her words,
within the same verse, is significant in this respect and contains

---

[1] Jb 30:30. Edouard Dhorme, *Le Bible,* Bibliothèque de la Pléiade (Paris:
NRF–Gallimard, 1959), 1305.

a hint of challenge: "I am black but lovely, daughters of Jerusalem"! Her fundamental beauty has not been touched by her sorrows. And the Bridegroom will soon agree, finding only grace in her. And is it not sufficient indeed for her to please the Bridegroom in order to be beautiful? Since her darkened face does not repulse the one she loves and does not prevent her from being loved, how could she not be beautiful, beautiful because she is loved, simply beautiful because he looks at her? Yes, marred as I am, if I am willing to expose my face to the eyes of the Bridegroom, his look does change me. The Bridegroom necessarily transforms what he sees. "What brings about the return of beauty", says Gregory of Nyssa, "is to go back to the true beauty from which one had gone away."[2]

This is a theme that John of the Cross in particular develops masterfully. Paraphrasing our verses of the Song, he makes the Bride invoke the Lord her Bridegroom:

> Do not despise me anymore. If you found that my complexion was dark, now you can look at me since you have looked at me and have thus given me grace and beauty. . . . For, before you had looked at me, you saw in me the ugliness of sin and the imperfections and lowliness of my natural condition. . . . Ever since you looked at me, taking away this dark and ugly complexion that made me unworthy of being seen, now you can well look at me, and more than once, because not only did you take away my dark color with your first glance, but you made me worthier of being seen since your loving glance left in me grace and beauty. . . . This is precisely what the Bride in the Song is telling to the daughters of Jerusalem, when she says, "I am black but lovely, daughters of Jerusalem", i.e., do not wonder, daughters of Jerusalem, that the King gives me such favors and has brought me into his rooms because even though I myself was black and did not deserve his favor, I am still beautiful for him since he looked at me, and, for this, loved me. . . . You can therefore, my God, look at me now and have a high regard for the one you had looked at once since, through your first

[2] Saint Gregory of Nyssa, *In Canticum Canticorum*, Homily 4, PG 44, 831C.

glance, you left graces in her for which she deserves not only one but many glances from your eyes.[3]

All powerful and transfiguring look of the beloved! What is essential is to remain in this look. Therefore it is impossible to despise and depreciate oneself because one cannot see oneself anymore but through the loving and transfiguring look.

1:5 *I am black but lovely, daughters of Jerusalem,*

Like the chorus in ancient tragedy, the daughters of Jerusalem enable the bride of the Song, here and throughout the Poem, to reveal the depths of her heart. Faithful companions, they share her anguish, her search, her questioning, or they startle her. The attitude of the chorus with regard to the Bridegroom is quite different. If he happens to give orders or to ask questions, the chorus never echoes his soul, for the soul of the Bridegroom in the Song has neither emotion, nor trouble or hesitation. He has no moods.

The daughters of Jerusalem have, in any event, a very important role, not at all secondary or episodic in the Song. They are addressed and questioned seven times: four times by the Bride (1:5; 3:11; 5:8, 16) and three times by the Bridegroom (2:7; 3:5; 8:4). And they talk on their own as a chorus in the drama seven times also (1:8; 3:6–11; 5:9; 6:1, 10; 7:1, 2).

In fact they represent the nations of the world, as we have already noted about the maidens of the Prologue (1:3). Their group, forming the only chorus of the drama (for there are no other choruses, no other voices for us in the Song), can be seen near the Bridegroom and his love, as the genuine third person of the Poem, just as, through the entire Bible, the pagan nations were near Yahweh and Israel. With the exception of the watchmen, whom we will meet twice without hearing their voices and whose reactions always show a lack of understand-

---

[3] Saint John of the Cross, *Cantique spirituel,* Stanza XXV, *Oeuvres complètes,* Bibliothèque européenne (Paris: Desclée de Brouwer, 1958), 635–636.

ing (3:3) and even brutality toward the bride (5:7–6:1), the daughters of Jerusalem always testify — even if there is a hint of irony and scepticism in their words — to a great deal of compassion. Israel in exile would also know this dual attitude of the pagan nations, and so does Jesus during his Passion when he sees among the merciless soldiers the weeping daughters of Jerusalem (Lk 23:28).

Without their intervening directly at the beginning of this first poem, the bride thinks that she saw in their eyes a certain contemptuous pity at the sight of her sorrows. Let them not bemoan her fate too much since, black as she is, she is loved and therefore beautiful!

And in order to stress very precisely that she is at the same time black and beautiful, she compares herself to the tents of Kedar and to the pavilions of Salmah.

1:5 *like the tents of Kedar,*
like the pavilions of Salmah.

Kedar and Salmah are two sites in northern Arabia. Why were these towns chosen? One could say: simple poetical choice. These two names ring very true. It can well be the case. But one must note that Kedar means above all black and somber; remember that the tents of the desert's nomads, "the camp where Kedar lives" (Is 42:11), are made of woven black goats' hair. The parallel drawn here by the Bride between the color of her face and the tents of Kedar is thus all the more easy to explain in that she herself is stranded like the nomads, without a dwelling, exiled and also burned by the sun. "This is worse than a life in Meshech, or camping in Kedar", as the psalmist was already lamenting (Ps 120:5). Yes, but the Bride knows that she is also as gracious, as beautiful and as light at the same time as a white pavilion in the sunshine! Black to be sure, like the tents of Kedar, but white and beautiful like a pavilion of Salmah! Thus the colors of the night and the colors of the day, the colors of joy, are united in her face.

One could also think in a more direct way, as does Origen, that if the tents of Kedar brought to mind the stay of Israel in the desert when she was a nomad in the desert of Exodus, the white pavilions of Salmah recall the brilliant colors of the draping adorning the inside of the Temple during the days of glory of Solomon's kingdom (the poet of the Song making a pun on the words *Salmah* and *Shlomo,* or Solomon). It would therefore be in fact the whole destiny of Israel, the unhappily exiled daughter and happily beloved daughter, a tried and glorious people, mirrored in the face of the Bride, which is as black as the tents of Kedar and yet as beautiful as the pavilions of Salmah.

The beloved is moreover not as black as she had been saying at first. Her face is rather tanned, bronzed, golden, as expressed by the diminutive *sheharhoreth* (from the root *shahor,* meaning black or dark brown), which she uses now. This is why, daughters of Jerusalem:

1:6 *Take no notice of my swarthiness,*
   it is the sun that has burned me.

She stresses the reasons for her complexion being so dark. For it must be known that she was not always thus. By birth and original condition, she was a noble and free maiden, endowed with a dazzling face. Then she had to undergo the trial of servitude. And the difficult labors to which she was subjected under the sun of exile did burn her skin.

It must be noted in passing that the Bride is suffering now because of the deterioration of her beauty, though there is never the slightest reservation (on either her part or anyone else's) about the beauty of the Bridegroom, which is rather strange in itself if this is a purely secular work of literature, in which beauty is essentially the attribute of women. But it does make good sense if the Bridegroom of the Song is Yahweh.

The Fathers of the Church apply what the Bride is saying here about herself not only to the individual soul—as Saint

John of the Cross does in the passage of the *Spiritual Canticle* we quoted before—but also to the Church, the new Israel, and the genuine bride of Christ. Origen devotes no less than thirteen columns in his great commentary to these words of the Bride: "I am black but lovely, daughters of Jerusalem". "The Church", he explains, "comes from the pagan world, from the gentiles, and is black. But by welcoming the Word made flesh, she became beautiful and dazzling. 'I am black, indeed,' " Origen has the Bride say, " 'because of my low birth, but I became beautiful through penance and faith, for I received in myself the Son of God, I received the Word made flesh, I came close to him who is the splendor of glory and the radiance of holiness. And I became beautiful.' "[4]

There is a very similar interpretation in Saint Ambrose, though when Origen stresses above all the transfiguration of our humanity due to the very fact of the Incarnation of the Word in human flesh, Ambrose sees more specifically the passage from the state of being a sinner, which was ours, to that of God's child through baptism. "The Church," he writes in *De Mysteriis,* "who is wearing these white robes since the bath of her new birth, says in the Song of Songs 'I am black but lovely, daughters of Jerusalem'. Black because of the frailty of human nature, lovely because of grace; black because she is made of sinners, lovely because of the sacrament of faith. Seeing her robes, the daughters of Jerusalem are stunned and exclaim, 'Who is this one who rises up all white?' She, who used to be black, how did she become white all of a sudden?"[5]

As far as Saint Bernard is concerned, when the bride confesses "I am black but lovely," she means above all that she is at the same time in solidarity with the world of men's sins and wholly sanctified in her belonging to the Bridegroom. It is therefore the very condition of the Church in this world that is expressed in this verse: the Church in her dual solidarity and communion with God and mankind. "The Church is black",

---

[4] Origen, *In Canticum Canticorum,* PG 13, 111.

[5] Saint Ambrose, *Des sacrements, des mystères,* Book V (Paris: Cerf, 1961), 175.

Bernard explains, "because she dwells in the tents of Kedar, a rough place for warriors, a long sojourn in misery. This is the effect of a long exile in hardship and, in a word, of this body, which is at the same time heavy and frail. . . . Under the tents of Kedar, she cannot be exempt from stains, wrinkles or other dark features. . . . But Christ came to take upon himself this darkness, so as to give back to his bride all her radiance. . . . Christ wrapped himself in the night by taking the form of a slave and the robe of human nature. . . . He whose beauty is far beyond that of all the children of men is indeed hidden in his passion, subjected to the agony of the Cross, the agony of death, so as to return light to the children of men. He gives up all his beauty and thus earns for his admirable bride a Church without stain or wrinkle. . . . I therefore recognize the tent of Solomon but all the more do I worship Solomon himself under this darkened tent."[6]

When he was writing with such warmth, Bernard might well have remembered that admirable passage in which Saint Gregory of Nyssa, eight centuries earlier, had put these words in the mouth of the Bride in his homilies on the Song: "Do not be surprised by the fact that though I was black due to my sin and akin to darkness due to my works, I was loved [by my Bridegroom] because he made me beautiful through his love by exchanging his beauty for my deformity. Taking upon himself the stain of my sins, he communicated to me his own purity and made me share in his own beauty. He made me lovable, though I had been ugly at first, and then he loved me. . . . This is why the beloved does not allow the souls she instructs to despair of becoming beautiful when they look at their past life; rather, they ought to look at her and learn from her example that the present can become a veil covering the past. . . . Even if you are the tents of Kedar, by the fact that the prince of the power of darkness dwells in you—since the word Kedar means darkening—you will become Solomon's tents

[6] Saint Bernard, *Sermons sur le Cantique des Cantiques, Oeuvres mystiques,* Sermon 28 (Paris: Seuil, 1953), 337ff.

since King Solomon will have made his dwelling in you. . . . Thus will the foreigners become citizens; the Babylonians, inhabitants of Jerusalem; the courtesans, virgins; the Ethiopians, dazzlingly white; and Tyre will become a city from on high."[7]

Later on, the reaction of Saint Francis de Sales to this same verse, though it is inspired by a quite different consideration, is thereby no less beautiful or deep. If the Bride is black, he says, the reason is the sadness caused by her compassion for the pitiful state of Jesus in his Passion; and if she is beautiful at the same time, it is because she knows that, at the very cost of his suffering, she is the only beloved one: "I am black with pain through compassion; . . . the anguish of my beloved has discolored me. For how could a faithful lover see such torments in the one she loves more than her own life without becoming all chilled, haggard and shriveled with pain? The nomads' tents are always exposed to the abuse of the elements and of war; they are almost always wrinkled and covered with dust; and I, exposed to the sorrow that I received through compassion from the unique travails of my divine Savior, am all covered with distress and pierced with pain. However, since the pains of the one I love come from his love, they make me suffer in compassion and delight me out of kindness in the same measure. For how could a faithful, loving soul not be extremely happy when knowing that she is so loved by her heavenly Bridegroom? For this reason, therefore, the beauty of love resides in the ugliness of pain."[8]

However, when the Bride says that the sun has burned her, she does not give the full explanation nor the first cause of her miseries: Well, why would you go to face this harsh sun? she could be asked. Why did you thus expose yourself to a burning sun in this fiery desert and then come to complain about having lost the whiteness of your complexion? And she answers:

[7] Saint Gregory of Nyssa, *In Canticum Canticorum*, Homily 2, 789–792.

[8] Saint Francis de Sales, *Traité de l'amour de Dieu, Oeuvres*, Bibliothèque de la Pléiade (Paris: NRF-Gallimard, 1969), 272–273.

1:6 My mother's sons turned their anger on me,

Here are the real, the truly guilty ones: my mother's sons. Yes, but how unnatural and twisted this language is! Why say "my mother's sons" when it would have been simpler to say "my brothers"? At times, people say that the language is less prosaic and typically oriental and that this style is found elsewhere, for instance in the psalms (cf. Ps 69:8: "I am a stranger to my brothers, unknown to my mother's sons."). But, in fact, in order to understand the phrase in this context, we have to recall with the Jerusalem Bible that Israel is descended from Abraham, who came from the land of Ur in Chaldea (cf. Gn 11:28, 31). There is, therefore, Chaldean blood flowing in the veins of Israel. Israel or, in other words, the Bride has in common with the Chaldeans of the time one great ancestor: Israelites and Chaldeans are brothers in Abraham. But the Chaldeans of Nebuchadnezzar are precisely the enemies who have now despoiled Jerusalem and led Israel to her exile. How could these accursed Chaldeans be my brothers? At the most, sons of my mother!

For they turned against me, they dragged me into exile and reduced me to servitude:

1:6 they made me look after the vineyards.
    (Because it is true, and I admit it)
    Had I only looked after my own!

Very frequently, Israel is called the vineyard of Yahweh in Holy Scripture. And every Jew surely knew by heart the song of Isaiah: "Let me sing to my friend the song of his love for his vineyard. My friend had a vineyard on a fertile hillside. He dug the soil, cleared it of stones, and planted choice vines in it." The key to the apologia is given at the end of the poem: "the vineyard of Yahweh Sabaoth is the House of Israel, and the men of Judah that chosen plant" (Is 5). The entire land of Palestine had been given to this vineyard so that it could take root and grow (Ps 80:9–12). But, through her faults and infidelities, Israel lost her beautiful inheritance. Her vineyard was taken away, according to the prophecies of the same Isaiah: "Now I will tell you what I will do with this vineyard: I will tear off its hedge; it will be grazed upon; I will knock down its fence; it will be trampled." And a sad echo is to be found also in Psalm 80. In another text, probably even older, Yahweh says through the prophet Hosea: "I will lay her vines and fig trees waste" (Ho 2:14). The parallel between the Song and this verse of Hosea is all the more stunning in that the same characters are involved—a husband and his unfaithful wife. It is the same context of the covenant and of the uprooted vine.

Therefore, instead of tilling her own vineyard and working for herself, Israel is sentenced to go to a foreign land. Exiled, she has to work in the "vineyards" of Nebuchadnezzar's Chaldeans, i.e., to accomplish the hard labor inflicted on her by her merciless oppressors, because she does not know how to keep her own vineyard! "Oh how sad", says Gregory of Nyssa, "are those who are wise enough to understand when they hear this phrase: 'I did not take care of my own vineyard'. . . . How did she become a prostitute, Zion, the faithful city?"[9]

The poor exile, the sad caretaker of foreign vineyards, rises from the depths of her exile and from her pain, lifting up her eyes toward her beloved:

1:7 *Tell me then, you whom my heart loves:*
Where will you lead your flock to graze,
where will you rest it at noon?

The evocation of the mother's sons who rose against her and brutally enslaved her can only lead the bride to return quickly and with a whole heart to her only recourse, her beloved: "you whom my heart loves". This is how she calls him, in the secrecy

---

[9] Saint Gregory of Nyssa, *In Canticum Canticorum*, Homily 2, 880B.

of her heart. For her, this is his true name, the only one she could indeed give him. "Thus I name you", Gregory of Nyssa makes her say, "since your name is above any other name; it is inexpressible, inaccessible. . . . This name, revealing your goodness toward me, shows the love of my heart for you. For how could I not love you, you who loved me when I was black?"[10] "Here," Origen has already noted, "the Bride calls the Bridegroom with a new name. That is because she knows quite well that he is the son of love; better yet, he is love itself, that is, God. It is therefore his name, as it were, that she utters when she says here, 'you whom my heart loves'. She does not say: the one I love, but the one my soul loves. This is not a mere delight but a love coming from her whole soul, her whole strength and her whole heart."[11] In fact, the Hebrew word is *nefesh*, i.e., my whole being, my whole life.

1:7 *Tell me then, you whom my heart loves:*
   Where will you lead your flock to graze?

Thus the beloved is a Shepherd. He was Bridegroom and King. And now he is also the Shepherd who pastures his flock. How can one not be struck by the fact that these three titles thus brought together by the Song are those that God gives to himself through the whole of Scripture? It is noteworthy, especially in the great prophetical texts of the exile as well as in many psalms, that the three names of God as King, Bridegroom and Shepherd of his people are often associated, as is the case here in the Song and as Jesus applies them to himself.

But these biblical words must come even more clearly to the soul of the exiled Bride when she is appealing with such expectation to her beloved Shepherd: the very words in which Yahweh in Ezekiel promises to come himself to put an end to her exile and bring her back at last with him in a great rest. "As a

---

[10] Ibid., 801AB.

[11] Origen, *In Canticum Canticorum*, 120.

shepherd keeps all his flock in view when he stands up in the middle of his scattered sheep, so shall I keep my sheep in view. I shall rescue them from wherever they have been scattered during the mist and darkness. . . . I shall gather them together from foreign countries and bring them back to their own land. . . . There they will rest. . . . I myself will pasture my sheep; I myself will show them where to rest. . . . I mean to raise up one shepherd, my servant David, and to put him in charge of them, and he will pasture them; he will pasture them and be their shepherd. I, Yahweh, will be their God, and my servant David shall be their ruler" (Ezk 34:12–15; 23–24).

What joy will the Bride know when, freed from her oppressors, she will sing again the verses expressing her happiness and peace near the Shepherd she found again, near her true David, her beloved prince: "Yahweh is my shepherd, I lack nothing. . . . To the waters of repose he leads me. . . . You prepare a table before me under the eyes of my enemies" (Ps 23). But without waiting any longer, I beg of you, answer me:

1:7 *where will you rest it* [your flock] *at noon?*

For in truth I am pining for that hour when the sun at its zenith will shine in its fullness, without any hint of decline. Then will end this day of clouds and darkness, the exhausting way of a "people that walked in darkness" (Is 9:1); then "your light will rise in the darkness" (Is 58:10).

Tell me, then, you whom my heart loves, where will you rest your flock at noon? This is the first and, in fact, the only question asked by the Bride to her Bridegroom in the entire Song. But is it not also the only question that man is asking? Is there for him another genuine expectation, in this life, than that of the Kingdom? Saint Bernard notes that it is also through a question, and indeed the same one, that the first disciples approach Christ: "Master," they asked him, "where do you live?" Not: "Where are you going?" or "What do you demand?" or "What are you teaching?" But: "Where do you live so that we can live always with you?" (cf. Jn 1:38). There is no other appeasement to our waiting.

What poignant tones will the Gregorian chant be able to give one day, in the liturgy for the dead, to the prayer of the Bride in the Song: *"Requiem aeternam dona eis, Domine, et lux perpetua luceat eis";* eternal rest in perpetual light!

The ardent aspiration of the Bride, who wants to join her Shepherd and rest with him at noon among his flocks, brings, as can be imagined, many commentaries from the Fathers. In these verses uttered by the Bride, they hear a long complaint of mankind exiled and divided, struggling in the night and lifting its eyes toward Jesus, the Good Shepherd, and toward the Kingdom of peace and pure light that he promised. More precisely, for Origen, noon is the time when God, dispelling at last the obscure night of the faith, unveils to the soul all the treasures of wisdom and knowledge, in a rest which is that of eternal contemplation. It is the time when the sun of justice, the Word-light, will be the only one to draw all eyes. The Bride does not aspire to anything else: "I do not seek, in truth," Origen has her say, "other times to pasture: evening or morning or sunset. But this is the only moment that I seek, when in the fire of the day you are revealed in the fullness of light, in your dazzling majesty. . . . If you do not tell me so, I will err here and there, and while looking for you, I will stumble on the flocks of other shepherds. Now I blush in the presence of others and veil my face because I am a very beautiful bride and I do not uncover my face for anyone but you whom I have loved for so long."[12]

As far as Saint Augustine is concerned, noon is the time when the incarnate Word, who has been hidden under the infirm flesh of his body, the sick flesh of his Church, radiates in his glory. "He pitched his tent in broad daylight, i.e., in full view of everybody. His tent is his flesh; his tent is his Church.

---

[12] Origen, *Homélies sur le Cantique des Cantiques,* Homily 1:8 (Paris: Cerf, 1966), 97.

It is pitched in broad daylight."[13] Noon is the time when Jesus is crucified in full view and, according to John's testimony, the time of his glory. "The hour [when] the Son of Man [is] glorified" (Jn 12:23). Such is also the time for which she who had been black longs in the night, "until my darkness", she says in Saint Augustine, "becomes the light of noon under your eyes."[14]

But the most beautiful analysis of the Bride's prayer is undoubtedly that of Saint Bernard in his thirty-third sermon on the Song. For Bernard, the entire history of the world is like a single day. Before the advent of Christ, there was darkness; the Incarnation was the dawn announcing the day; then came the sunrise of his hidden childhood, and later the day was still dark during his public life; the Resurrection saw the sun of glory rise and illumine the earth; but one must wait for the eternal Kingdom in order to contemplate the noon sun.

> I beg you, the Bride says, show me where you pasture your flock, where you rest at noon, i.e., the whole day, for this noon is a full day that does not know what evening is. And the day spent in your house is better than any other because it does not have any sunset, though perhaps the day had a morning, when this holy day illumined us for the first time through the merciful compassion of our God, who brought to us from on high the visit of the rising sun. Truly, Lord, we received your mercy in the midst of your Temple when, amid the shadows of death, the light of the morning rose for us, and we saw as early as the dawn the glory of the Lord. So many kings and prophets had wished to see it who did not see it, for it was still dark and the morning had not yet come with your promised mercy. . . . First there was a certain dawn on that day, when the sun of justice was announced to the earth by the archangel Gabriel and when a virgin conceived God in her womb. . . . The dawn lasted until the Lord himself appeared in his glory and talked to men. During that whole time, his light appeared to be rather weak, truly like that of dawn, so that most people did not know that the day had

---

[13] Saint Augustine, *Commentaire de la première épître de saint Jean* (cf. SC 75) (Paris: Cerf, 1966), 161.

[14] Saint Augustine, *Confessions*, Book X, 5(7); PL32, c. 782; CCL 27, 158.

started. . . . And the sun still hid its rays, not pouring them out on the earth yet. . . . The light was so wavering, so tiny, that it appeared more like a faraway dawn than like the presence of the sun. Yes, it was a dawn and quite a foggy one, all of Christ's life on earth, until having reached sunset, then sunrise again, the glory of his solar presence chased away the dawn and the night was swallowed up in the triumph of the morning. . . . For the first day of the week, very early, they came to the tomb as the sun had just risen. This was surely morning since the sun was rising; but it was especially luminous because the Resurrection gave it a particular radiance and a light that was purer than usual. . . . Dispelling then the mists of infirm flesh, he put on the stole of glory. Then the sun rose and little by little cast its rays on the earth, starting to manifest more clearly its light, more strongly its warmth. Let it increase its strength indefinitely, let it multiply and extend its radiance on the entire course of our mortal life—for it will be with us until the end of time; it will never attain the glory of noon; it will never be seen in this world in the fullness with which it will appear one day. . . . Then will it be really noon, immutable sun, perfect light, end of the shadows, drying up of the marshes, . . . eternal solstice in which the day will never set, illumination of noon, spring weather, charm of the summer, abundance of the fall and, to forget nothing, quiet and leisure of winter, unless you prefer winter never to come back. . . . Teach me, O you whom my heart loves, where is this place of light, peace and perfection so that my exalted spirit can see you in your absolute radiance, pasturing your flock in the richest meadows and enjoying a safe rest. . . . On this earth, the Shepherd tends his flock, but he cannot sate it; and he cannot rest since he must stand and watch because of the fears of the night. Here there is neither pure light, perfect rest, nor safe haven. For this reason, show me where you tend your flock and where you rest at noon. . . . What is my condition, in fact, when I compare it to the happiness of those who are filled with the goods of your house, sit at your table and rejoice in your sight? . . . All things, surely, are given here to me except perfection. . . . When then will you fulfill me by showing your face to me? It is your face, Lord, that I am seeking. Your face is my noon.

I know where you pasture your flock without resting; but tell me where you pasture it at rest. I even know where you lead your flock at the other hours of the day, but I would like to know where you keep it at noon. For at this time of my mortal life and in this place of my exile, I am accustomed to graze and to pasture others under your care, in the Law, in the prophets, in the psalms that tell about you, and also in the Gospel's pastures. I take my rest in the company of the apostles, and I often went begging a pittance for me and my own here and in the life of the saints, their writings, their words. But more often yet, for this was closer to me, I ate the bread of pain and drank the wine of affliction. My tears were my food day and night, while they repeated endlessly: Where is your God? In truth, at times, I was fed at your table for you had the goodness to set it for me in the presence of my foes. . . . I know therefore these pastures, and I went there often under your staff. . . . But, I beg you, teach me now what I do not know. . . . This is why I ask you where you rest at noon, i.e., in broad daylight, so that I will not err anymore and go astray with the wandering flocks of your companions. For they are vagabonds, having no certainty of truth, always trying to learn without ever attaining the knowledge of truth. . . .

Such are the words of the Bride.[15]

Words that are indeed lofty and sublime. Would we be lowering their tone by thinking that, in what the Bride will say later, one can discern a lesser purity of intention? For, if she longs for this rest, it is also, as she admits:

1:7 *That I may not wander like a vagabond*
    beside the flocks of your companions.

In the preceding verses, we had already heard her complaining that her mother's sons, in their rage against her, had put her in charge of their vineyard. This is the same idea, with the symbolism of the flock. The two themes of vineyard and flock are often used together in the Bible. Thus in the beautiful psalm (80) of pleading for the return: "Shepherd of Israel, listen, you

---

[15] Saint Bernard, *Sermons*, Sermon 33, 395ff.

who lead Joseph like a flock. . . . Bring us back. . . . There was a vine. . . . Why have you destroyed its fences? . . . Visit it, protect what your right hand has planted" (Ps 80: 1, 3, 8, 12, 14–15). Because she did not know how to guard her vineyard, Israel must work in the vineyards of her enemies; because she did not know how to remain in the flock of the good Shepherd, Israel is condemned to watch over their flocks. And the antithesis is painful between these two verses: "Where will you lead your flock to graze" (the flock of the good Shepherd) and "that I may not wander like a vagabond beside the flocks of your companions."

Errant and vagabond the Bride will remain as long as she does not return to her land and her home, to Mount Zion. Jeremiah, when he addresses Israel in exile, talks in the language of the Song: "How long will you hesitate, disloyal daughter?" (Jr 31:22). Israel, who was dragged into exile because of her infidelities, resembles perfectly—the image is striking and dramatic—an errant woman, a vagabond, a woman wandering far from her home. But today her only desire is to go back to the Shepherd, the Bridegroom, to him of whom Jeremiah says: "He who scattered Israel gathers him, he guards him as a shepherd guards his flock" (Jr 31:10).

Is it necessary to point out the identity of these companions from whom the Bride wants to get away? "The flocks of your companions", she says. They are obviously none other than the sinister mother's sons, of whom she spoke earlier. These are the foreign kings who oppress her, shepherds of their peoples just as Yahweh is of his own, and thus "his companions", his colleagues, as it were. For her infidelity to her good Shepherd, Israel-the-Bride is sentenced to serve the flocks of the shepherds of Babylon.

The very style of this whole passage attests to the wretched choice made by the Bride; the contrast is impressive between the stable images of happiness with Yahweh (pasturing flock, rest, noon) and the images of the exile's instability (to err, foreign flocks, vagabond). Let us stress again, in conclusion of this verse 7, that it offers an important testimony to the influence of prophetic literature on the Song. Yahweh—King, Shepherd and Bridegroom—has a vineyard and a flock: Israel. But the deceiving vineyard had to be removed and plucked out; the unfaithful flock had to be scattered. However, Israel will not always remain errant and in exile. One day, she will recover, with the return to her Shepherd, endless rest in the noon light of the Kingdom.

The Bride voiced her suffering and prayers. Now she is silent, and the daughters of Jerusalem, whom she had first addressed, respond to her:

1:8 *If you do not know this, O loveliest of women,*
   follow the tracks of the flock,
   and take your kids to graze
   close by the shepherds' tents.

The Bride was quite mistaken when she feared that the daughters of Jerusalem would deride her because of her complexion ("I am black but lovely, daughters of Jerusalem, . . . Take no notice of my swarthiness"). The daughters of Jerusalem do not show the slightest contempt for her. On the contrary, they find her "loveliest of women". There is in these words more than admiration: recognition that among all the nations of the earth, the Bride-Israel, even chastised by God and exiled, is the only one chosen by God and, for this reason, the loveliest among her companions. We already hear, in this first chorus of the Song, an echo of what God himself said to his beloved Israel in Ezekiel 16: "You grew more and more beautiful. . . . The fame of your beauty spread among the nations, since it was perfect" (Ezk 16:13–14).

It is however true that certain commentators, such as Father Bea, think that the "loveliest of women" seems to be said here (just as in 5:9 and 6:12) with a certain hint of irony by the daughters of Jerusalem *(ab eis dici videtur cum quadam ironia).*[16]

---

[16] Cardinal Augustin Bea, *Cantique des Cantiques,* v. I, 8 (Rome: Biblical Institute).

Agreed, you are the loveliest, but you must not exaggerate. Poor Bride, we are rather inclined to admire her too much!

But "O loveliest of women" what a strange question you are asking us! You ask us where your Bridegroom is resting at noon? How is it that you do not know this? And the chorus tells the Bride what she had told herself a hundred times: the place where Yahweh rests with you is the Holy Land; it is Jerusalem! Follow therefore the tracks of your flocks, for the way to follow is the reverse of the one you took when going into exile. And look, here on the ground, you can still see the footprints of your steps; Jerusalem is at the other end! The chorus speaks to the Bride with the same language that Jeremiah uses when he watches the departure of the exiles: "mark the road well," Jeremiah warns, "the way by which you went. Come home, virgin of Israel, come home to these towns of yours" (Jr 31:21).

Therefore, let the Bride prepare immediately to lead again her flocks, i.e., the children of her people who are like the kids of the mother ewe on the mountain of Zion. Let her go back, the chorus says, "close by the shepherds' tents", i.e., close to the very dwelling of the kings of Judah, Jerusalem. There she will regain her dignity, her freedom and her perfect beauty together with the Bridegroom. The chorus could not formulate a more explicit or more pressing invitation to this return and full conversion.

Now, suddenly, without the slightest preparation and for the first time, we hear the voice of the Bridegroom himself. Here he is answering the long invocation of his Bride:

1:9 *To my mare harnessed to Pharaoh's chariot*
     I compare you, my love.

1:10 *Your cheeks show fair between their pendants*
     and your neck within its necklaces.

1:11 *We shall make you golden earrings*
     and beads of silver.

Where does the Bridegroom come from? How did he suddenly appear? some are asking. In truth, this sudden appearance is quite in conformity with the entire biblical revelation, as is the spiritual experience of God's manifestation. "It is proper to the Creator", says Saint Ignatius Loyola, "to enter, to exit, to cause motions in the soul, drawing it whole into the love of his divine majesty. I say: without cause, without any feeling nor any previous knowledge of any object."[17] All through the Song, we see the Bridegroom appear and disappear in such an abrupt way, mysteriously, as Jesus does so often in the Gospel and in his relationships with us.

Though it must be said that the first words of the Bridegroom are even more surprising than the suddenness of his appearance: "To my mare harnessed to Pharaoh's chariot I compare you, my love." Would not the tenderness and delicacy of the Bridegroom enable him to find for his first love words—since these are love words, and they are indeed meant for his Bride—that would be more intimate or at least more human? "To my mare . . . I compare you".

One exegete exclaims: "In the idylls of the desert tent, the Bride is often compared to a mare, the royal desert mount, more supple and more vivacious than a horse. . . . [This is] a graceful image of style, a felicitous evocation, expressing in the oriental way the charm of the bride. . . . Besides which, the modern commentator believes himself entitled to add that the wonderful trappings that the desert men like to put as adornments on the heads of their mares are perfectly in tune with the jewels about the face of a woman."[18]

Let us say that there can be consideration and even reverence on the part of the Bridegroom when, from the outset, he compares his beloved to a mare! But is it really here a poetic image on the part of the Bridegroom, a mere evocation of the proud and graceful beauty of his beloved? One would have to admit

[17] Saint Ignatius Loyola, *Exercices spirituels,* Christrus no. 5 (Paris: Desclée de Brouwer, 1960), 174–175, no. 330.

[18] Denis Buzy, "Le Cantique des Cantiques", in Louis Pirot and Albert Clamer, *La Sainte Bible,* vol. 6 (Paris: Letouzey, 1943), 71.

that he does this in a strange way. Why, for instance, does he say "to my mare" and not "to a mare I compare you", as one would expect in an ordinary comparison? And why must it be said that this mare is harnessed to the chariots (and the word is plural in the text) of Pharaoh? The untamable pride, the nobility and the liberty of the mare that are so vaunted seem to be thus somewhat affected.

In fact, we are here in the context of Exodus, as Origen points out as early as 240 A.D. The chariots of Pharaoh and all his cavalry had been drowned in the Red Sea after having been overwhelmed by God's cavalry, God's "mare". Now the very same overwhelming superiority over her adversaries is promised today to Israel. Here is how Origen makes God, the Bridegroom of Israel, speak: "Just as in the past, in Egypt, when Pharaoh, pursuing my people Israel, was advancing on his chariot at the head of his cavalry, my own cavalry overtook him from afar, overcame him and threw him into the sea; thus today again you, my Bride, are superior to all women, equal to what I made of you in my cavalry, which, compared to that of Pharaoh, is infinitely stronger and more beautiful."[19] And, more explicitly perhaps, in his first homily on the Song, Origen comes back to the same interpretation of the passage: "Why did I compare you [my Bride] to my mare among the chariots of Pharaoh? Don't you know that the Bridegroom is a rider, as the prophet put it? Thus you are compared to my cavalry among the chariots of Pharaoh because just as my cavalry, that of the Lord, who throws into the waves Pharaoh and his captains, his riders, his horses and his chariots, shows itself superior to that of Pharaoh, so also are you superior to all women, you my Bride, you, O ecclesial soul, compared to all those who are not so."[20]

However, it seems that we should not limit ourselves to see in this passage of the Song the mere expression of the superiority in beauty and strength of God's mare to that of Pharaoh,

[19] Origen, *In Canticum Canticorum*, 129.
[20] Origen, *Homélies*, Homily 1: 10, 100–101.

for the beauty of the mare is still, at this point, disfigured and outraged. The face of the Bride who is exiled in Babylon can only sadly resemble her face when she was a captive in ancient Egypt, "harnessed to the chariots of Pharaoh", i.e., enslaved to all kinds of chores, laden with the chains and collars of work imposed on her by the Egyptian oppressors. The very plural "chariots" that we encounter here—and that would not make much sense for only one mare, one particular woman—is on the other hand quite understandable if the mare thus harnessed is the people of Israel, condemned to pull the chariots, just as they tend the vineyards of the Chaldeans.

But what is admirable in the eyes of the Bridegroom is that his beloved manages to remain beautiful even in chains and under the yoke of her slavery. "Your cheeks show fair between their pendants and your neck within its necklaces." Strange adornment, which the Bride manages to use as an enhancement for her beauty and a heart-moving device. It reminds us of the poem written by Brasillach in his prison and read by Pierre Fresnay: "And here I go, like a black king, adorned with my iron jewels."[21]

Now, instead of the iron rings, necklaces and armlets that are still holding her captive, the Bridegroom is going to place rings and necklaces that will be at the ears and neck of his beloved pure jewels of gold and silver: like those I had once given to you, do you remember? How beautiful you were then, when as a young Bride you were fulfilled and covered with jewels by your Bridegroom: "I loaded you with jewels, gave you bracelets for your wrists and a necklace for your throat. I gave you rings for your nose and ears; I put a beautiful diadem on your head. You were loaded with gold and silver" (Ezk 16:11–13). Well, what you are going to get now will be even more wonderful!

[21] Robert Brasillach was a hero of the French Resistance during the Nazi occupation of World War II. Pierre Fresnay was one of the greatest French actors of the French theater and movies during and after the same period.—Trans.

We are reminded of the return of the prodigal son. It is almost the language that Jesus puts on the lips of the father, who is overwhelmed at the sight of his son's rags and replaces them immediately with festive robes: "Quick!" he said. "Bring out the best robe and put it on him; put a ring on his finger [the ring of the covenant!] and sandals on his feet" (Lk 15:22). What a kinship between the song of Jesus and the song of the Bridegroom in our text!

All the very ingenious and poetic subtlety of our passage lies therefore in this: the very same image is used on three different planes. Its features apply at the same time to a mare, a captive woman in exile, and a beloved Bride. Necklaces, rings and earrings (in the very literal translation of Father Bea) are at the same time the harness of a mare, the irons of a captive, and the jewels worn by the Bride at her neck, nose and ears. These words do indeed apply very well to all three dimensions of the image. Lastly, the very word *mare* seems very judiciously chosen since it depicts a noble, free and proud animal with a beautiful stance but also because of the rings, the necklace and the buckles that attach her, the condition of servitude of the Bride kept by force and "harnessed to Pharaoh's chariot", while the use of the possessive "my mare" suggests with what love the bride is loved, more than ever.

And in the last verses we see the very insignia of servitude being transformed into the jewels of the covenant.

1:11 *We shall make you golden earrings*
and beads of silver.

Yahweh says in Psalm 81: "I . . . relieved your shoulder of the burden, your hands could drop the laborer's basket; you called in your trouble, so I rescued you" (Ps 81:6–7). And we also read in Isaiah: "For the yoke that was weighing on him, the bar across his shoulders, the rod of his oppressor, these you break as on the day of Midian" (Is 9:3). The vision of the Song's author goes further. Yoke and collar are not exchanged here. Nor are jewels substituted for them later. The very instruments of servitude become adornments of beauty. And to her who was a harnessed mare the Bridegroom now gives for the first time her real name: "my love".

This name is given to each of us, no matter how pathetic our failures. There is no servitude that lasts forever. "The almighty, the all powerful," writes Isaac of Stella, "having taken a feeble and insignificant bride, made a queen out of that servant, . . . and she who was crouching at his feet, he took and placed next to himself."[22]

No matter how low we fall, the marks of our sins, the irons and the shackles that entrapped us, can be changed through the grace of the merciful Love into the jewels of the covenant. And out of our very scars, God creates our beauty. The sin is not only forgotten or "blotted out" as people say at times; it is forgiven, i.e., it becomes a theme of celebration of merciful Love. John of the Cross says: "The wounds coming from another cause (i.e., our sins) become then wounds of love."[23]

The whole Trinity is at work in this metamorphosis. "We shall make you golden earrings", the Bridegroom says (not "I will make you"). This "we" is in fact the three Persons of the Holy Trinity speaking; they are at work in the transfiguration of the Bride as had been the case on the first day of her creation: "Let us make man", they had said. The Bride, in order to be so unfairly fulfilled, to experience such a wonderful thing, must only have humility in response to the munificence of the Bridegroom. Nothing else is required, as Thérèse of Lisieux understands while meditating on these "beads of silver" that the Bridegroom inlays on the golden jewels. She confides to Mary of the Trinity: " 'One day I was particularly struck during my prayer by this passage in which the Bridegroom tells his beloved: we will make you golden chains with silver beads. What

---

[22] Isaac Stella, Sermon XI; PL 194, 1728C.

[23] Saint John of the Cross, *Vive flamme d'amour*, Stanza II, *Oeuvres complètes*, Bibliothèque européenne (Paris: Desclée de Brouwer, 1958), 743.

a strange thing', she told me! 'We could understand it if the Bridegroom were to say: we will make you silver necklaces inlaid with gold or golden necklaces inlaid with precious stones; for generally one does not adorn a precious jewel with an inferior metal. Jesus gave me the key to the mystery. He made me understand that the gold necklaces were love, charity, but that these gold necklaces were not pleasing to him unless they were adorned with silver, that is, with simplicity and the spirit of childhood. Oh!', she added, very moved, 'who could tell the value God finds in this simplicity since it alone is considered worthy of enhancing the radiance of charity?' "[24]

To the long complaint, the long desire, the long wait of the Bride, the Bridegroom has thus responded. But, as Gregory of Nyssa notes here, "instead of accomplishing this first arrival in a frightening fire, consuming the mountain from top to bottom, his attitude is on the contrary full of sweetness and graciousness for the joy of the Bride."[25] His first words were only those of compassion and admiration. But now that the two of them are together for the first time, there is such a wonder of love, of happiness in both of them, that they surrender together in an endless celebration of their love.

The Bride starts the song:

1:12 — *While the King rests in his own room*
my nard yields its perfume.

The first name she gives to the Bridegroom, now that he is present, is not: "O you whom my heart loves" but "the King". She does not yet dare to call him beloved, as Saint Bernard notes: "She will call him 'my beloved' as early as the next verse; but she starts her song with respect, veneration and a

---

[24] "Carnet rouge" of Mary of the Trinity, no. 16–22 of the Testimony at the Beatification Trial of Thérèse of the Child Jesus; cf. *La Bible avec Thérèse de Lisieux* (Paris: Cerf/Desclée de Brouwer, 1979), 107–116.

[25] Saint Gregory of Nyssa, *In Canticum Canticorum*, Homily 3, 809A.

humble awareness of herself."[26] The one she loves is for her, first of all, the King of majesty, whom she adores.

It is equally significant that each time the Bride calls her beloved "King", it is in reference to the Temple, the house where he dwells within her. "The King has brought me into his rooms", she had said at the beginning (1:4). "While the King rests in his own room", she says now. The two expressions are parallel. "Rooms" and "room" are both used to mean the Temple.

What the French version of the Jerusalem Bible translates as "enclosure" can be rendered in several other possible ways. But all the translations suggested for the Hebrew *masseb* have this in common: they refer to a round space, an enclosure, a round room, a round banquet hall and, by extension, the banquet itself; or else, if we follow the Latin Vulgate, the sofa on which the guests are seated in a circle: *Dum esset Rex in accubitu suo* (*accubitus*: sofa, bed of the Bridegroom).

It can therefore be understood why the French version chose to translate *masseb* as enclosure. The King, who is Yahweh himself, resides now in Jerusalem in the midst of his people, in the midst of a city surrounded by hills ("Jerusalem! Encircled by mountains"—Ps 125); Yahweh the King is in the very enclosure of the Temple (very clearly called *masseb* in 2 Samuel 23:5). And the Bride wonders at finding herself together with him, in the intimacy of their common dwelling, within the walls that surround her and protect their home.

The translation is all the more felicitous in that "enclosure" can also be understood as "sheepfold". Thus Jesus says in John, "And there are other sheep I have that are not of this fold" (Jn 10:16). But in the last analysis, whether one translates the word *masseb* as enclosure or sofa or banquet, the meaning is not fundamentally different, and all these various connotations have to be retained. What matters is the idea, the feeling, that the Bride has: wherever she is, she is now always wrapped in the

---

[26] Saint Bernard, *Sermons*, Sermon 42, 466.

protective tenderness of the Bridegroom and totally surrendered to him. "The time has come now", Paul Claudel writes,
"for possession. In this embrace of the Bridegroom between
the arms of the Bride that the Latin expresses with the word
accubitu, I see someone lying or huddling or, in the ancient
fashion, reclining at a table: . . . *Dum esset Rex in accubitu suo*.
This is how he takes possession of a soul; this is how he seizes
this prey created by his own hands to teach her love through
his touch."[27]

To her King, whom she contemplates now in the Temple,
seated with her at the banquet of their wedding and greeting her on the sofa of his rest for their definitive marriage,
the Bride offers her nard: "my nard", she says, "yields its
perfume."

The nard that belongs most specially to the Bride and that
we will encounter a second time in the third poem (4:14) was a
very costly perfume, extracted from a plant originating in India whose fragrance was exquisite. "My nard", says the Bride.
She might as well say: my life! For this is in fact her whole being, the very essence of her being that is poured out at the feet
of the King. To her King, who has just called her "my love"
and has promised to cover her with gold and silver jewelry, she
does not respond with words of gratitude. Her first and genuine response can be given fully only by her life: my nard, myself, my life, silently and lovingly poured like nard spilling out
of a broken vase; what other response can I give you? "Just as
cassia must be broken to yield its perfume", Malraux writes,
paraphrasing a Shakespearean verse. And quite close to the
Bride of the Song, Thérèse of Lisieux writes:

> To love you, Jesus, what a fecund loss!
> All my perfumes are yours forever.[28]

---

[27] Paul Claudel, *Paul Claudel interroge le Cantique des Cantiques* (Paris: NRF-
Gallimard, 1948), 41.

[28] Saint Thérèse of the Child Jesus, "Vivre d'amour", *Poésies* (Paris: Cerf/
Desclée de Brouwer, 1979), 99.

It is impossible here not to bring to mind, following Origen—though did not Saint John already think about this?—Mary of Bethany pouring on Jesus' feet a very costly ointment (Jn 12:3). This is the only time such a word is found in the New Testament, and it is quite likely from the Song, since the scenes are so close to each other. Mary poured out her perfume as a sign of her life surrendered to the one who would soon surrender his life for her. "The house", it is written, "was full of the scent of the ointment." The whole house, the whole Church, the whole world were penetrated with the perfume of Mary, as had been Jerusalem and the Temple, "the whole enclosure of God", with the nard of the Bride. "In the house that was filled with the fragrance of the perfume, the Lord does indeed teach us", says Gregory of Nyssa, "to see the whole world and the whole earth: since it is said that wherever this Gospel would be proclaimed (Mt 26:13), the fragrance of the perfume would be poured out together with the proclamation of the Gospel."[29]

Meditating at the same time on the gesture of the Bride in the Song and on that of Mary of Bethany, her younger sister, Saint Bernard sees the nard poured by both of them in a surrender and offering of their whole being at the feet of the beloved as the symbol of humility united to love; "loving humility", as Saint Ignatius Loyola writes in his Spiritual Diary, i.e., the mingling of humility with the tenderness that is proper to a great love. "These words, 'my nard yields its perfume', do not mean anything else", writes Saint Bernard, "than that my humility was rewarded with grace! Not my wisdom, my nobility, my beauty because they were nothing in me; but the only thing I had, humility, yielded its customary perfume. . . . Thus the King, when he was resting in his room, i.e., in his high chamber, felt the perfume rising up to him while he was resting in the bosom of the Father. For the

---

[29] Saint Gregory of Nyssa, *In Canticum Canticorum*, Homily 3, 825B.

Son is always in the Father, taking his rest in the inn of paternal mercy."[30]

In his commentary on the Song, Claudel writes a passage of extraordinary intensity to describe this gift of the soul that surrenders, breaks up and is poured out like a perfume in God's embrace: "In this embrace, under this strong, patient, penetrating, intelligent demand, the soul feels itself surrendering and dilating little by little, and its intimate essence, so long repressed, compressed and hardened, is unfolded and breathed out. . . . My nard, she says, that which is in me the most intimate, the most personal, I was about to say the most animal, that which enables the animals themselves to identify one another, the testimony that my very self gives spontaneously through the means of this vital spirit torn away from my flesh. Here I am, says the Bride, in the arms of the one I love in an odor of sacrifice. And the house was filled with the scent of the ointment."[31]

As soon as the Bride says "my nard yields its perfume", she forgets herself and seems to have no attention or breath except for the perfume—infinitely stronger and more penetrating than hers—yielded by the Bridegroom:

1:13 *My Beloved is a sachet of myrrh*
lying between my breasts.

1:14 *My Beloved is a cluster of henna flowers*
among the vines of Engedi.

Just a moment ago, she was calling her Bridegroom "the King": "While the King rests in his own room". She calls him now "my beloved", *dodi,* a word significantly made of the same consonants as the name of David. Thus the name of the

---

[30] Saint Bernard, *Sermons,* Sermon 42, 474–475.
[31] Claudel, *Paul Claudel,* 42.

beloved on the lips of the Bride suggests by itself that the prince of her heart is the true messianic King awaited and desired by a whole nation. This is the first time she gives him this name, which is used twenty-eight times in the Song. She had said, more discreetly and indirectly (1:7), "you whom my heart loves"; more daringly and freely, she calls him now "my beloved" (*dod, dodi*) and will not call him otherwise. The expression had appeared once in Isaiah, and indeed the precision was suggestive, in the overture to the famous song of the vineyard: "My friend (*dodi*) had a vineyard" (Is 5:1). The Bride of the Song joyfully adopts the name, and her King lets himself, obviously happily so, be called by her by this little pet name that is also his long before he reveals in Saint John that his full name is love.

And, as she had said that the King was in his enclosure, the Bride now adds, more intimately and also more daringly, that her beloved rests between her breasts. Her heart is thus the true dwelling of her Bridegroom. Saint Bernard notes very well this daring passage: "Before," he says, "he was a King, and now the beloved; he rested in his royal dwelling ['his enclosure'], and here he is between the breasts of his bride. . . . The respectful address gives way to a friendly name, and he who was far away took only a moment to come closer."[32] We thus pass, in one gesture as it were, from the language of humble and profound adoration to that of simple familiarity in a way that is natural and dear to contemplate: adored Lord and Bridegroom who is simply loved very much.

We see Origen entering into a profound admiration for this verse of the Song: " 'My Beloved is a sachet of myrrh lying between my breasts.' He made of my breast the house in which he rests. . . .[33] The King takes his rest in this soul. . . . He is pleased with lying there and resting. It was to her that he had

[32] Saint Bernard, *Sermons*, Sermon 43, 477.
[33] Origen, *In Canticum Canticorum*, 142.

said: 'My Father and I will come; we will have supper with him and will make our dwelling in him.' Where Christ rests with the Father, where he lives, can he not always rest also? Happy spaces that contain this soul! Happy room, this heart where the Father, the Son and of course the Holy Spirit, take their rest; where they have supper and make their dwelling."[34]

"My Beloved is a sachet of myrrh". Myrrh is a kind of gum, a resin secreted by a plant, and is very sought after because its perfume is spellbinding, penetrating, dizzying even. Myrrh symbolizes the attraction of the Bridegroom just as nard in the preceding verse symbolized that of the Bride. In Psalm 45, it is also said of the Bridegroom that "myrrh and aloes waft from your robes" (Ps 45:8). But the robes of the Bridegroom are not the only ones to be filled with this perfume. He himself is the essence of the perfume, the sachet of myrrh. "You exhaled your perfume", Saint Augustine says in his *Confessions*; "I breathed it in, and now I sigh for you."[35]

Was the author of the Song, in writing of the Bridegroom that he is a sachet of myrrh between the breasts of the bride, remembering what Isaiah had said about the sachets or scent boxes that the beautiful women of those days adroitly hid in their garments (Is 3:18–23)?

This is what Gregory of Nyssa thinks, and he draws from this a magnificent extrapolation: "It is said that worldly women . . . take perfumes that they hide in the folds of their garments. This is something similar to what the noble young woman dares to do in the Song. I have a sachet, she says, that I hang from my neck on my breasts and with which I perfume my whole body, . . . not just simply any of the spices that produce a pleasant fragrance, but the Lord himself, who has become myrrh in the sachet of my conscience and dwells in my very heart."[36]

[34] Ibid., 138–139.
[35] Saint Augustine, *Confessions*, Book X, 27(38); PL 32, 795; CCL 27, 175.
[36] Saint Gregory of Nyssa, *In Canticum Canticorum*, Homily 3, 825D–828A.

And in truth the Bridegroom dwells nowhere else but in the depth of his Bride's heart. Constantly breathed in, rising up from her breast and, as it were, mixed with her own breath, he is the secret radiance of her whom he loves. We read in Gertrude of Helfta, a Cistercian mystic of the thirteenth century, that one night, seizing her crucifix and pressing it tenderly against her heart, she said, "My beloved is for me a bouquet of myrrh", and in her heart a voice responded, "He will rest on my breast."[37]

In the Book of Hosea, Yahweh had said brutally to his unfaithful wife: "Let her rid . . . her breasts of her adultery" (Ho 2:4). Isn't the beloved of the Song, brought back to her Bridegroom, using here the language of fidelity instead of her formerly erring heart, when she sacrificed to her lovers, to her idols? Between her breasts, at the heart of her life, there are no more adulteries. From now on, there is only her God and his love breathed in day and night.

We can assuredly add with the Jerusalem Bible that the Bride, when she says "between my breasts", is also thinking about the presence of Yahweh in the midst of his city, between the hills of Zion, in this Temple where the fragrance of the offerings and sacrifices rises again toward him from the heart of the city. All the more so since one can stress the symmetry between "the King rests in his own enclosure [or room]" (that is precisely Jerusalem and the Temple) of verse 12 and "my beloved is . . . lying between my breasts" of verse 13. Let us simply say that we have in these words, "between my breasts", a striking phrase, with a thousand harmonies of the *Deus interior intimo meo* ("God who is more interior to me than my deepest self") of Saint Augustine. The Bride asked where the Bridegroom led his flock to the noon rest (1:7). And here she is, daring to give the answer herself: the rest of the Bridegroom is in me, between my breasts, his true temple, his real enclosure.

[37] Saint Gertrude of Helfta, "Le héraut de l'amour divin", III, XLII, *Oeuvres spirituelles* (cf. SC 143) (Paris: Cerf, 1968), 193.

For Saint Bernard, the bouquet of myrrh (he uses the word "bouquet" for what we call "sachet") represents more particularly Jesus in his life on earth. Jesus who was poor, despised and suffering (this is evoked by the slight bitterness connected to the penetrating fragrance of myrrh). Jesus in the very bitter distress of his Passion especially, which was constantly in Saint Bernard's mind: "From the start of my conversion . . . I did take care to hold against my heart this bouquet composed of all the sufferings of the Lord. I first put in it the poverty of his childhood; the fatigue of his preaching and long walks; his temptations during the fast; his tears of compassion; the nights of vigil and prayers; the traps of his hecklers; and, at last, the dangers of the false brothers, the insults, the spittle, the slaps, the mockery, the nails and so many other sufferings that the forest of the Gospel, as you well know, grew for the salvation of the human race. Among my branches of fragrant myrrh, I took good care not to forget that myrrh he was given to drink on the Cross or that which was used to anoint his body before the burial. . . . My entire high philosophy today consists in fact in knowing who Jesus is and that he was crucified. Therefore I do not ask, as the Bride does, where he rests at noon since I crush him joyfully against my heart. I do not seek to know where he pastures his flock, for I see him, my Savior, on the Cross. To know him at noon is certainly more sublime; to hold him against my heart is sweeter. . . . That is why he will stay on my heart."[38]

The meditation of Saint Bernard refuses to consider Jesus only in his glory, in the dazzling rest of his noon. His tenderness demands a constant return to the simple earthly face of Jesus, to the holy face. Teresa of Avila writes in her autobiography that "Saint Bernard was delighted by the humanity of Jesus." We have just seen that. And Teresa adds: "We too must enter into ourselves through this door if we want the sovereign majesty to reveal great secrets to us. . . . One must not look

for another way, even if we are at the height of contemplation."[39] What a deep wisdom on the part of the Madre!
She always distrusted very much the so-called sublime ways
that claim to lead to God without the mediation of the humble,
poor and suffering humanity of Jesus. Following in her footsteps, Thérèse of the Child Jesus always prefers the myrrh of
the beloved to all other perfumes. She draws strength, she confides, from its very bitterness: "The hill of myrrh strengthened
us through its bitter fragrances."

To myrrh the Bride of the Song adds henna:

1:14 *My Beloved is a cluster of henna flowers*
     among the vines of Engedi.

Now that she dares to say it a first time, how happily she repeats it, this name "beloved"! But can she express what he is
for her soul? There are no words for this! One needs all the subtlety of the perfumes. Only the intangible nature of the perfumes can evoke the elusive beloved. Therefore, attempting
always to express the same penetrating intoxication, she adds:
"My Beloved is a cluster of henna flowers among the vines of
Engedi." According to Father Abel, "The yellow and white
flowers of henna, gathered in a bunch (which enables one to
compare them to clusters), give off an extremely strong, sweet
and penetrating perfume."[40] The Bride is clearly on the look-
out for the headiest perfumes, the most spellbinding ones:
nard, myrrh, henna of Engedi.

Engedi is a small town on the west side of the Dead Sea and
is mentioned in the Book of Joshua in its description of the
Holy Land (Jos 15:62). "In the midst of an amphitheater of
jagged rocks," Father Abel writes, "Engedi is accessible only

---

[39] Saint Teresa of Avila, *Autobiographie*, 22:7, *Oeuvres complètes*, Bibliothèque européenne (Paris: Desclée de Brouwer, 1964), 150.

[40] Pére Marie-Félix Abel, *Une croisière autour de la Mer Morte*, 1911, 140–142;
quoted by André Robert and Raymond Tournay, *Le Cantique des Cantiques*
(Paris: Gabalda, 1963), 90.

to the goats; it is a charming and true oasis of greenery and water as the name suggests ('source of the kid')."[41] Once again, the themes of the vineyard and the flock are evoked together. The Bridegroom is now settled at the center of his vineyard, as he is in his enclosure among his flock. He is, in the heart of his beloved Bride, source and perfume all together: henna in the vines of Engedi, at the source of the goat kids.

This interpretation is confirmed by the very structure of the stanza. The parallel is indeed clear, on the one hand, between "my Beloved is a sachet of myrrh" and "my Beloved is a cluster of henna flowers" as it is also between "lying between my breasts" and "among the vines of Engedi." "Between my breasts" and "among the vines of Engedi" both refer to the soul of the Bride, which has become the dwelling of her beloved.

In the exchange between the two lovers, she had the first stanza, one made up entirely of perfumes—myrrh and henna; the Bride is herself pure perfume. Yet she had thought, in all good faith, that the nard she yielded was her own. She discovers that in fact her perfume is his and only his. "While the King rests in his own room"—such then was the source of the unutterable perfume she yielded! The nard of her love draws its aroma solely from the gift made by the Bridegroom, as Origen understands so profoundly: "The Bride is now with the Bridegroom, and she anoints him with her perfumes. And what a surprise for her: the nard, which earlier had no fragrance when it was in her sole possession, starts now to give off a fragrance after having touched the body of the Bridegroom to the extent that it is not so much the Bridegroom, one could say, who was perfumed by the nard but rather the nard by the Bridegroom. . . . And it is from the perfume of the Bridegroom that the nard then gives its fragrance to the Bride when she says: "my nard yields its perfume." It is as if she were saying: my nard, with which I anointed my Bridegroom, now

41 Ibid., 140–142.

comes back to me, bringing in itself the fragrance of my Bridegroom. . . . And there is no reason to be surprised that Christ, who is at the same time a source—from him comes the living water—and bread—he gives life—is also nard and therefore gives perfume. And this nard makes those who have been anointed with it one with Christ."[42]

"Indeed, we cannot love you", as William of Saint-Thierry puts it, "unless this love come from you. . . . You were the first to love us and the first to love those who love you. But we love you with the ardent love you put in us, . . . and your love is the Holy Spirit."[43] As Saint Paul writes to the Romans: "the love of God has been poured into our hearts by the Holy Spirit which has been given us" (Rm 5:5).

At the feet of her beloved King, the bride lets her soul breathe freely. She has not yet said anything directly to him since he is present. He is the one who has to open their first dialogue of love. Rather than dialogue, one should speak of a duet since the two voices that are now rising respond to each other only to sing the same song.

1:15 —*How beautiful you are, my love,*
how beautiful you are!
Your eyes are doves.

1:16 —*How beautiful you are, my Beloved,*
and how delightful!

The same theme on either side. How could it surprise us? "If there are two lutes that have the same sound and chord, one next to the other," Saint Francis de Sales writes, "and if one plays on one of the two instruments, the other, even if untouched, will still ring like the one on which one is playing: the harmony between them, as if through natural love, creates this

---

[42] Origen, *In Canticum Canticorum*, 140–141.

[43] William of Saint-Thierry, *Traité de la contemplation de Dieu* (cf. SC 61bis) (Paris: Cerf, 1968), 90–97.

agreement."[44] Saint Augustine had already said, pointing more clearly to the true author of this harmony, "If two flutes filled with the same breath are in harmony, how could there be a dissonance between two voices filled with the same Spirit of God?"[45]

Two lutes, two flutes! Is it not quite striking that in this love song of our text not a single musical instrument is heard? None of those instruments that have such an important role in the psalms for instance. Neither the zither, flute, lute, trumpet, tambourine, cymbals nor harp of Psalm 150 is heard or even mentioned. Here, in fact, all the music is in the voices, in the two united voices of the beloved and his love. As if all the music in the world were called to blend in a beautiful concerto for two voices: the voice of the Word calling and man's voice responding to him through creation. It has been said about Bach's concerto for two violins that "it was the ascent of two penetrating melodies, seeking each other and finally mingling together like two souls united at the peak" (Bernard Gavoty). Thus it is also, but on a higher note yet, that the two united souls of the Bridegroom and his love communicate and praise each other.

William of Saint-Thierry, abbot of Signy in the Ardennes and a friend of Saint Bernard, deeply feels this mutual enchantment: "The Bride hears herself being called beautiful, and again beautiful, and loved; the Bridegroom is called beautiful and delightful and beloved. . . . Mingling together, enchanted with each other, praising each other in a tender concert, in harmony, in a familiar colloquy, the Bridegroom and the Bride are now savoring in anticipation the joy of mutual possession."[46]

What fascinates them both at first, one and the other, one in the other, is their beauty. This is the first word springing from

[44] Saint Francis de Sales, *Traité*, 715.

[45] Saint Augustine, *Commentaire*, 389.

[46] William of Saint-Thierry, *Exposé sur le Cantique des Cantiques* (Paris: Cerf, 1966), 215.

their lips in this first dialogue: "How beautiful you are . . .
how beautiful you are!"

1:15 —*How beautiful you are, my love,*
      how beautiful you are!
      Your eyes are doves.

Or, more literally, "Here you are. Oh you are beautiful, my
love!" This "here you are" is more than just an exclamation. It
is a cry. On the lips of the beloved, it is, as it were, an echo of
the cry of love and admiration of the first man facing the first
woman born from him: "This at last is bone from my bones,
and flesh from my flesh; this is to be called woman", the first
Adam had said. "Here you are, you are beautiful", says the
Bridegroom, the new Adam. And this repetition by the Bridegroom of this "how beautiful you are" bears witness to the
kind of trance that overcomes him when he sees the Bride. "To
be sure, these are not empty repetitions", Saint Bernard
writes, "but a confirmation of love."[47]

Let us say that the frequent repetitions of the Poem are one
of the beauties of the Song. The Song is said again and again,
as one likes to play Mozart repeatedly. The beautiful theme
begs to be heard again for the pleasure of the ear and the encore
is enchanting, spellbinding. Thus love is always returning to
the same tunes. Fifteen times, like here, the Bride will be told
that she is beautiful and nine of these by the Bridegroom himself as an echo to the word he had uttered on the sixth day of
creation, when man emerged so handsomely from his hands:
"God saw [that] it was very good" (Gn 1:31). "The Song",
notes Father Urs von Balthasar, "is the book of the Bible in
which the adjective *beautiful, yafe,* is used the most frequently
to describe human appearance."[48] And God is the first one to
wonder at and be caught by the human being's beauty. We are

[47] Saint Bernard, *Sermons,* Sermon 45, 489.
[48] Hans Urs von Balthasar, *La gloire et la croix,* vol. 3 (Paris: Aubier, 1974),
489.

totally overwhelmed and say with the psalmist, "What is man
that you should spare a thought for him?" (Ps 8:4). But God
answers with these words that Gregory of Nyssa puts in his
mouth: "You came to me. . . . Therefore you became beautiful, changed as it were into my own image through some kind
of mirror. . . . You became beautiful as soon as you approached my light, drawing to yourself, through this very approach, a share in my beauty."[49] And, as an echo of these
words, Saint Catherine of Siena says in her Dialogues, when
she hears the Lord confiding to her inner soul, "When I created
[man], . . . I looked into myself and was seized with love for
the beauty of my creature."[50]

To the one whose beauty ravishes him, the Bridegroom
gives the name "my friend" (Hebrew ra'eyah, ra'eyati). If the
Bride, when she addresses the Bridegroom directly, calls him
always and only "my Beloved"—he has only one name because he is unique; he has only one name because he is Love—
the Bridegroom, on the other hand, gives to her whom he
loves thirty-two different names, to be precise! What is strange
is that among these names, one does not find "beloved". The
word ra'eyah translated generally as "beloved" should be more
precisely rendered as "friend" or "companion". But the word
dod does not have a feminine counterpart, at least in the Hebrew of the Song; it is a word reserved for the Bridegroom.
From poem to poem, however, the name of "friend" will take
on a more and more profound and singular resonance.

The glory of the friend's beauty seems to come from the
eyes. This first time, the Bridegroom is attracted only by her
eyes, source of light, life and transparency of the soul, mirrors
of intelligence and radiance of the beloved's whole being. Will
not Jesus say one day: "The lamp of your body is your eye.
When your eye is sound, your whole body too is filled with
light" (Lk 11:34)? It is also the light, gestures and life in the

[49] Saint Gregory of Nyssa, *In Canticum Canticorum*, Homily 4, 834B.
[50] Saint Catherine of Siena, *Le dialogue*, tran. Hurtaud, Dialogue 167 on
Providence (Paris: Téqui, 1976), 328ff.

look of the Bride that charm the Bridegroom of the Song. "Your eyes", he says, "are doves." This is not a comparison. The Bridegroom does not say, "Your eyes are like doves." But "your eyes are doves": vivacious, agile and pure doves. Yes, your eyes have the simplicity, the innocence, the purity, the grace, the shimmering mobility of doves at play.

Truth to tell, Israel in exile had been compared, especially by Hosea, to a bird: "they will come speeding from Egypt like a bird" (Ho 11:11). However, it was not always to the glory of Israel. Perhaps the word *candid* would, in the biblical tradition, be the one that applies best to Israel the dove! *Candid,* a word whose meaning is quite ambiguous because it can signify at the same time naiveté, as in Ho 7:11, when God says that Israel is like a silly, witless dove, or purity and faithfulness, and this is always the meaning it has in the Song. The ambivalence of the dove symbol appears also in Jonah (Jonah means dove in Hebrew), who represents Israel as first rebelling, then being faithful to her prophetic mission. Lastly, as is the case in all civilizations, the dove is a symbol of peace, as in the dove bringing an olive branch after the punishment of the flood — peace found anew in regained fidelity. Stanza XXXIV of Saint John of the Cross' Spiritual Canticle thus paraphrases our text when it reads: "The white dove returned to the ark with its branch. It is over! The turtledove has joined her dear companion on the green riverbank."[51]

As could have been foreseen, Origen, in his great commentary, is attracted by the dove. He immediately thinks about the Holy Spirit, who, during Jesus' baptism, manifests himself in the form of a dove. If the Bride is so beautiful, it is because she now possesses the Holy Spirit, whose love enlightens the eyes of her intelligence and of her heart. Therefore, she in her turn can exclaim now that she has new eyes, eyes capable of discerning the beauty of Christ: "How beautiful you are, my Beloved". The beauty of the beloved, foreshadowed by the

---

[51] Saint John of the Cross, *Cantique spirituel, Stanza XXXIV,* 663.

fragrance of his perfumes, is now emerging from its darkness, and, thanks to her new eyes, the Bride discovers it with wonder: "How beautiful you are, my Beloved". If, indeed, no one can say "Jesus is Lord" except in the Holy Spirit, as Saint Paul affirms (I Co 12:3), who could say to God, "How beautiful you are, my Beloved" if not also in the Holy Spirit? If his eyes were not doves like those of the Bride in the Song? Here is what Origen writes:

> The Bridegroom now proclaims that she is beautiful, and beautiful not only as she was before among women because, he adds without explanation and in an absolute way, "Here you are, you are beautiful!" But if until now he had not praised her face, I think it was because she did not yet possess the look of spiritual intelligence. However, now he tells her: "Your eyes are doves." . . . It is as if he were telling her, "Your eyes are spirit because they see spiritually, they understand spiritually", . . . which explains that now, as if it were for the first time, the Bride seems to consider attentively the beauty of her Bridegroom because the eyes with which she sees him now are dove eyes. Now she sees the beauty and the splendor of the Word of God because it is not possible to discern and recognize the magnificence of the Word without having first received dove eyes, i.e., spiritual intelligence. . . . Indeed, those who are content with believing in the Bridegroom but who are not yet able to discern how great the beauty of God's Word is are saying: "Without beauty, without majesty [we saw him], no looks to attract our eyes" (Is 53:2). On the other hand, she whose beauty has increased to the extent that she is the greatest among all the other maidens . . . can truly say: "How beautiful you are, my Beloved, and how delightful!"[52]

To analyze in a somewhat didactic way this great passage of Origen, we will say that there are four essential features of the Bride's beauty.

First of all, it is not her creation, it is the creation of the Bridegroom. "Here you are, you are beautiful!" Such a word

---

[52] Origen, *In Canticum Canticorum*, 145–147.

is indeed creative, a sacramental word, creating beauty. Saint Augustine understands it: "What then is this love that makes the loving soul beautiful? God, who is always beautiful, who never loses his beauty, who never changes: he loved us first, he who is always beautiful. And what were we when he loved us if not ugly and disfigured? But he did not love us to leave us to our ugliness but to change us and, disfigured as we were, to make us beautiful. How then can we become beautiful? By loving the one who is eternally beautiful. The greater the love in you, the greater your beauty."[53]

More precisely, the beauty of the Bride is made of that of her Bridegroom. "Freed from her carnal passions," Saint Gregory of Nyssa says, "the soul, now living in the Spirit, receives the testimony that she is, in his eyes, the image of a dove."[54] The exact symmetry of the two sentences, carbon copies of each other as it were—"How beautiful you are. . . . How beautiful you are, my Beloved"—expresses already in itself the kinship of the two faces: "your God will be your splendor" (Is 60:19).

The Bride receives the revelation of her beauty only in the eyes of the one she loves. She knows that she is beautiful only through him, only through this "how beautiful you are!" that he is the first to utter.

Lastly, she herself could not say, "O you, how beautiful you are" (which indeed she had not yet said; the word beauty appears for the first time in the Song on the lips of the Bridegroom) had he not given her eyes, his own eyes, the eyes of the dove of the Holy Spirit. Just as she could not yield her perfume before having received it from him, she cannot wonder about his beauty until he has given her his own eyes.

Like the Bride of the Song, the young Carmelite novice Françoise de Sandoval had undoubtedly received such eyes. She was twenty years old. One day, when Saint John of the Cross, who was staying at Béas, asked her how she spent her

[53] Saint Augustine, Commentaire, 397.
[54] Saint Gregory of Nyssa, In Canticum Canticorum, Homily 4, 833D–836A.

prayer, she replied that she admired the beauty of God. The saint was so happy with this answer that for several days he kept saying admirable and very lofty things about the beauty of God. And, inspired by this love, he composed five stanzas on the topic, starting thus:

> My friend, let us rejoice
> and let us go to see you in your beauty. [55]

In the commentary of Stanza XXXVI, the word *beauty*, repeated twenty times in fifteen lines, again bears witness to a kind of intoxication, an almost wild emotion overwhelming the saint, as if he could not tear himself away from the theme and pull away from the spell of a note repeated endlessly. And we are carried away with him:

> My friend, let us go to see you in your beauty: let us be alike in beauty, and let this be in your beauty, so that when we see each other, you are the only one to appear beautiful, and let each one see himself in your beauty; and so it will be if you transform me in your beauty.
>
> And I will see you in your beauty and you will see me in your beauty; and you will see yourself in me in your beauty and I will see myself in you in your beauty. And I will be like you in your beauty, and you will be like me in your beauty.
>
> And my beauty will be your beauty, and your beauty will be my beauty. And I will be you in your beauty, and you will be me in your beauty: because your very beauty will be my beauty. [56]

Was there ever a lover possessed by such an intoxication? But could any love in this world have contemplated such a beauty? To be sure, as Gregory of Nyssa puts it: "The other objects of the world might well, for those who seek the senses, appear to be beautiful. . . . But how could something that has no consistence have any beauty? You alone are truly beautiful since you are the very essence of beauty; you are always the same.

[55] Saint John of the Cross, *Cantique spirituel*, Stanza XXXVII, 497–498.
[56] Ibid., 669–670.

You are eternally what you are. You do not blossom at one
moment to lose your bloom at another. The charm of your
beauty stretches as far as the eternity of your life."[57]

1:16 *How beautiful you are, my Beloved,*
     and how delightful!

She does not repeat, as the Bridegroom had done: "how beautiful you are!" But she associates to the beauty of the Bridegroom the taste, the deep sweetness he always awakens in her:
"how delightful!" Or, more precisely, how delectable and
tasty! Association between beauty and taste is also found in the
royal epithalamium: "Of all men you are the most handsome,
your lips are moist with grace" (Ps 45:2); and in Psalm 34:
"How good Yahweh is—only taste and see!" (Ps 34:8).

   Moreover the beloved does not fear to use in her reply the
most exclusive of all tender words: "my Beloved," she says,
and, this time, not speaking about him in the third person as
was the case in the preceding stanza but addressing him directly. This, to the great astonishment and happiness of Saint
Bernard: "Here is the beloved. The master and the King are
gone. He has been stripped of his rank; all fear is dispelled.
Love does away with display. Just as Moses once spoke to God
as a friend and God answered him, so here between the Word
and the soul a familiar conversation starts as if between two
neighbors. . . . He calls her 'friend', tells her that she is beautiful, repeats this, and she replies in the same vein. . . . 'Here
you are, how beautiful you are, my Beloved, how admirable!'
See what heights the Bride has reached, what summit of intelligence she attained to dare call the Lord of all things her beloved and, as it were, her property. Note that she does not only
say "Beloved," but "my Beloved," as if he belonged personally to her. She must be favored with a great wisdom to become so daring and have the audacity to see him not only as her

[57] Saint Gregory of Nyssa, *In Canticum Canticorum*, Homily 4, 836B.

master but as her friend, he who is the sovereign of the universe. . . . As once with Moses [he for his part] talks to her face to face; and she sees God openly and not in enigmas or figures. . . . Her eyes contemplate the King in his beauty not as a monarch but as a beloved. Another [Isaiah] was able to see him on a high throne, and yet another [Moses] testifies that he saw him face to face. But I think that the unique privilege of the Bride in the Song is this: others have seen a master and she her beloved."[58]

Saint Bernard is right to admire. The Bride needs a certain daring to thus call her Lord simply "my Beloved". But this should also be the audacity of us all. This is what he expects from each one of us. And the Bride shows us well what path we must take in her footsteps: we must go, like her, from admiration to love, from "how beautiful you are!" to "how delightful!" The great school of love is indeed admiration, as Bossuet explains in a surprising passage about this particular verse of the Song: "The first disposition of a heart that wishes to love is a certain admiration . . . .; it is the first wound that holy love inflicts upon the heart. A dart comes through the glance so that the heart is always occupied with the beauties of Jesus Christ and says with the Bride, without uttering a word: 'How beautiful you are, my Beloved, how beautiful and pleasant!' This admiration for the Bridegroom draws the soul to a certain silence that overwhelms all things and is busy with the sole beauties of its beloved; a silence that hushes all things to the extent that it even hushes holy love. It does not allow it to say, I love or I want to love, lest it become intoxicated by talking about itself: so that all that is done by this blessed admiration is to let itself be drawn by the charms of Jesus Christ."[59]

---

[58] Saint Bernard, *Sermons,* Sermon 45, 489–494.

[59] Jacques Bénigne Bossuet, "Lettres de piété," *Lettres* (Paris: Plon, 1927), 250. Applying to Jesus, in his entire life, this same verse of the Song ("How beautiful you are, my Beloved"), Saint Augustine paraphrased it thus: "He is beautiful on earth as the Word is beautiful in the presence of the Father; and

Surrendering to this blessed admiration, the Bride of the Song forgets the limits of her desires. And talking about the whole earth, stretching beyond sight around them, she invites the Bridegroom to lie down with her as on the bed of their wedding night:

1:16 *All green is our bed,* she says.

All this fresh and green earth that they see, as if it were an endless lawn, is for their marriage. This is their wedding bed. And she daringly says: our couch, our bed. Everything is theirs to be held in common and first of all this land in the spring, this beautiful Palestine to be sure, but also all the earth of God, on which their wedding will be consummated. "Let the earth produce vegetation", God had said during the creation (Gn 1:11). Yes, God's whole earth, as it was on the first day, is given to them for love. All creation is the immense park of their happiness. Francis of Assisi, in the Canticle of the Creatures, will not speak differently. The love of the Bridegroom, far from enclosing one in an intimacy that shuts out the rest of the world, is always opened, in the Song as in the entire mystical tradition, to the entire universe. The closest union with the Bridegroom has this consequence: it always puts one in communion with the world and all of mankind. It is noteworthy, in this respect, that though nothing is more personal, more intimate than the Song, nothing either is more universal and more cosmic.

Responding to the Bride's description of a world that would, as it were, have only one season, the spring, the Bridegroom enlarges infinitely the vision of the green bed by rep-

---

beautiful on earth, dressed in human nature; he is beautiful in the womb, beautiful in the arms of his parents, beautiful in the miracles and in the scourging; he is beautiful in surrendering his soul, and beautiful in taking it back; he is beautiful on the Cross, beautiful in the tomb, beautiful when back in heaven."
Saint Augustine, *Enarratio in Psalmum XLIV*; PL 36, 495.

resenting the house as made of fragrant and indestructible materials, strong as eternity: the definitive Temple, untouched by time or weather, that will be the house, the home, of their union:

1:17 — *The beams of our house are of cedar,*
      the paneling of cypress.

The Bride spoke about "our bed" with a disconcerting simplicity, which could be explained and excused only by her great love. He replies in the same tone. Of course, he consents wholeheartedly to make a bed out of this earth. He will rest on it. He will unite completely with mankind by becoming flesh in the Virgin Mary. "The bride calls 'bed' the union of human nature with divinity."[60] And more explicitly yet, Saint Augustine and Saint Gregory the Great say about this same verse of the Song: "The bed of the Bridegroom was the womb of the Virgin. For in this virginal womb they united together, the Bridegroom and the Bride, the Bridegroom Word and the Bride flesh."[61] "When, in the mystery of the Incarnation, the heavenly King celebrated the wedding of his Son by giving him Holy Church as a bride, the womb of Mary served as a nuptial bed for the Bridegroom."[62] The Bridegroom adds, however, that this union will then lead the one he loves to his house, which he already calls tenderly "our house". "The beams of our house", he says, "are of cedar, the paneling of cypress."

The author of the Song is obviously talking about the Temple, just as he saw all the Holy Land in the bed of greenery. The beams of cedar, the paneling of cypress are the woods that Solomon had ordered from Hiram of Tyre for the construction of the Temple and for his forest house (cf. 1 K 5:22–24; 7:2–8).

[60] Saint Gregory of Nyssa, *In Canticum Canticorum*, Homily 4, 836D.
[61] Saint Augustine, *Commentaire*, 117.
[62] Saint Gregory the Great, quoted by Henri de Lubac, *Méditation sur l' Église* (Paris: Aubier, 1953), 291.

However, we can already see, in the prospect opened by the Temple, the house where God and man will finally be together "to rest . . . at noon", to lie eternally in the unity of love: the house of the Father that, for Jesus the Bridegroom, becomes indeed "our house", as the Bride had joyfully foreseen since the Prologue: "The King has brought me", she had said, "into his rooms".

Paul Claudel, in his commentary on the Song, enters into the symbolism of the cedar and the cypress. The latter, in contrast with the passing green bed of the earth, bespeaks the "fragrant and incorruptible" character (Gregory of Nyssa) of God's definitive house with man. "The cedar, which is exalted in the Bible, is the most sacred of all trees; it gives an indestructible wood, a surviving matter, brought forth by long growth and meditation in high places. . . . And what is the meaning of these panelings that, we are told, are of cypress? . . . Between us and the entire contingent and passing spectacle of the world is interposed this thought of eternity contained in the cypress. press. . . . Our dwelling is an adoring house of good odor."[63]

It is richly significant that the green bed is evoked by the Bride while the Bridegroom speaks of the house of cedar and cypress. The Bride offers her earth as a bed where the Bridegroom can rest his humanity; as for him, he offers to the one he loves his eternal house. Solomon, in the Book of Kings, builds the house of God, the Temple. And again, it is the new Solomon, the true son of David, who presents humanity, his bride, with the house he had "prepared . . . since the foundation of the world" (Mt 25:34) — a dwelling that, as we know, is finally himself.

Thus we can foresee in the Bridegroom of the Song, as it will be revealed one day in Jesus, the presence of the Holy Trinity, and can apply to him what Saint Hilary of Poitiers says about the three Persons: "Eternity is in the Father (the beams

---

[63] Claudel, *Paul Claudel*, 46.

of our house are of cedar); beauty in the image ("How beautiful you are, my Beloved"); delight in the gift (how delightful, sweet and charming you are!).

Now the Bride utters the following verses:

2:1　*I am the rose of Sharon,*[64]
　　　the lily of the valleys.

"Now," Chouraqui points out, "since she has seen herself in the pure mirror of her lover, the Bride has the true revelation of her beauty: not anymore a woman of flesh and blood but a flower offered in the unanimous offering of nature that she incarnates."[65]

Indeed the Bride speaks here and depicts herself as the rose of Sharon and the lily of the valleys. Continuing the evocation of spring in Palestine ("green is our bed", she had said), she brings now for his admiration the spring flowers that she is offering. In fact she herself is the flower. And it might well be as Ernest Renan and Jean Guitton inferred: she utters here some humble protest; after the Bridegroom has promised to bring her to his house of cedar, she is objecting, as it were: "The house you offer me is too beautiful! The bed of the fields would suit me better; you, my beloved, talk about high cedar and cypress. But I am only a poor rose of the plain and one of these

[64] In Hebrew: *Ani Habezeleth HaSharon, Shoshanath HaAmakim.* The original and traditional English translation has been kept here; it would be quite difficult if not impossible to give a faithful translation of the flowers' names. According to *Harper's Bible Dictionary* (pp. 562 and 889), "The rose of Sharon is probably not a true rose, but a bright red tuliplike flower *(Tulipa montana)* today prolific in the hills of Sharon." "The lily of the valleys of the Song of Solomon (2:1–2) is not our common lily-of-the-valley but most likely the sweet-smelling blue hyacinth *(Hyacinth orientalis)* common in fields and rocky places." — *Trans.*

[65] André Chouraqui, *La Cantique des Cantiques* (Paris: Presses Universitaires de France, 1970), 46.

beds that grow hidden at the bottom of the valleys." There might also be a hint of blushing humility in the words of the Bride, but such modesty would only add to her grace!

For, in fact, she identifies with the whole of spring, in the kingdom of flowers. The rose and the lily are not chosen by chance. They are the spring flowers par excellence, and this is the Holy Land in its most beautiful season, the earth adorned as a bride of God—("you shall be called 'My Delight,' " says Isaiah) (Is 62:4). The narcissus (or rose), *habezeleth,* makes an immense golden carpet covering the entire plain from winter until the month of March, and Sharon, meaning the plain, gives its name precisely to the large coastal band of land between Jaffa and Caesarea. Thus the Song, once again, shows its Palestinian origin. As to the lily, called here shoshana, it is not our lily, which is extremely rare in Israel and moreover is not a spring flower. Lastly, the lily is white, while the flower described in the Song is clearly red, as will be seen later in the comparison which otherwise would be barely comprehensible: "His lips are lilies" (5:13); "your lips are a scarlet thread" (4:3). The Song is quite likely referring to the red anemone, which covers the countryside and the bottom of the valleys of Palestine from February to April.

Such is the bed of the Bride. Indeed it is humble. She does not have a palace to offer with beams of cedar and paneling of cypress. Only the bare ground, and, moreover, this ground, not the high mountains of the Sinai or Hermon, but the flat plain and the low valley. Not even a plain planted with high trees but one strewn with wild flowers. Yes, but this is also a royal bed covered with red and purple, the one that had been given to her during the creation by the King her Bridegroom. Such is the bed of the Bridegroom now, such is the Bride herself with whom he is going to unite (it is significant that the narcissus or rose and the lily have the feminine gender in Hebrew).

Saint Bernard even thinks that he can see what Jesus would admiringly say one day about the lily of the fields (Mt 6:28).

It was in fact about his bride that he would say: "Look at the lilies of the fields. See how beautiful and strong they are among the weeds. If God watches thus over a flower that lives today and will be thrown into the fire tomorrow, he will watch even better over the one he loves, his bride."[66] Would Jesus then have seen in the lilies of the field his bride, as he would see in the ripe ears of corn the crowds waiting for him (Jn 4:35)?[67]

However, the description of spring in the Holy Land is not meant only to make us admire the beauty and the humble and ardent desire of the Bride. In the Song, as in the prophets, spring also symbolizes the conversion and return to grace of Israel, its re-creation after the trials of winter and exile. In this respect, the conclusion of the Book of Hosea, in which the restoration of the covenant is described precisely as a renewal of spring, is quite probably in the background of our passage of the Song: "I will fall like dew on Israel," God says; "he shall bloom like the lily" (Ho 14:6). For each one of us also, a conversion, whatever the past has been and whatever our age, is always a return of the spring. No winter of sin can be an obstacle to this spring of love.

The Bridegroom catches on the wing, as it were, the floral theme of his beloved, by exalting and magnifying it:

2:2 — *As a lily among the thistles,*
      so is my love among the maidens.

It is true, my beloved, that you are humble and small like the red anemone of the Galilean spring, but you are also splendidly

---

[66] Saint Bernard, *Sermons*, Sermon 48, 514.

[67] Many of these so appear, especially in the Gospel of John, in veiled references by Jesus to the Song. And "it is not impossible", as Father de Lubac notes, "that Saint Paul himself had explicit awareness [of similar parallels]. When he wrote in the Epistle to the Ephesians that Christ wanted to have in the Church 'a bride all resplendent, without stain or wrinkle' or when he spoke to the Corinthians of his 'divine jealousy', perhaps he remembered precisely the corresponding verses in the Song and wanted to show their scope." *Méditation*, 309.

beautiful! "In truth, Solomon in all his glory was not as magnificently dressed as you are" (cf. Mt 6:29). For among all the
maidens, i.e., all the nations of the world, I see no one who is
as beautiful as you are. Compared with you, they are at most
thistle flowers, i.e., with more thorns than grace! See how God
admires and prefers! "Indeed, when the Bridegroom came to
my bed," as Gregory of Nyssa has the Bride say, "I became,
rising above the plains of my nature, a flower more beautiful
than all the others in the beauty of its color and the excellency
of its perfume."[68]

But what can be said then about the Bridegroom? What
homage can be made to him? Echoing the compliment she has
just received, keeping the same rhythm and cadence, the Bride
in her turn sings:

2:3 — *As an apple tree among the trees of the orchard,*
  so is my Beloved among the young men.

Faithful to her first theme of spring, the Bride responds, but
this time she picks up the tune that the Bridegroom had given
to her: " 'You are more beautiful than all the other flowers of
spring', you said, my beloved, but you are the most beautiful
tree of spring, the most radiant, the most flower-studded of the
orchard: an apple tree in blossom, promising an infinity of
fruits." In fact, the apple tree is somewhat surprising here; it is
not very common in Palestine. But being a rare species, it is all
the more precious. Indeed, the Bride could not compare the
one who is unique in her eyes to some common variety!

But there must be some premonition in the mind of the
Bride when she chooses the apple tree to praise her beloved. In
the very name of the apple tree, there is something satisfactory
to her: the Hebrew word *tappuach* derives from a verb meaning
to breathe, to exhale. The Bride, who is always so sensitive to

---

[68] Saint Gregory of Nyssa, *In Canticum Canticorum*, Homily 4, 840C.

the perfumes of the one she loves, spontaneously compares the beloved to a tree whose flowers are very fragrant. Moreover, as Origen points out: "The fragrance of the perfumes, though it is sweetly breathed out and pleasing to the sense of smell, is not always sweet to the taste. But there is one thing that is sweet to the senses of both smell and taste, at the same time delightful to the palate by its savor and fragrant in the air I breathe: the apple."[69]

The bride is undoubtedly sensitive to the beauty of the apple tree in the spring, as Marcel Proust would be one day of May in Normandy: "The apple trees were in blossom as far as the eye could see, dressed as if for a ball but with their feet in the mud, oblivious to the fact that the most wonderful pink satin ever seen under the shining sun was being spoiled. The faraway line of the sea on the horizon gave them a sort of Japanese background as seen on some engravings."[70]

We also know that apples had a privileged place in the great paintings of Botticelli, Chardin, Cézanne; the apple for these painters, who loved beautiful forms, seems to conjure, through its round shape as well as its colors, the earth itself. Thus the apple tree manifests, through the beauty of its flowers as well as the taste of its fruits, what the Bride had said in her first ecstasy: "How beautiful you are, my Beloved, and how delightful!"

It is probably no accident that the penetrating perfume of the apple, its round and colorful beauty, the sweetness of its taste have frequently been associated with love. The apple is a love fruit. It is significant, for instance, that popular tradition has seen in the apple—even though it was not named—the fruit of "the tree beautiful to look at and whose fruit is good to eat", which is the first tree mentioned in Holy Scripture.[71] The fact

[69] Origen, *Homélies,* Homily 2:6, 125.

[70] Marcel Proust, *Á la recherche du temps perdu,* vol. 9 (Paris: NRF-Gallimard), 232.

[71] Gn 2:9; *La Bible,* introduced by Pierre de Beaumont (Paris: Fayard-Mame, 1981), 26.

remains, in any case, that the Song mentions the apple four times, always in connection with love: "restore me with apples, for I am sick with love" (2:5); "your breath sweet-scented as apples" (7:9).

But, above all, the apple tree is so exalted in the Song because the tree has very beautiful flowers and excellent fruits and because it links the spring of the flowers and the autumn of the fruits. It is thus counted above all the sterile trees of the forest, green oaks and terebinths especially, which Israel was tempted to venerate; in the same vein, the Bridegroom transcends all vain idols, as Origen understands: "All the trees of the forest are indeed sterile when compared with the Word of God. All that you could imagine would only be brushwood in comparison with Christ. In his presence, all is fruitless. And what can be called fecund when he is here? Even those trees that seem to bend under the weight of their fruits bear witness, when compared with him, to their sterility. Which is why, like the apple tree among the trees of the forest, my beloved is the most beautiful among the young men."[72]

Needless to say, though Gregory of Nyssa does, the Bridegroom is also infinitely more beautiful than his love, no matter how graceful she is: "For the lily she is has only beauty and perfume, . . . while the grace of the apple tree . . . at the same time rejoices the eye by beauty, seduces the smell by its perfume, and fulfills the taste by its sweetness. . . . The Bride also sees perfectly well the difference between herself and her Lord: he has at the same time grace for our eyes since he made himself our light; perfume for our smell; and life for those who eat him, for the one who eats him will live"[73] (Jn 6:57–58).

Such are the reasons, and there are undoubtedly others, for which the Bride, when her Bridegroom praises her as a lily among the thistles, responds, in the same tone, that he himself,

---

[72] Origen, *Homélies*, Homily 2:6, 125.
[73] Gregory of Nyssa, *In Canticum Canticorum*, Homily 4, 844A.

compared with the other young men, is like the apple tree among all the other trees. He is the tree of life in the midst of the garden of paradise!

But it is not enough for the Bride to admire the beautiful tree of her beloved. She also yearns to rest in his shade and taste of his fruit. She who has suffered so much when burned by the sun of exile, who exhausted herself "wander[ing] like a vaga-bond beside the flocks" of the foreigners after having vainly sought the protective shade of the terebinths ("you prostituted yourself under any green tree" is a verse that recurs frequently and sadly in the prophets), she now desires only the shade of her beloved apple tree:

2:3 *In his longed-for shade I am seated*

It is true that the shade of the apple tree is rather meager; it is a tree that, above the Bride, has the form of her friend. So often in Scripture, the psalmist invokes thus the protective sweet-ness of this shade: "hide me in the shadow of your wings" (Ps 17:8); "I take shelter in the shadow of your wings" (Ps 57:1); "I rest in the shade of Elyon" (Ps 91:1). After the burns the sun inflicted on her in exile because of her unfaithfulness, after the wounds caused by the fiery darts of her persecutors, what freshness and security she finds when she is again in the shadow of Yahweh, according to his promise: "They will come back to live in my shade" (Ho 14:8)!

This shade is all the more necessary to eyes that are still too weak. How could they look at the blazing Bridegroom? The light of his face is dazzling and unbearable "when his ardor", writes Gregory of Nyssa, "is not filtered by the cloud that the Lord unfolds as a shield, as it is said in Isaiah: 'the glory of Yah-weh will be a canopy and a tent to give shade by day from the heat' "[74] (Is 4:5–6). "This shade is therefore well named," Saint Teresa of Avila avers in her turn, "for we cannot see him in this

[74] Ibid., 796A.

world. But the resplendent sun is behind this cloud. And, by means of love, it lets us know that his majesty is more united to us than we could express."[75]

Of this protective and sweet shade where she finally enjoys rest, of this shadow still veiling somehow in her eyes the excessively burning radiance of the face of the Lord her Bridegroom, the Bride will one day also know the fruitful power when she will be told: "The Holy Spirit will come upon you, . . . and the power of the Most High will cover you with its shadow" (Lk 1:35). The shadow of the Spirit covers and fecundates the Virgin Mary, who thus becomes, more than the *shehina* of the desert covered by the cloud, the real tabernacle of God. What riches of meaning there were for Mary, when she carried Jesus in her womb, in the words uttered here by the Bride of the Song: "In his longed-for shade I am seated and his fruit is sweet to my taste", with the admirable connection of these two words *shade* (of the Spirit) and *fruit* ("and blessed is the fruit of your womb, Jesus").

2:3 *and his fruit,* the beloved already whispers,
    is sweet to my taste.

Linked to the theme of perfect rest in the protective and sweet shadow of the beloved apple tree comes quite naturally that of the love fruit savored together. "The sons of men take shelter in the shadow of your wings", says the psalmist: "they feast on the bounty of your house" (Ps 36:7–8). The coolness of the shade appeases and relaxes little by little the limbs of the Bride, and at the same time desire comes to its conclusion with the fruit that satisfies thirst and hunger. "I longed", the bride says in the second homily of Origen, "to rest in his shade. But as soon as he protected me with his shade, I was also fulfilled with his fruit. And I say: his fruit is sweet to my taste."[76]

[75] Saint Teresa of Avila, *Pensées sur l' amour de Dieu, Oeuvres complètes,* Bibliothèque européenne (Paris: Desclée de Brouwer, 1964), 5:4, 593.

[76] Origen, *Homélies,* Homily 2:6, 127.

The heart is not expecting anything anymore. It has tasted the fruit of the tree of life, the beloved apple tree of the friend. And this fruit, instead of having the bitter aftertaste of sin (the contrast with the text of Genesis is striking), gives the sweetness of a pure and faithful love that is a blessing. "Approach me," says Wisdom (i.e., the Word, the Bridegroom himself), "you who desire me, and take your fill of my fruits" (Si 24:19). For the Bride, this is the banquet of Wisdom. And it is absolute happiness near the one who is all for her: beauty, perfumes, rest, love fruit, and life fruit.

Saint Teresa of Avila, reading this passage of the Song of Songs, expresses quite well what it means for her in her experience of contemplation: "I sat", she writes, "in the shade of him whom I desired, and his fruit was sweet to my taste. It seems that the whole soul feels itself engulfed and protected by a shade, a kind of divine cloud. . . . It feels a sort of rest, so that the mere obligation to breathe is tiring. . . . It does not need to move a hand nor to get up , . . . for cut, cooked or even eaten, the Lord himself gives the fruit of the tree to which she compares her beloved. Thus she says that his fruit is sweet to her taste. And here is all her delight, without any work of the soul's faculties under the shadow of the Divinity."[77] Thus contemplation is already a foretaste of the Kingdom and of its banquet, as Saint Augustine noted, for "what we desire avidly to eat and drink, we already taste and touch now, even if it is with a touch of our lips."[78]

The interpretation given by Saint Teresa of Avila to these verses of the Song is the one that all mystics give spontaneously. Of course, such an interpretation is quite different from that of the exegetes of the naturalistic school, who understand—as they do all along—the words of the beloved to have a carnal meaning. And it is undoubtedly the language of the most vehement passion, appealing to the senses and running

[77] Saint Teresa of Avila, Pensées, 5:4, 593.
[78] Saint Augustine, Sermons, 21, 2; PL 38, 142; CCL 41, 277.

therefore the risk of being totally misunderstood. Teresa of Avila was quite aware of this: "It will seem to you", she says (in a page already partially quoted in our Introduction), "that in these songs certain things might have another style. Our stupidity is such that this would not surprise me. I heard certain people say that they would rather avoid listening to them. Merciful God, how great is our stupidity! Just as venomous things turn everything they touch into poison, when the Lord makes us listen here to what the soul possesses—the soul that loves him—we are still capable of giving it a meaning in conformity with the weak sense of God's love, which is ours."[79] Saint Augustine had already warned: "Many passages in the Song of Songs, if they are accepted in the flesh, do not bring a fruit of light and charity but an inclination to sensual desires."[80] The error of the naturalistic school is precisely to interpret the meaning of the Song "according to the flesh", i.e., in a sensual way.

Now we must say in opposition—and once and for all, which is why we must stress this somewhat—how the language of the senses, in Scripture generally but certainly especially in the Song of Songs, can be put to the service of pure love and even become its most transparent expression, even at the risk, when uttered, of provoking laughter, as Origen already expected when preaching about the Song: "He who cannot grasp and understand the things that pertain to the Spirit of God, if he hears our explanations, will certainly make a mockery of them and declare them to be inanities without ground. . . . For such men, the fragrance of the Song of Songs becomes a smell of death unto death. . . . But for those who look at the invisible and spiritual goods as more real than the physical objects under our eyes, such interpretation as we propose gains all its value."[81]

[79] Saint Teresa of Avila, *Pensées*, 1:3, 562.
[80] Saint Augustine, *De Spiritu et Littera* IV, 6; PL 44, 203.
[81] Origen, *In Canticum Canticorum*, 97B.

Origen is undoubtedly the first to have noticed that, in parallel with the body, the soul also has senses of a sort: "In man," he says quite explicitly, "besides the bodily senses, there are five other senses which need to be exercised";[82] to wit: sight, smell, taste, hearing and touch, which are properly spiritual and through which the soul has a certain experimental knowledge, diversified according to each sense, of divine things. "Thus," Origen writes, "the soul has a sense of sight to contemplate supernatural objects, a hearing capable of distinguishing voices that do not resound in the air, a taste to savor the living bread come down from heaven, . . . in the same way, a smell, leading Paul to speak of the perfume of Jesus, and also a sense of touch, which John had since he told us that he touched with his own hands the Word of God."[83] Following Origen, Gregory of Nyssa says just as clearly: "We have two kinds of senses, those of the body and those of the spirit."[84]

It may seem strange to hear these writers speak of approaching God through the senses of the soul because we practice most often a prayer that is far too abstract and cerebral. But if Christ became flesh, and not only Spirit, it was in order to be reached also by all the senses of the soul, which correspond indeed to those of the body,[85] without any possible ambiguity, because they are interiorized, purified, decanted, unified, and, so to speak, spiritualized. Father Donatien Mollat, whose words on John are rightly admired, can write in full confidence: "The Word made himself visible, audible, tangible. It is through the senses that revelation came to men, that divine life was communicated to them, and it is in this way that they receive and welcome it. . . . The use of sensory language to ex-

---

[82] Ibid., 96.

[83] Origen, *Contre Celse,* I–II (cf. SC 132) (Paris: Cerf, 1966), 201–209.

[84] Saint Gregory of Nyssa, *In Canticum Canticorum,* Homily 1, 780C.

[85] Saint Gregory of Nyssa says that there is an analogy between the activities of the soul and the senses of the body. Ibid., 780C.

press the experience of communion with God in Christ is one of the characteristic features of Johannine spirituality. It is within the logic of the Incarnation."[86]

This is a point that Origen, and after him all the great mystical tradition, has stressed very strongly: "Christ", he comments, "becomes the object of each sense of the soul. He calls himself the true light, to enlighten the eyes of the soul; the Word, to be heard; the bread of life, to be tasted; he is also called oil of anointing and nard because the soul is delighted by the perfume of the Logos. He became the Word made flesh, tangible, substantial, so that the inner man would be able to grasp the Word of life."[87]

Saint Augustine might have known these lines of Origen when he wrote, in his commentary on the Gospel of John, "If the senses of the body have their pleasure, does not the soul also have pleasures? But if the soul does not have its own pleasure, why is it written in Psalm 36:7–9: "The sons of men will take shelter in the shadow of your wings. They feast on the bounty of your house, you give them drink from your river of pleasure; yes, with you is the fountain of life, by your light we see light"?[88]

In a similar vein, Saint Ignatius Loyola, who is not generally blamed for giving an excessive place to senses and sensitivity, asks a retreatant, in the meditation on the Incarnation or the nativity, "to sense and taste through smell and taste the infinite sweetness and gentleness of the Divinity."[89] And how rich is the orchestra of the senses that John of the Cross calls to magnify the obscure night of the faith! To underestimate the importance of the spiritual senses in the contemplative experience is to cause grave damage to the self, as Saint Teresa of Avila ad-

---

[86] Donatien Mollat, "Jean l'Évangéliste", *Dictionnaire de spiritualité,* vol. 8 (Paris: Beauchesne, 1974), c. 217–224.

[87] Origen, *In Canticum Canticorum,* 142.

[88] Saint Augustine, *In Joannem,* 26, 3; PL 35, 26, c.1608.

[89] Saint Ignatius Loyola, *Exercices spirituels,* 77, no. 124.

mits: "It was very bad for me", she says, "to ignore that it was possible to see something with eyes other than those of the body."[90]

The painters of icons could teach us much in this respect. Instead of using a human model, as did the painters of the Renaissance in their workshops, in order to paint, for instance, a transfigured Jesus, the icon painters first stayed long hours in inner contemplation, letting the eyes of the soul be slowly penetrated by his face. Thus the icons are at the same time so human and so transcendent.

All the senses of the soul can contribute equally to unite us to God, as Saint Augustine attests in a famous passage of the *Confessions*. This passage of Augustine has, moreover, the great merit of stressing very precisely what separates the experience of the carnal senses (of which he had a certain knowledge before his conversion) from the experience of the spiritual senses: "O God," he asks himself, "what do I love in loving you? It is not the beauty of the bodies, nor their perishable grace, nor the radiance of the light so dear to my eyes, sweet melodies with their varied sounds, sweet smells of flowers, perfumes, aromatic spices, manna, honey nor limbs made for carnal embraces. No, this is not what I love when I love my God. . . . And yet, there is a light, a voice, a perfume, a food, an embrace that I love when I love my God. It is the light, the voice, the perfume, the embrace of the inner man in me, where there shines in my soul a light that is not limited by space, where melodies are heard that time does not drive away, where perfumes are wafting that are not scattered by the wind, where one tastes a food that cannot be devoured by any voracity and embraces that are never sated. This is what I love when I love my God."[91]

[90] Saint Teresa of Avila, *Autobiographie*, 7:7, 46.
[91] Saint Augustine, *Confessions*, Book X, 6(9); PL 32, 782–783; CCL 27, 159.

On the other hand, one must note that when we deliberately refuse to "apply", according to the Ignatian meaning of the term, the senses of our soul to the things of God, the consequences are likely to be quite serious. First, evangelization of the depths of the being—the source of our affectivity, the very roots of the unconscious—would never occur. Our love of God would remain purely cerebral. In consequence, our personality could not be truly unified in Christ. We would inevitably live a sort of inner divorce, the head belonging to the Lord while the heart would necessarily go to other objects with the disasters that this could provoke both on the psychological plane and on the spiritual one. Lastly, one should admit that only through the development of the senses of the spirit can we achieve a true purification of our sensitivity, as Origen indicates very clearly in his commentary on the Song. As he points out, it is only when we apply to the very person of Jesus our different senses that we can, little by little, become detached from carnal seductions. And this is far more efficacious than through a simple discipline of voluntary deprivations because, as he explains, "the eye, if it reaches the contemplation of the glory of the Word, the glory of the only Son coming from the Father, will not want to see anything else; and the ear will not want to hear anything but the Word of life that saves; and he whose hand has touched the Word of life will not want to touch anything fragile and perishable; and he whose taste has savored the Word of life, his flesh and the bread come down from heaven, will thereafter be incapable of tasting anything else; and later he will not want any other food, for, in this bread capable of having all tastes, he will find all the desirable savors."[92]

As Marie-Nöel puts it so expressively: "O my God, by dint of eating and drinking you, God, will one day be my instinct."[93]

---

[92] Origen, *In Canticum Canticorum*, 95.

[93] Marie-Noël, *Notes intimes* (Paris: Stock, 1959), 137.

However, the Bride—whom we have somewhat neglected, though we never forgot her!—has not been fulfilled. As if she were dreaming aloud and awake, she whispers to herself:

2:4 *He has taken me to his banquet hall,*

He has taken me. Again, as we saw previously, she does not have the initiative. She who was independent for so long is now completely surrendered to her beloved, letting herself meekly be led by him.

And the beloved takes her to his house, "the banquet hall", the house of love's intoxication, where the feast is going on eternally. The Bride, already in the Prologue, had been taken to the King's rooms and was praising "love above wine" (1:4). She says here, more realistically: "He has taken me to his banquet hall" (literally "house of wine"). "House", "banquet hall" and "house of wine" are in fact one and the same thing, and we might as well write "cellar" in our translation, as André Robert does; *Beth-Hayyain,* however, is literally the "house of wine", the banquet hall[94] where wine is served in superabundance as we will see. It is here and now and not by desire and in dream only that the Bride is taken. "Her ardent thirst", says Ruysbroeck, "finds at last in the cellar the wine that her lips were seeking."[95] After having tasted near her Bridegroom the fruit of love in the garden, in the shade of the apple tree, she lets herself be led by him to the inside of his house; she sits at the table near him, and now she drinks from his intoxicating cup: "Yahweh, my heritage, my cup", she can say with the psalmist (Ps 16:5).

How far has the Bride already gone, led by her beloved, if we pay careful attention to her progress! After a first time of mere admiration at the sight of the beautiful apple tree, she

---

[94] Paul Joüon, *Le Cantique des Cantiques* (Paris: Beauchesne, 1909), 155.

[95] Jan van Ruysbroeck the Admirable, *Oeuvres choisies* (Paris: Perrin, 1947), 157.

rested under its protective and sweet shade; then she delighted in the tasty fruit; now she is intoxicated by the shared cup, in this "nuptial communion" as Theodoret of Cyrrhus says: "In consuming the flesh of the beloved (symbolized by the fruit) and his blood (symbolized by the wine), we enter", he writes, "into nuptial communion".[96]

The Jerusalem Bible then puts on the lips of the bride the following verse:

2:4 *and the banner he raises over me is love.*

In fact, the exegetes are not always in agreement about the meaning of this translation. In the dictionaries, the first meaning of the Hebrew *degel* is, quite literally, banner, military flag, insignia. Thus the majority of the exegetes adopt the same interpretation as does André Robert: "and the banner he raises over me is love." This means that for the Bride, i.e., for Israel, the very love of Yahweh, her Bridegroom, accompanies her, sustains her, and also protects her victoriously in all her combats, as well as being the insignia rallying all the peoples.

One could rebut this translation, as do Fathers Joüon, Bea, de Vaux, Buzy et al., in the following way: if *degel* seems in fact to have a primitive meaning of standard or military insignia, it never had it in the Bible. In the entire Bible, *degel* has only one meaning: that of battalion, corps and army (*degalim*—the plural form—is synonymous with *Sabaoth*). It is thus quite literally that Father Joüon translates: "and his army against me is love."[97] And in Latin, Father Bea, very much in conformity with the version of the Septuagint and Saint Jerome: *"Et exercitus ejus contra me est amor."* The "above me", which is used by Dhorme and Robert out of sheer necessity, is in fact and without any doubt an "against me": his army against me is love!

---

[96] Theodoret of Cyrrhus, *In Canticum,* 3, 11; PG 81, 128B.
[97] Paul Joüon, *Le Cantique des Cantiques,* 156.

Thus one sees clearly the connection with all the previous context. Taken by the Bridegroom to the "house of wine", the Bride, victim of an excess of wine, wavers and faints. The cup of love is too strong for her. Saint Bernard understands this very well: "the words and the sight of the Bridegroom inflamed her so much that she is like a drunken woman; as if her surprised maiden companions ask her for the cause of her intoxication, she answers that it is quite natural to be somewhat tipsy after having been in the wine cellar."[98]

John of the Cross, though, is undoubtedly the one who entered best into this state of the soul that is astray and wavering after having drunk too deeply from the love cup: "In the secret of the cellar, I drank from my beloved, and when I came out on this great plain, I did not know anything anymore, and I lost the flock that I had been following." And thus it happened indeed, as Saint John of the Cross explains, to "the soul that drinks of God. . . . Through understanding it drinks the wisdom and science of God; through will, it drinks an extraordinarily sweet love; through memory, it drinks the pleasures and delights kept in mind, . . . and the drink of the very sublime wisdom of God that it drank there makes the soul oblivious to all the details of the world. It seems that all its past science and all its worldly understanding were, compared with this knowledge, pure ignorance."[99]

At last, love overcomes her strength. And she who had been unfaithful, who could ignore all oracles and prophetic threats, must now surrender to the all-powerful love of her beloved though he has no other weapon or army against her than his very love, which conquered in the end. "His army against me is love." The God of the armies has, in the last analysis, only one weapon. It is neither thunder, nor the sword of justice, to which too many preachers had recourse. It is love. God does not conquer our hearts except through the excess of love.

[98] Saint Bernard, *Sermons,* Sermon 49, 522.
[99] Saint John of the Cross, *Cantique spirituel,* Stanza XVIII, 612ff.

That this however is a real battle, at the same time inexorable and tenderly fought—as, in the past, was the struggle of Yahweh's angel against Jacob (Gn 32:25–32)—is felt in the very complaint of the Bride: *amore langueo,* she moans, and we have to translate, "I am wounded by love" (rather than "I faint" or "I am sick with love") since the Hebrew *halath* means to be wounded. The Bride does not vacillate only from drunkenness. She is not only unsteady and lost. She is incurably wounded. A Moslem mystic of the fifteenth century says in a wonderful way: "He whose illness is called Jesus cannot be cured." This is already the case with the Bride of the Song. Lost, fainting and wounded, she must call for help:

2:5 *Feed me with raisin cakes,*
   restore me with apples,

Whom might she be imploring thus, asking for such strange remedies? To whom does she turn in her distress? Toward the very one who, unbelievably, is overwhelming her! Yes, it is Love—causing her to be delirious, tormenting her and wounding her—that she begs to "feed" her and "restore" her. In asking to taste even more of his fruit, to drink more from the cup of intoxication, to see him increase the assaults that exhaust her, the Bride sees the only appeasement for her sufferings. Because he is the only one, as she well knows, the one who wounds is also able to heal her. "The malady of love", says Thérèse of the Child Jesus, "is cured only by love."

Paradoxical love that wounds and heals by wounding even more and that Saint John of the Cross attempts to express through the violence of his words: "The wound made by an iron heated in the fire of love cannot be healed by any other medication except by the same cautery that made it and will cure it. Because each time the cautery of love touches the wound of love, it enlarges the wound, and, in this way, the more it wounds, the more it binds and heals. For the one who loves is all the more healthy in that he is distressed; and the cure brought by love is to distress and to add one wound on top of the other, and in the end the wound becomes so large that the whole soul is turned into a wound of love. . . . Oh happy wound caused by the one who alone knows to heal!"[100]

Happy wound that makes the beloved languid and strengthened at the same time.

> *Feed me,* she moans, *with raisin cakes,*
> *restore me with apples,*

Raisin cakes, contrary to those that Israel was offering to her idols when she was unfaithful—"they turn to other gods and love raisin cakes" (Ho 3:1)—are to be likened, as the very continuity of the text suggests, to the wine of the banquet hall where the Bridegroom took the Bride, while the apples are of the apple tree under whose shade she sat and ate fruits. Thus, by getting even more intoxicated on this wine poured by love, by eating even more of its fruits, which are those of love, the Bride, fainting under the excessively violent blows that are dealt her, will find remedy and salvation. Let no one imagine that she is complaining when she says:

2:5 *for I am sick* [wounded] *with love.*

For if she moans in this way about being wounded, Saint John of the Cross observes that she does not complain! "She does not complain of the wound, for the more distressed the lover is, the more he is rewarded. Her complaint is rather that having wounded her heart, he did not heal her by killing her, for the wounds of love are so sweet and so pleasant that if they do not lead to death, they cannot satisfy the soul. . . . And in this vein she says: 'Why don't you heal this heart since it received its wound from you? And having stolen it, why do you leave

---

[100] Saint John of the Cross, *Vive flamme d'amour,* Stanza II, 743.

it thus and do not take away what you have robbed?' . . . It is
as if she were saying: Why have you struck [this heart] until it
is distressed with love; why don't you heal it by finally killing
it with love? And since you caused the wound by love's malady, now bring about the healing by love's death."[101]

The theme of the love wound is found very frequently in
mystical literature: "The sweetest thing about love", says
Hedwig of Antwerp, a thirteenth-century Beguine, "is its
violence. . . . The most severe wound is a sovereign balm.
. . . To languish for it is our strength. . . . Its hardest blows
are its sweetest consolations. . . . Its consolations enlarge our
wounds."[102] Even though she was still in the world and busy
all day with the concerns of an important business, Marie de l'
Incarnation, in the seventeenth century, was also very familiar
with the anguish and joy of this wound: "I was pining with
love, and yet I enjoyed love", she writes in her *Relations*;
". . . I don't know how I should put it: one suffers, one lan-
guishes, one enjoys."[103] Teresa of Avila goes so far as to say
that she is dying "of not dying."[104]

It is here, in the Song, that we have the true starting point;
we hear it here for the first time, as we find undoubtedly in
Origen the first analysis: "If a man has once burned with the
faithful love of the Word of God; if, to speak like a prophet, a
man has one day received the sweet wound, the sweet pain
'from the best arrow'; if anyone, one day, has been pierced
with the dart of love to the extent that later on, day and night,

[101] Saint John of the Cross, *Cantique spirituel*, Stanza IX, 565.

[102] Quoted by Élisabeth de Miribel, *La liberté souffre violence* (Paris: Plon,
1981), 241.

[103] Guy-Marie Oury, *Marie de l'Incarnation*, vol. 1 (Québec; Abbaye de
Saint-Pierre, Solesmes: Presses de l'Université Laval, 1973), 127.

[104] "I live without living in myself, and thus I hope to die of not dying."
Saint Teresa of Avila, *Poésies, Oeuvres Complètes*, Bibliothèque européenne
(Paris: Desclée de Brouwer, 1964), 1067.

he sighs with desire and knows nothing else, wants nothing else, is attracted by nothing else except to desire it, want it and hope for it, such a one can rightly say: 'I am wounded with love.' "[105]

These lines reveal the profound soul of Origen, and we can understand this very well in the way he lets himself be caught by the same verse of the Song in his second homily: "How beautiful and how loving it is to receive the wound of love! One is wounded by the dart of carnal love, another by some earthly passion; but as for you, expose your limbs and offer yourself to the choicest dart, to the beautiful arrow, since God is the archer. Listen to what the arrow itself says in Isaiah: 'He made my mouth a sharp arrow, and hid me in the shadow of his hand' (Is 49:2). . . . How happy the one who is wounded by this arrow! Had they not been wounded with this wound, those who talked among themselves, saying, 'Was not our heart burning in us while he opened the Scriptures for us on the way?' and if someone is wounded by our word today; if today someone is wounded by the reading of divine Scripture; if he can say, 'I am wounded with love', does not the same thing apply perhaps to him? But why say 'perhaps' since it is obvious?"[106]

In Holy Scripture, we were used so far to hear Israel, the bride of Yahweh, lament because of wounds that were quite different. Until now, wounds caused by her adultery and infidelity made her sick, as the very words of the Bridegroom attest in the Book of Jeremiah: "Your wound is incurable, your injury past healing. . . . Why bother to complain about your wound? Your pain is incurable. So great is your guilt, so many your sins, that I have done all this to you" (Jr 30:12–15). But today, even though she is wounded by the hand of the same

[105] Origen, *In Canticum Canticorum*, 162.
[106] Origen, *Homélies*, Homily 2:8, 133–135.

archer, the arrow is not the same; on the contrary, "she praises the archer for his dexterity," writes Gregory of Nyssa, "admiring him for having done so well in aiming the arrow that sunk into her heart. . . . And in the heart that it penetrates [the arrow] introduces the very archer that cast it. . . . O beautiful and sweet wound, through which life enters, opening as it were a door for itself through the wound of the arrow!"[107]

But how could the Bridegroom himself, in his turn, not be torn when he sees his dearly beloved fainting under his blows, wounded by his love? He is with her in an instant. He takes her in his arms, sustains her, consoles her, and embraces her: thus Adam will be seen one day in the arms of Jesus on the northern portal of the cathedral of Chartres. And the Bride sighs blissfully:

2:6 *His left arm is under my head,*
his right embraces me.

How totally she surrenders in these hands! Powerful and at the same time tender hands; hands of her Lord and hands of her Bridegroom. Hands that carry her and embrace her. Double gesture of her loving God! As a mother with her infant, he holds the head with his left hand, while the right grasps and embraces.

"May it please God that in me too", Origen implores, "the Bride feel this tightest embrace of the Bridegroom and that, in my turn, I may say: 'His left arm is under my head, and his right embraces me.' "[108]

Now the bride is resting. And the Bridegroom, alone, concludes the whole song by an adjuration to the daughters of Jerusalem not to disturb this sleep:

[107] Saint Gregory of Nyssa, *In Canticum Canticorum,* Homily 4, 852AB.
[108] Origen, *Homélies,* Homily 1:2, 77.

2:7 —*I charge you,*
      daughters of Jerusalem,
      by the gazelles, by the hinds of the field,
      not to stir my love, nor rouse it,
      until it please to awake.

Would this stanza, uttered by the Bridegroom as if with a finger to his lips, be merely an amiable and poetic conclusion, the
last coda of a first musical movement? Here is one who was
drunk with a strange intoxication, who was fainting and ends
up sleeping. She rests now near her beloved. Let nothing disturb her peace!

The evocation of the gazelles and the hinds is so graceful that
it might indeed be only a pretty lullaby, an invitation to sleep,
as many exegetes have understood it. Unless these pleasant animals are named here, others think, only to symbolize the
fauna of the Holy Land, just as the rose (or narcissus) and the
lily stood for its flora. Unless, as yet others think, gazelles and
hinds belong to the vocabulary of love and stand only for the
gracefulness and charm of the woman, as we might be led to
think by the words of the Book of Proverbs: "Find joy with
the wife you married in your youth, fair as a hind, graceful as
a fawn" (Pr 5:18–19).

If we do not go any further than these various interpretations, it seems that we remain at the very surface of the text.
Many, indeed, are the elements leading us to see in this stanza
nothing but a simple and affected formula of amorous incantation. First of all, it will appear twice more in the Song, and
each time at the conclusion of a poem (3:5 and 8:4)—here, notably, as a very clear conclusion of the first poem. Such a lo-
cation already bespeaks its importance. Then we must stress
that the stanza opens with a very solemn form of adjuration—
"I charge you"—and therefore there is no reason to treat it
lightly. Lastly, the repetition—"not to stir my love, nor rouse

it"—shows an insistence to which we cannot be insensitive. It is easy to see that this key word is the conclusion of the first poem.

Now these words, this stress, cannot help but bring to mind certain recollections. It is the very expression of return and conversion in the Bible, as in this verse of Isaiah: "Awake, awake! To your feet, Jerusalem! You who from Yahweh's hand have drunk the cup of his wrath. The chalice of stupor you have drained to the dregs" (Is 51:17). And in Isaiah, as in the Song, it is in a context of intoxication that the word *awake* is repeated. But in Isaiah it is an angry intoxication, and in the Song, one of love.

Do we hold the key for which we were looking? Whether we deal with the Song or the prophets of exile, the situation is the same: Israel has not yet completely returned to God. Full of ardor and faith in some ways, she remains undecided on the whole, hesitating before taking the decisive step of return and union. Yahweh bluntly told her one day: "Ephraim is a half-baked cake" (Ho 7:8). "As long as our will retains whims that are opposed to the divine union, fantasies of 'yes' or 'no', we remain children, we do not walk with the giant steps of love; for the fire has not yet burned the whole alloy, the gold is not pure, we are still seeking ourselves."[109] Such indeed does the Bride seem at this point: she is not ready for the ultimate decision. She indeed loves the Bridegroom with unequalled passion, but this love cannot yet be fully achieved. She drank at length from the cup of love but did not have the strength to sustain such an intoxication. Her constancy does not match her ardor.

However, one should not be surprised if God, in spite of her weakness, has already been able to shower her with such exceptional favors. Indeed it is not rare to see God freely grant his graces to the most insignificant of his novices, to beginners

---

[109] van Ruysbroeck, *Oeuvres choisies*, 157.

who are very far from the level of the grace they receive: "I re-call a person", says Saint Teresa of Avila, "to whom in three days the Lord gave such goods as seemed impossible to me. . . . The same thing happened to another one in three months. They were both young. . . . I spoke about these two, and I could mention others so that you could understand that if I wrote that the Lord rarely grants such favors without having subjected souls to long years of trial, there are still some such other souls."[110]

Moreover, Teresa invokes her own testimony in her auto-biography. She tells about her confessor—when she was a young nun and, as she says, quite imperfect—being so amazed by the lights she then received in prayer that he already saw her at the highest peak of perfection. "My confessor then started with a holy determination to treat me as a strong soul, which is what I must have been in his understanding of my pray-er. . . . But no matter how advanced I was in God's favors, I was only a beginner in virtues and mortifications."[111]

In fact, graces in prayer, even the highest ones, are not the sign of the sanctity of a life but rather one's absolute surrender to God's will in complete self-denial.

However, it is not God's way either to hasten things. In the last stanza, he addresses all the nations: he will never do any-thing to force the heart of his Bride. Never will he compel her to rush her return, even by one hour. Very solemnly, and in everybody's presence, he swears "by the gazelles, by the hinds of the field"—i.e., in the last analysis, by himself, if we man-age to perceive with André Robert a clear assonance for the Hebrew ear between "gazelles [and] hinds of the fields" *(ayy-aloth Has'doth)* and "God of hosts" *(Elohe Sabaoth)*. Thus, pa-tiently the Bridegroom will wait as he commits himself to the

[110] Saint Teresa of Avila, *Pensées*, 6:12, 599.
[111] Saint Teresa of Avila, *Autobiographie*, 23:8–9, 159–160.

free awakening of her who, awake or asleep, will always be "his love" *(ahavah)*:

> *daughters of Jerusalem,*
> *[do] not . . . stir my love, nor rouse it,*
> *until it please to awake.*

The Spring of Betrothal

Second Poem

Chapters 2:8–3:5

The Bride

I hear my Beloved.
See how he comes
leaping on the mountains,
bounding over the hills.
My Beloved is like a gazelle,
like a young stag.

See where he stands
behind our wall.
He looks in at the window,
he peers through the lattice.

My Beloved lifts up his voice,
he says to me,
"Come then, my love,
my lovely one, come.
For see, winter is past,
the rains are over and gone.
The flowers appear on the earth.
The season of glad songs has come,
the cooing of the turtledove is heard
in our land.
The fig tree is forming its first figs
and the blossoming vines give out their fragrance.
Come then, my love,
my lovely one, come.
My dove, hiding in the clefts of the rock,

in the coverts of the cliff,
show me your face,
let me hear your voice;
for your voice is sweet
and your face is beautiful."

THE BRIDEGROOM

Catch the foxes for us,
the little foxes
that make havoc of the vineyards,
for our vineyards are in flower.

THE BRIDE

My Beloved is mine and I am his.
He pastures his flock among the lilies.

Before the dawn wind rises,
before the shadows flee,
return! Be, my Beloved,
like a gazelle,
a young stag,
on the mountains of the covenant.

On my bed, at night, I sought him
whom my heart loves.
I sought but did not find him.
So I will rise and go through the City;
in the streets and the squares
I will seek him whom my heart loves.
. . . I sought but did not find him.

The watchmen came upon me
on their rounds in the City:
"Have you seen him whom my heart loves?"

Scarcely had I passed them
than I found him whom my heart loves.

I held him fast, nor would I let him go
till I had brought him
into my mother's house,
into the room of her who conceived me.

The Bridegroom

I charge you,
daughters of Jerusalem,
by the gazelles, by the hinds of the field,
not to stir my love, nor rouse it,
until it please to awake.

The Spring of Betrothal

At the end of each poem, we believe that the lovers are finally
united. But in the next poem, we see the renewal of desire,
then of waiting and of seeking until there is a new union. This
will continue as long as this life goes on; there is no end to our
waiting, our desire and our search for God. And the union,
even though it progresses from one poem to the next, from
one conversion to the next, will be achieved definitively only
in the Kingdom. In the Song, we progress as if on a mountain
path, returning indefinitely above the same point of view, in a
spiral without any apparent progress. Yet, each time, we have
come a little closer to the summit. Gregory of Nyssa, in his
first homily, already observes this: "God, through the voice of
Solomon, teaches our reason, in the present philosophy of the
Song of Songs, how to climb by successive stages toward
perfection."[1]

2:8 *I hear my Beloved.*
   See how he comes
   leaping on the mountains,
   bounding over the hills.

2:9 *My Beloved is like a gazelle,*
   like a young stag.

The Bride joyfully exclaims: "I hear my Beloved." From afar,
very far, she is warned of his coming. She already recognizes
him by his step, even before hearing his voice. It is said of
Adam and Eve that the very first time they perceived God's
coming, they recognized his footsteps: "[They] heard the

---

[1] Saint Gregory of Nyssa, *In Canticum Canticorum*, Homily 1, PG 44, 765.

sound of Yahweh God walking in the garden" (Gn 3:8). In Hebrew, the word is the same as here.[2]

The Bridegroom of the Song is not strolling! He runs,
"leaping on the mountains, bounding over the hills." Of
course, these mountains and hills are those of Jerusalem.
"Jerusalem! Encircled by mountains" (Ps 125:2). The anxious
bride was scanning the mountains for months to see whether
her beloved was not coming to join her at last: "I lift", she
sighs, "my eyes to the mountains; from where is my help to
come?" (Ps 121:1). But the beloved comes from a higher plane,
from this "mountain of the Temple of Yahweh", of which Isaiah had spoken," [which] shall tower above the mountains and
be lifted higher than the hills" (Is 2:2). Leaving his eternal
dwelling, he bounds; "[he] comes out of his pavilion like a
bridegroom, exulting like a hero to run his race. He has his rising on the edge of heaven, the end of his course is its further
edge, and nothing can escape his heat" (Ps 19:5–6).

Thus his arrival, and his rapid step is that of a dance because
it is the step of love. "Leaps rather than steps!" says Origen.[3]
He runs, he leaps, he jumps. What haste and what joy in joining her whom he loves! For him, there is no obstacle impossible to overcome when he joins her. But, as Origen points
out, is this not always the case with him? When the Bride
"reads the Scriptures today, when she leafs through the writings of the prophets, does she not also see him leaping across
the lines of the inspired text and run out of them to meet her?"[4]

She imagines him then as now, vivacious and light like a gazelle or rather a young stag: he has its freedom, agility, energy
and gracefulness. His haste, truth to tell, is that of a messenger
bringing the news that is expected for such a long time: "How

---

[2] Gn 3:8 *VeYeshmeou et Kol Yahweh Elohim Mithalekh beGan:* And they
heard the voice of Yahweh God, strolling in the garden. Sg 2:8: *Kol Dodi hine
Ze ba:* And here comes the voice of my Beloved. — *Trans.*

[3] Origen, *In Canticum Canticorum,* PG 13, 166.

[4] Ibid., 170.

beautiful," Isaiah says about him, "on the mountains, are the feet of one who brings good news, who heralds peace, brings happiness" (Is 52:7).

He runs, unable to hold back any longer, so strong is his love. "On the summit of the mountains, the wounded deer appears," Saint John of the Cross sings, "for, seeing that his bride is wounded with love, and hearing her moan, he too is wounded with love for her. . . . Thus he hastens immediately to her side to console her and caress her . . . and seems to be saying: 'O my bride, if you are wounded with love for me, I too, like the deer, through your wound am wounded with love for you.' "[5]

The Bride, who has first heard from very far away the footsteps of the beloved on the heights of the mountains, understands suddenly that he is inexplicably here. For him, there is no such thing as distance!

2:9 *See where he stands*
behind our wall. He looks in at the window,
he peers through the lattice.

While he showed daring and power when hastening to her, he is discreet and reserved now that he is present. He holds back and as if in hiding, behind the wall. Then he comes a little closer. He watches through the window for the moment when he will be able to enter. As a true lover also, he spies, through the thin lattice *(HaHarakim)*, the least gestures of her whose image is always with him. There is a truly striking contrast between this almighty one so joyously leaping over the mountains and the so humble and deferential waiting at the door of my life, him whose glance penetrates my very depths but who never wants to force the entrance of the soul—all the ardor of love, with the humblest respect. Saint Irenaeus loved to say

---

[5] Saint John of the Cross, *Cantique spirituel*, Stanza XIII, *Oeuvres Complètes*, Bibliothèque européenne (Paris: Desclée de Brouwer, 1958), 584.

that if many centuries had to elapse before man could be able to welcome the incarnate Word, many years also were needed for the Word of God to become familiar little by little with our humanity and to adjust, as it were, to our flesh. Isn't it already suggested in the successive approaches of the Bridegroom in the Song?

Meanwhile, the Bride has not lost sight of each of the steps of her Bridegroom, every one of his gestures. "See", as Saint Bernard has already pointed out, "with what pious subtlety the vigilant Bride discerns the approach of the Bridegroom and then notes his slightest gesture. He comes, he hastens, he approaches, he stands, he looks, he speaks. None of his gestures escapes the experienced Bride. . . . Even though he is hidden behind the wall, she felt his presence and guessed that he was watching her through the window and lattices. And now, to reward her for this religious vigil, he speaks."[6]

2:10 *My Beloved lifts up his voice,*

"And he spoke so softly", Saint John of the Cross writes, "that his voice immediately covers any other voice and overcomes all the noises of the world. For it is an extraordinarily powerful and inner voice."[7] He says:

2:10 *"Come then, my love,*
      my lovely one, come."

All God's desire for man is in this pressing call of the Bridegroom, a repeated call—"Come then, . . . come"—with the tenderest words of love—"my love, my lovely one". Love and loveliness, loveliness and beloved. So beautiful because she is loved. "Come", says the Bridegroom. Apparently, "the vig-

---

[6] Saint Bernard, *Sermons sur le Cantique des Cantiques, Oeuvres mystiques,* Sermon 57 (Paris: Seuil, 1953), 587.

[7] Saint John of the Cross, *Cantique spirituel,* Stanza XIV, 591.

ilant Bride", who was so good at discerning the successive approaches of her Bridegroom, has not yet moved; she is still very languid. She sees, she hears, but how difficult it is to act!

"Come . . . come", says the imploring voice of the Bridegroom, the same voice that will order the son of the widow to tear himself from the sleep of death: "I tell you to get up" (Lk 7:14). However, the Bridegroom does not force himself on her. He does not want to compel. "Come," he says, "come of your own will, not with regrets and out of necessity but on your own."[8] This is an invitation, not an order. It is "come" and not "go" that the Bridegroom says—the same invitation extended one day to the first two disciples: "Come and see"[9] (Jn 1:39).

But to what does the Bridegroom invite her in such a pressing manner? Simply to celebrate with him the season of love, the beautiful season of the year, the season of his beautiful betrothed, spring, time of the exodus from Egypt (Ex 13:4) and of the entrance into the promised land (Jos 4:19), the time of the Passover, his true birthday. The delights of the Palestinian spring are thus also those of the Bride herself, though she seems to have some difficulty in tearing herself away from the long winter she just experienced.

[8] Saint Gregory of Nyssa, *In Canticum Canticorum*, Homily 5, 876D.

[9] Here we have the imperative of the verb *halakh* (to go): Go! And the literal translation of 2:10, as of 2:13, would be, "Go to yourself!" But Joüon points out that this is in fact an ethical dative form that should be translated as "Go away!" To translate it thus with André Chouraqui and more precisely by "Go away toward yourself!", which has such a Socratic tone, would make the word we translated as "Come" attractive in itself and apparently grammatically correct. But the context does not allow this. Would it not be strange indeed that, after having told her "Go away!", the Bridegroom then becomes so urgent when drawing his love to himself and manifests such a strong desire to 'see her face and hear her voice', while she, on her part, expresses such pain when her Bridegroom goes away? Cf. Paul Joüon, *Grammaire de l'Hébreu biblique* (Rome: Pontifical Bible Institute, 1923), no. 133; "Introduction", *Cantique des Cantiques* (Paris: Beauchesne, 1909), no. 109, which is followed by Robert, Osty, TOB.

2:11 *For see, winter is past*, the Bridegroom sings,
the rains are over and gone.

2:12 *The flowers appear on the earth.*
The season of glad songs has come,
the cooing of the turtledove is heard
in our land.

2:13 *The fig tree is forming its first figs*
and the blossoming vines give out their fragrance.

Winter—the time of trial and exile—is past. It was also the time
of a sleeping and torpid soul. Here comes the spring! The
spring of renewal and conversion, the spring of love arising
with the coming of the Bridegroom, a rather extraordinary
spring which clearly goes from January to May and even leaps
joyfully into summer, the long spring of a loving God! It is
bursting out everywhere: with the first flowers that make such
a beautiful carpet of the Holy Land: "The flowers appear on the
earth." Vine and fig tree are not chosen by chance. In addition
to being the two trees grown by all the local peasants, and in
whose shade they rest in perfect Solomonic peace (cf. 1 K 5:5),
they appear here above all as a very tactful reminder of the first
love that started in the desert: "It was like finding grapes in the
wilderness when I found Israel, like seeing early fruit on the fig
tree when I saw your fathers" (Ho 9:10). And already we hear
the first songs of the birds, and the first are, of course, the love
birds: "The cooing of the turtledove is heard in our land." As
the Lord had said in Ezekiel: "Your time had come, the time
for love" (Ezk 16:8).

The entire creation is thus associated with the awakening of
the Bride: flowers on the mountains and in the valleys, songs
of birds, songs of men. There is always this correspondence in
the Bible between the whole world and the destiny of man, for
better and for worse. After the first sin, we see thorns and
weeds. But after the return of Israel to the first love of her
youth, everything takes on the color and the music of the

spring: "There is no creature", as Paul Claudel puts it, "for which the moment has not come to open itself to God now and to receive love."[10]

One phrase is especially moving when it comes from the mouth of the Bridegroom. He says: "in our land." It is because our land, with his coming, with the Incarnation, is also his. Now we share the same country. Saint Bernard felt this: "This is the second time that the heavenly Bridegroom speaks about the land. And he speaks so tenderly that you might think he were a creature of this earth, . . . It is very sweet to hear the God of Heaven say 'our land'. . . . 'In our land' — this does not have the ring of sovereign words, but of companionship and friendship. . . . He claims our earth not as his fief but as his motherland. And why not? He receives from it his Bride and his very body. . . . As Lord he rules over it; as Creator, he rules over it; as Bridegroom, he shares it."[11]

However, not only does the Bridegroom invite his love in almost supplicating words—twice he says "Come" from verse 10 to verse 13 inclusive—to enjoy with him this spring in the Holy Land, which is that of their love and their covenant. But he also begs her not to delay in showing her face to him, in letting him hear her voice:

2:14 *My dove, hiding in the clefts of the rock,*
    in the coverts of the cliff,
    show me your face,
    let me hear your voice;
    for your voice is sweet
    and your face is beautiful.

Until now, in the whole of Holy Scripture, the Bride—Israel—was the one who so ardently desired to hear and see the Bridegroom. "Show me your glory, I beg you", Moses implores

[10] Paul Claudel, *Paul Claudel interroge le Cantique des Cantiques* (Paris: NRF-Gallimard, 1948), 69.

[11] Saint Bernard, *Sermons,* Sermon 59, 610ff.

(Ex 33:18). And the psalmist: "My heart has said of you, 'Seek his face.' Yahweh, I do seek your face; do not hide your face from me" (Ps 27:8–9). What is new in the Song is that the Bridegroom implores the one he calls his dove to show her face and to let him hear her voice. Instead of staying secluded in her reserve and withdrawn into herself (like the timid and fearful dove in the clefts of the rock), she bravely decides to return to her Bridegroom, not averting her face but turning it toward him, not silent but responding to his call. To use the words of Origen: "Let her not stay inside the house anymore, but let her go out and meet him on the way."[12] We always dare so little; we are so stubbornly closed and withdrawn into ourselves. And this is not generally out of humility!

Thus Saint Francis de Sales understands this passage very well when he writes this paraphrase: "Let us go, arise, says the Bridegroom, get out of yourself, fly toward me my dove, my very beautiful love. . . . Come my very dearly beloved, and to see me more clearly, come to the window through which I am looking for you; come to contemplate in my heart the gap cut in my side when my body, like a demolished house, was so sadly destroyed on the tree of the Cross. Come and show me your face."[13]

What is noteworthy in this commentary of Saint Francis de Sales is that the cleft of the rock is at the same time the retreat of the fearful and sleepy dove and the opening in the side of the Bridegroom, through which he reveals himself to her and welcomes her. A very ancient mystical tradition has always seen in the cracks of the rock the new retreat where the Bride must now dwell, passing from her poor refuge within herself, where she had been hiding, to this very deep cave in the body of Christ, our "rock" (1 Co 10:4), which is the wound in his

[12] Origen, *In Canticum Canticorum*, 180.
[13] Saint Francis de Sales, *Traité de l'amour de Dieu, Oeuvres*, V: Bibliothèque de la Pléiade (Paris: NRF–Gallimard, 1969), 12, 600.

Heart (Jn 19:34). "How can one not see," writes Saint Bernard, "through these openings, the secret of his Heart that is bared in the wounds of his body?"[14] And Saint John of the Cross invites us to stay in these openings: "We will go up to the high caves of rock that are deeply hidden. In these caves the soul wants to go deeper and deeper, to be absorbed, to get intoxicated, to be deeply transformed in the love that the knowledge of the mystery will give to it and to hide in the bosom of her beloved. The latter, indeed, invites her in the Song of Songs to enter into the gaps of the stone, into the caves of the wall."[15]

And what supplicating terms he uses! It is truly in him that loving passion appears to be the most ardent, as we can hear in these tender names given to his beloved: my beloved, my love, my dove; the repeated call to come; his haste to see her face and hear her voice; the beauty he finds in her face; the sweetness he hears in her voice. Truly, how can one understand that the Word of God, voice of the Father, can find some sweetness in our voice and that he who is "the radiant light of God's glory" (Heb 1:3) can be sensitive to the beauty of our face? "Show me your face," he says, "let me hear your voice."

However, great and wild as it is, the love of the Bridegroom is without delusions. He is not blinded by passion. He knows that his Bride is very shy and fearful, still very much a prisoner of herself. She is quite ready, "like a silly, witless dove" to which the prophet Hosea compares Israel, to return again to Egypt or Assyria to ask for their help, rather than to her Bridegroom (Ho 7:11). We already know that the Bride has the sweetness and simplicity—praised by Jesus—of the dove (Mt 10:16), but she is also naive; and her love, while ardent, is still a frail and threatened love. Hence the extreme anguish of her Bridegroom when he thinks about the perils to which she is exposed:

[14] Saint Bernard, *Sermons,* Sermon 61, 631.
[15] Saint John of the Cross, *Cantique spirituel,* Stanza XXXVI, 671ff.

2:15 *Catch the foxes for us,*
      the little foxes
      that make havoc of the vineyards,
      for our vineyards are in flower.

Who are these nefarious foxes? First, they represent, on the historical plane, all those nasty and detested little neighbors who in their cowardice took advantage of the fact that Israel was in exile after the ruin of Jerusalem to come and loot the land and settle in a country that did not belong to them. Deuteronomy already gives a good list of them (Dt 20:17), and this is echoed in the Lamentations of Jeremiah: "because Mount Zion is desolate; jackals roam to and fro on it" (Lm 5:18).

But the vineyard of Yahweh Sabaoth is not only the Holy Land, it is each of our lives. And just as there are many foxes and jackals who come to make all kinds of mischief where the vines are in flower and then bear fruit, trampling on the plants and eating the grapes, there are also thousands of little enemies, in and out of ourselves, attempting to compromise and sabotage the work of the Lord, especially when love is still new, weak and poorly rooted. "Catch the foxes for us, the little foxes that make havoc of the vineyards." Saint John of the Cross stresses this image of the foxes: "We are dealing with a multitude of diverse thoughts, . . . with many motions and various attractions that come by their subtlety and vivacity to annoy the soul and trouble the sweetness and inner quiet it is enjoying. We are also dealing with demons who, jealous of the peace of the soul and its inner recollection, represent to the spirit horrors, troubles and fears—all these things that are called foxes. For, just as these nimble and shrewd little animals hop around and destroy the flowers of the vine when it blossoms, thus do the demons who are full of ruse and malice."[16] Not that they are so terrible in themselves! Gregory of Nyssa

---

[16] Ibid., Stanza XXVI, 638–639.

sees them as "little foxes that are shrewd and pathetic".[17] But one must take into account the frailty of the Bride. At the moment indeed "they are little foxes," Saint Francis de Sales says, "but do not let them grow; because if you wait, when you will want to catch them, they will already have spoiled everything."[18]

But the Bride feels so secure, so well protected and defended by the Bridegroom, who is now with her, that without bothering anymore about the little foxes, without paying too much attention to the wise warning of her Bridegroom, she thinks only about her blessed surrender to him:

2:16 *My Beloved is mine and I am his.*
He pastures his flock among the lilies.

John of the Cross in the passage of the Ascent copied by Thérèse of Lisieux has the Bride say: "Leaning my face over my beloved, I forgot myself; everything vanished for me, and I surrendered, letting all my concerns get lost among the lilies."[19] "My Beloved is mine and I am his"—this is all the Bride is capable of saying and repeating. In her mouth, this is the sunny song of happiness, of perfect reciprocity in union: "It is a continuous renewal of the covenant between my soul and its beloved", Marie of the Incarnation is able to say. "O God, how great is this union! It is a mixture of love and love, and one can say with God: 'My Beloved is mine and I am his.' "[20] This is the expression of the covenant so often used by the prophets: "You shall be my people and I will be your God"

---

[17] Saint Gregory of Nyssa, *In Canticum Canticorum,* Homily 5, 881A.

[18] Saint Francis de Sales, Letter 60 to the nuns of the Monastery of the Filles-Dieu, *Correspondance,* Bibliothèque européenne (Paris: Desclée de Brouwer, 1980), 99.

[19] Saint Thérèse of the Child Jesus, *Lettres* (Paris: Cerf/Desclée de Brouwer, 1977), Letter 108, 177.

[20] Guy-Marie Oury, *Marie de l'Incarnation,* vol. 1 (Québec/Abbaye de Saint-Pierre, Solesmes: Presses de l'Université Laval, 1973), 127.

(Ezk 36:28); "I will be their God and they shall be my people" (Jr 31:33). It is repeated and transposed here by the Bride in terms of conjugal love. To express the love of his people for him, Jesus will use similar phrasings: "I know my sheep and my sheep know me" (Jn 10:14; cf. also 6:56; 17:23).

Such is also the dream of the Bride, a slightly premature dream, though she does explain quite clearly through the order of the words she uses that in this union all the initiative comes from her Bridegroom. And because he was the first to love her (1 Jn 4:19), because he first belonged to her, she therefore belongs so totally to him. This is enough to make her happy. "See, Theotime," writes Francis de Sales, "how the holy Shulamite is content to know that her beloved is with her or on her breast or in his pasture or anywhere else, as long as she knows where he is! Thus she is a very peaceful, calm and restful Shulamite. And this rest is at times so deep in its tranquility that the whole soul and its faculties remain as if asleep, without any motion or action of any kind."[21]

Her beloved is with her; more, he is here, and indeed this is enough for her: "[Pasturing] his flock among the lilies," the Bride says. He is again in the heart of his land. The Holy Land in festive attire with flowers like a carpet of lilies ("I am . . . the lily of the valleys", the Bride had said; 2:1) forms the bed on which the Bridegroom and his Bride are resting. And the Good Shepherd of Israel with his two staves, "goodwill" and "union" (Zc 11:7), is today among his own; he is pasturing his flock; his sheep that had been scattered are now gathered with him among the lilies of the Holy Land. Surrendering totally to her beloved, the Bride enjoys the deepest peace.

How can we then explain the sad words that follow?

2:17 *Before the dawn wind rises,*
before the shadows flee,

---

[21] Saint Francis de Sales, *Traité*, VI:8, 633.

return! Be, my Beloved,
like a gazelle,
a young stag,
on the mountains of the covenant.

How can she cry "return!", she who a moment ago was saying, "My Beloved is mine and I am his"? Is this the effect of
some confusion in the text? In fact, we have here one of these
passages of the Song in which spiritual experience in its joy and
pain is rendered very precisely. The time of perfect rest in
irrevocable and fulfilled possession of the beloved is not for
this life: first because the Bride is weak, frail and inconstant,
subject to those "intermittencies of the heart" as Proust calls
them[22]—on fire now and icy the next moment—and also because the Bridegroom, for his part, never lets himself be completely caught. He could never be kept forcefully by our
mastery and possession. It is even good for him to escape us at
times and in the most unexpected way so as to increase in us the
regret of his absence and therefore the desire of his presence.
Such is his paradox! "By fleeing, he lets himself be discovered. . . . Hiding himself, he unveils his secrets to us; re-
fusing himself, he surrenders."[23]

William of Saint-Thierry writes very subtly about these
games of divine love: "The Bridegroom often seems to play
with the Bride the game of passionate love, and he always tears
himself violently from the arms of his love in order to surrender again to the whim of her desires. At times, he goes out and
away as if for a definitive retreat, so as to be sought out more
ardently. At other times, he returns and comes to her, as if for
a perpetual stay, to invite her more tenderly to kiss him. At

[22] Marcel Proust, *Sodome et Gomorrhe, À la recherche du temps perdu,* Bibliothèque de la Pléiade (Paris: NRF-Gallimard 1978), 751–781.
[23] Élisabeth de Miribel, *La liberté souffre violence* (Paris: Plon, 1981), 241,
quoting Hadewijch of Antwerp.

other times yet, he stands behind the wall and looks through the window to excite the desire of the Bride by letting himself be seen, though not fully so, with a sweet face, or by letting her hear, from however afar, his invitations and calls. But then, once the fire has been well kindled in the heart of the beloved, he goes away for good and vanishes. He is neither seen, heard nor felt. The bride, unable to detain the fugitive, begs him therefore to come back at least from time to time: return, my beloved, be like the gazelle or the stag."[24] Thus the psalmist was already sighing: "God, you are my God, I am seeking you, my soul is thirsting for you, my flesh is longing for you, a land parched, weary and waterless" (Ps 63:1–2).

The entire admirable seventy-fourth sermon of Saint Bernard on the Song, a kind of long confession of his heart, bears witness in the same way to a very deep experience of these comings and goings, these arrivals and unforeseeable departures of the Bridegroom. "Who will enlighten for me the mysteries of these ups and downs and explain to me the comings and goings of the Word? . . . The Word of God, who is God himself and the Bridegroom of the soul, comes to the soul, then leaves it at whim. . . . One can seek him only when he is absent and call him back at the moment he goes away. . . . Once the Word of God is gone and until he comes back, the soul has only one voice, one continuous cry, a restless desire, a perpetual 'come back'. . . . Perhaps the Bridegroom has left on purpose so that it can call him with more fervor and retain him better when he comes back? It did happen in fact, on a certain day, that he feigned a departure not because he had decided to go but to hear it say: 'Stay with us, Lord, for evening is coming' . . . He wants it to hold him back when he passes by and to call him back when he is absent. He visits the soul at daybreak; then tries it by suddenly withdrawing. And if he goes

[24] William of Saint-Thierry, *Exposé sur le Cantique des Cantiques* (Paris: Cerf, 1966), 369.

away, this too is a way of giving himself. . . . I confess, not without some indiscretion, that I have thus received the visit of the Word several times. And if he entered often into my soul, I did not feel it each time. I felt his presence, I remember it; and, at times, I was able to foresee his coming; but never have I had a precise awareness of his entering or going out; . . . no motion on his part announced his arrival. . . . Yes, here is the sign of his departure: my soul is irresistibly seized with sadness until he comes back, and each time he warns my soul, which is the mark of his return. . . . As long as I shall live, I will use in a familiar way to call him back this very phrase of the Bride: 'return!' And each time he escapes me, I will repeat this call. I will not cease to cry, as it were, after him, to proclaim the desire my heart has for him. . . . I beg him to come back full of grace and truth, i.e., as he always is, as he was yesterday and the day before yesterday. In this he seems to me to resemble very much the gazelle and the stag: he has the eyes of a gazelle and the grace and joyful leaps of a stag."[25]

The Bride would love him to regain at that moment the gazelle and young stag's pace that he had when he came to her. "My Beloved is like a gazelle, like a young stag", she had said when he came running from the mountains and the hills. "Be, my Beloved, like a gazelle, a young stag," she says now; yes, as you were before! "Indeed, these animals", as Claudel notes

[25] Saint Bernard, *Sermons*, Sermon 74, p. 761ff. Remarkably, there is a parallel between these words of Saint Bernard and those of Origen in his first homily on the Song: "[The Bride] looks for the Bridegroom, who showed himself and then vanished. This happens frequently through this Song, and he who has experienced such things can understand. Often, as God is my witness, I felt that the Bridegroom was coming close and that he was with me as much as he could be. Then he suddenly went away, and I could not find what I was looking for. Again, I start to desire his coming, and, at times, he does return. And when he has come back, when I hold him in my hands, there he goes again, fleeing from me, and once he has vanished, I go back seeking him. This happens often until I truly hold him." *Homélies sur le Cantique des Cantiques,* Homily 1:7 (Paris: Cerf, 1966), 75.

joyfully, "bring very well to mind the image of the beloved: his idea, in the mode of suddenness, inspiration, abrupt comings and goings."[26]

Thus the Bride is begging her beloved to come back and to do so not waiting for "the dawn wind [which] rises, before the shadows flee," i.e., before daybreak. For she ardently desires the return of the one she loves for the hour of covenant and union, for the wedding night. The symbolism of the night, in the Song as in spiritual life, is in fact polyvalent. At times, it is the night of absence—absence of the Bridegroom and thus of the light—because the soul has closed itself to the Bridegroom (as we will see at the beginning of the fourth poem); or else because the Bridegroom, by himself, for the progress of his love, has gone away (as in this second poem). Though the night can also be linked to the presence of the Bridegroom, who, even when he is very obviously present at the deepest level of life, remains hidden. Night is then that of union and wedding with the Bride and, with all her soul, she desires it and does not want to waste a moment, as we hear her express it here: "Before the dawn wind rises, before the shadows flee, return!"

It seems that, through these words, the Bride remembers particularly this very first night at the beginning of her history; that was the night of the covenant with the Bridegroom. Abraham had cut in half the victims of the sacrifice, and God, like a devouring fire, had passed between the two halves and had consumed them (Gn 15:1–21). Well, then, let Yahweh come tonight, also on the mountain of the covenant, i.e., on the hill of Zion, which has been abandoned for so long! Let him return to the heart of her life for a definitive union of covenant, and let the Bridegroom hasten for this union of love, as fast as a gazelle or a young stag!

But the Bridegroom has vanished as if forever! The Bridegroom is silent.

---

[26] Claudel, *Paul Claudel*, 100.

3:1 *On my bed, at night, I sought him*
whom my heart loves.
I sought but did not find him.

3:2 *So I will rise and go through the City;*
in the streets and the squares
I will seek him whom my heart loves.
. . . I sought but did not find him.

What a change in her who had exclaimed so joyfully: "All green is our bed" (1:16). Here she is, ready to say with the psalmist: "every night I drench my pillow and soak my bed with tears" (Ps 6:6). This is not the bed of her wedding night but of sickness and fever, on which she tosses without respite. "On my bed, at night, I sought . . ."

The Bridegroom, who had been hers—for a time she thought it would last forever—the beloved, who recently said that he found such sweetness in her voice, does not even seem to hear her call. He is insensitive to her complaint. He ran away mercilessly. Four times, in these sad verses, the word that describes the new activity of the bride appears: seek. "I sought", "I seek", "I will seek". And echoing it, at the end of each attempt, are these other despairing words: "I . . . . did not find him."

"And with him", writes William of Saint-Thierry, "vanishes also all the spiritual and divine beauty of the vines and the flowers. The fragrance of sweetness disappears with all its delights: joy of the flowers, fragrance of the vines, richness of the fruits. . . . The friend then loses the belief in friendship; the dove loses the beauty of her face and the sweetness of her voice; what is most beautiful loses the grace of divine resemblance. And what is left to her is her solitude; to the dove, her moaning; to beauty, the lonely woman. The clefts of the rock are closed again, the gaps in the wall closed up, no more a refuge for the dove whose heart is gone."[27]

[27] William of Saint-Thierry, *Exposé*, 347.

The polarity of "seek-find", which is at the core of this passage, is one of the major dualities in all of Holy Scripture. Chouraqui, a son of Israel, recognizes it without difficulty: "Nowhere can we see", he writes, "the most profound characteristic of the biblical revelation as clearly as here: the universe is the locus of a love drama. The lover and the beloved will for ever desire and call each other, lose and seek each other, find and embrace each other."[28]

In his prison of Toledo, John of the Cross knew a more desolating thing than the solitude of his cell: the absence of the beloved who escapes and whom he pursues endlessly: "But this is night!" repeats the refrain of the poem endlessly.[29]

The anxious search of the Bride is such that she forgets all prudence and reserve. She gets up ("So I will rise", she says resolutely; she does not need any more to implore "return!"; 2:17). She goes out alone in the middle of the night, without caring about her safety, in the squares and through the streets of the city. Thus she exposes her passion to the public. But what does she care about opinion or even the risks she might run? She wanders among the narrow market streets, in the large squares, exploring all nooks and crannies. Her search is fruitless. The one whom she has not found through the ardent imploration of her prayer could not be given back to her by the city of men. He is neither here nor there, and nothing and no one could bring him back to her. He is found only when he freely reveals himself of his own choice. Teresa of Avila does not fail to complain that this is too unjust, that she already has much to do and, by the same token, not enough time to devote to contemplative prayer: at least God should be there at those moments. But, on the contrary, he hides himself and remains silent! This is more than she can stand: "Well, then, God! Is it not enough for you to let me stay in this miserable life that I

---

[28] André Chouraqui, "Introduction au Poème des Poèmes", *La Bible* (Paris: Desclée de Brouwer, 1975), 24.

[29] Saint John of the Cross, *Poèmes,* VII, *Oeuvres complètes,* Bibliothèque européenne (Paris: Desclée de Brouwer, 1958), 927–928.

bear for the love of you, accepting to live here where everything prevents me from enjoying you, where I have to drink and sleep, and negotiate and deal with the world, as well as bear everything for the love of you? You well know, my Lord, what a tremendous torment this is for me. Must you also hide yourself in the rare moments that are left for me to enjoy you? How can your mercy tolerate this? How can your love for me accept this? I believe, Lord, that if it were possible for me to hide myself from you as you hide yourself from me, I believe, I think, that your love for me would not tolerate it. You are with me and you always see me. This is unbearable, my Lord; I beg you to consider that you are hurting one who loves you so much."[30] When the Madre complains. . . !

In her wild race through the city (through Jerusalem, through the whole world), the Bride has only one name on her lips: "him whom my heart loves." She has no other name for him. Four times in four verses, we encounter these words, spelling out at the same time all her tenderness and heartbreak. It is understandable that very often this passage of the Song was applied by the Fathers of the Church to the anxious search for Jesus by his mother through the streets of Jerusalem. Does she not also say on that day, she, the truly beloved of God, "My child, why have you done this to us? See how worried your father and I have been, looking for you" (Lk 2:48)?

However, the Bride is not satisfied with looking by herself and in all directions. She even asks the passersby. Here come the watchmen on their night rounds:

3:3 *The watchmen came upon me*
      on their rounds in the City:
      "Have you seen him whom my heart loves?"

Who are these watchmen? Would they be those of whom it is said by God in Isaiah: "On your walls, Jerusalem, I set watch-

---

[30] Saint Teresa of Avila, *Autobiographie*, 37:8, *Oeuvres complètes*.

men. Day or night they must never be silent" (Is 62:6–7)? Or
are they patrols of the occupying power making their night
rounds in the streets of the capital? What is certain is that the
Bride does not get any response from them. They show neither compassion nor interest nor even attention. It must be
said, of course, that she gives a rather peculiar description of
her spouse: "Have you seen him whom my heart loves?"
Which prompts Paul Claudel to say with a great deal of irrev-
erence: "Is this the kind of question one asks a policeman?"[31]
Saint Bernard had already shared his surprise: "As if these
watchmen", he says, "could know her thoughts, she questions
them about the one she loves. It is as if he had no name!"[32] But
how could the Bridegroom have for the others another name
than the one he has for her?

It might be worthwhile to dwell briefly, as M. Feuillet does,
on the link between the race of the Bride in the streets of Jerusalem in the Song and that other race of Mary Magdalen to the
empty tomb of Jesus on Easter morning. It is the same loving
search, the same wild haste, through the same city before daybreak; the same anguish, the same tears, the same questions
that are incomprehensible when thus posed to any passerby: "I
don't know where they have put him.". . . "Tell me where
you have put him" (Jn 20:13–15). Could the kinship between
the two scenes have escaped Saint John?

The watchmen making their rounds in the city are quite incapable of answering the Bride. The city does not shelter him.
No more than in her room will the Bride obtain the return of
the one she loves by wandering in the streets and the squares
and addressing herself to those whose mission is to watch over
the city. She must go beyond everything in order finally to
find him:

[31] Claudel, *Paul Claudel*, Bibliothèque européenne (Paris: Desclée de Brouwer, 1964), 284.
[32] Saint Bernard, *Sermons*, Sermon 79, 808.

3:4 *Scarcely had I passed them*
than I found him whom my heart loves.

"Scarcely had I passed them". Neither the world nor men nor even the Churchmen (the watchmen) can give me the presence of the Bridegroom. I must go beyond all things—to the mystery of a presence obtained only through total self-surpassing. Untiringly, in his commentary on the Song as well as in his Life of Moses, Gregory of Nyssa came back to the capital theme of all genuine spirituality: "The teaching Scripture gives us is, I think, the following: he who wants to see God will do so in the very fact of always following him. The contemplation of his face is an endless walking toward him. . . . There is only one way to grasp the power that transcends all intelligence. . . : not to stop while always searching beyond what has already been grasped."[33]

But the cry of the Bride must be heard now:

I found him whom my heart loves.

Where did she find him? It is not said. In fact, he was nowhere else than in her own heart. Nowhere but in her inmost self, and not outside of the self, that the Bridegroom inhabits, that he will always inhabit. Thus it is in her soul, going deeper and deeper in it in an endless search, that the Bride will find again the one she loves, insofar as he can be found. "It must be noted", Saint John of the Cross says, "that to find the Bridegroom, insofar as it is possible in this life, the Word in union with the Father and the Holy Spirit resides essentially in the deepest part of the soul, where he hides. . . . Thus the soul that must find him in a love union must detach its will from all created things, enter in deepest recollection within itself and there keep very loving and very affectionate relationships with God. . . . This is why Saint Augustine, addressing himself to

---

[33] Saint Gregory of Nyssa, *In Canticum Canticorum*, Homily 2, 801AB–805D.

God in the *Confessions,* tells him, 'Lord, I did not find you outside myself because I did not know how to look for you! I looked outside, while you are in me.'[34] God is thus hidden in the soul, and this is where the true contemplative must look for him, asking, 'Where did you hide, my friend?' "[35]

As suddenly and as mysteriously as he had vanished, the Bridegroom lets himself be discovered, without reason or cause and without foreseeable signs, according to his absolute freedom. What a happiness now in this cry: "I found him"! The bride does not say, "I found you again", for the discovery is always the first one and always new. For "he always comes for the first time", as Ruysbroeck points out, "as if he had never come before. . . . His arrival is always an eternal now."[36]

Find is also the word that the first disciples always send to one another—five times in the Gospel of John—and so many after them when they share their encounter with Jesus: "I found", "we have found".[37]

Ah, the Bride is again together with him, and she is not ready to let him go:

3:4 *I held him fast, nor would I let him go.*

She grasped him when she found him; and she will not let go of him whom she holds. At least this is what she claims. It is almost amusing to see how sure and proud of herself she is! One might be tempted to think that she seized him by force! And that she can dispose of him at her will! What does she intend to do now? Nothing less than drag him to the home of her mother:

[34] Saint Augustine, *Confessions,* Book X, 27 (38); PL 32, 795; and CCL 27, 175.

[35] Saint John of the Cross, *Cantique spirituel,* Stanza I, 527.

[36] Jan van Ruysbroeck the Admirable, *Ornement des noces spirituelles,* Book III, iii, *Oeuvres* (Brussels: Vromant, 1920), 212.

[37] Jn 1:41–45 (TOB).

3:4 . . . *nor would I let him go*
till I had brought him
into my mother's house,
into the room of her who conceived me.

This is a source of rejoicing for Saint Francis de Sales: "See, Theotime, this Bride thinks that she can do no less than keep the beloved at her mercy as a slave of love; she imagines that she is the one to lead him at her whim and take him to the dear home of her mother. . . . The Spirit, hurrying in loving passion, always gives itself an advantage over the beloved one."[38]

It is understandable that the Bride would now want to be alone with the one she loves. Was it however truly necessary for her to insist to such a degree, even to the point of indiscretion, even to asking him to lock himself up with her in "my mother's house" and again in "the room of her who conceived me"?

But we must never lose sight of the fact that the Bride is called Israel and that the sole desire of the Bride-Israel, exiled far from her homeland and from the Temple of Yahweh her Bridegroom, is to go back to Jerusalem, the beloved country of her birth, her "mother's house", and to see in his Temple, in the Holy of Holies of the Temple, in "the room of her who conceived me" at the very source of her life, the return of the King, her Bridegroom.

It is not enough though to see him coming only to her, to his people. She is asking for more. She wants in fact to bring the one she loves into "my mother's house, . . . the room of her who conceived me", to be begotten again by him, maternally as it were, in a "new birth". She feels quite keenly that in order to be fully his, to be truly one with him, she must be reborn from him, not only to link her life with him but to receive her very life from him. As Jesus tells Nicodemus, she has to be born again, to be "born from above", i.e., from him (Jn 3:3),

---

[38] Saint Francis de Sales, *Traité*, III:6, 500.

so that she can be both Bride and daughter. For such is the new couple of the new covenant, where the Bride is wife and daughter at the same time to the Bridegroom, as Eve was to Adam and as the Church is when emerging from the open side of Christ, her spouse, on the Cross (Jn 19:34–37).

The second poem should come to an end here, with this marvelous wish of the Bride that henceforth it will not be she who lives but her beloved in her, as Paul was one day to say to the Galatians (Ga 2:20). Alas, the desires of the Bride go faster than the complete conversion of her heart!

3:5 *I charge you,*
  daughters of Jerusalem, the Bridegroom says,
  by the gazelles, by the hinds of the field,
  not to stir my love, nor rouse it,
  until it please to awake.

This has already been the conclusion of the first poem: an invitation to respect the sleep of the Bride, though one could think at this point that it might be the sleep of union. Chouraqui does interpret it in such a way: "The union is consummated in wonder and in fulfillment."[39]

Unfortunately, the refrain, which comes back three times in the Poem on the lips of the Bridegroom,[40] still stresses the fact that perfect identification in love has not yet been reached. Indeed, the Bride has surrendered very sincerely and lovingly, and she desires to be one with her Bridegroom through this union. But how frail she still is! "The spirit is strong; the flesh is weak", Jesus says. Simon Peter protests: "I would give my life for you"—and this too is sincere, though we know what happens shortly thereafter. It is only at the end of the entire

[39] André Chouraqui, *Le Cantique des Cantiques* (Paris: Presses Universitaires de France, 1970), 54–55.
[40] As "the triple key of the poem's composition", Claudel notes; *Paul Claudel*, 98. Cf. Sg 2:7, 3:5, 8:4.

Song that the love of the Bride will be fully and definitively the victor. However, it does progress and deepen step by step.

This time again, the Bridegroom is not expressing any surprise or impatience. A whole life is needed, as he well knows, to achieve the work of conversion and divinization. He knows that the spring, though beautiful, is not the summer. He has the patience of a lover: "[Do] not . . . stir my love *(ahavah),* nor rouse it, until it please to awake."

The Summer of the Wedding

THIRD POEM

Chapters 3:6–5:1

THE CHORUS

What is this coming up from the desert
like a column of smoke,
breathing of myrrh and frankincense
and every perfume the merchant knows?

See, it is the litter of Solomon.
Around it are sixty champions,
the flower of the warriors of Israel;
all of them skilled swordsmen,
veterans of battle.
Each man has his sword at his side,
against alarms by night.

King Solomon
has made himself a throne
of wood from Lebanon.
The posts he has made of silver,
the canopy of gold,
the seat of purple;
the back is inlaid with ebony.

Daughters of Zion,
come and see
King Solomon,
wearing the diadem with which his mother crowned him
on his wedding day,
on the day of his heart's joy.

THE BRIDEGROOM

How beautiful you are, my love,
how beautiful you are!
Your eyes, behind your veil,
are doves;
your hair is like a flock of goats
frisking down the slopes of Gilead.
Your teeth are like a flock of shorn ewes
as they come up from the washing.
Each one has its twin,
not one unpaired with another.
Your lips are a scarlet thread
and your words enchanting.
Your cheeks, behind your veil,
are halves of pomegranate.
Your neck is the tower of David
built as a fortress,
hung around with a thousand bucklers,
and each the shield of a hero.
Your two breasts are two fawns,
twins of a gazelle,
that feed among the lilies.

Before the dawn wind rises,
before the shadows flee,
I will go to the mountain of myrrh,
to the hill of frankincense.

You are wholly beautiful, my love,
and without a blemish.

Come from Lebanon, my promised bride,
come from Lebanon, come on your way.
Lower your gaze, from the heights of Amana,
from the crests of Senir and Hermon,
the haunt of lions,
the mountains of leopards.

You ravish my heart,
my sister, my promised bride,
you ravish my heart
with a single one of your glances,
with one single pearl of your necklace.
What spells lie in your love,
my sister, my promised bride!
How delicious is your love, more delicious than wine!
How fragrant your perfumes,
more fragrant than all other spices!
Your lips, my promised one,
distill wild honey.
Honey and milk
are under your tongue;
and the scent of your garments
is like the scent of Lebanon.

She is a garden enclosed,
my sister, my promised bride;
a garden enclosed,
a sealed fountain.
Your shoots form an orchard of pomegranate trees,
the rarest essences are yours:
nard and saffron,
calamus and cinnamon,
with all the incense-bearing trees;
myrrh and aloes,
with the subtlest odors.
Fountain that makes the garden fertile,
well of living water,
streams flowing down from Lebanon.

THE BRIDE

Awake, north wind,
come, wind of the south!
Breathe over my garden,

to spread its sweet smell around.
Let my Beloved come into his garden,
let him taste its rarest fruits.

The Bridegroom

I come into my garden,
my sister, my promised bride,
I gather my myrrh and balsam,
I eat my honey and my honeycomb,
I drink my wine and my milk.
Eat, friends, and drink,
drink deep, my dearest friends.

The Summer of the Wedding

In the third poem there is a new point of departure within the Song. If anyone shares the sadness of Gregory of Nyssa because of the slowness of the Bride—"How can one fail to be sad", Gregory writes in his sixth homily, "if we consider that after having already risen in so many love ascents, . . . the soul does not seem yet to have grasped what it is seeking, . . . that it is still far from having reached the perfection of those who have not even taken the first step"—one must reply daringly with the very same Gregory that, in fact, the way of the Bride has not been a delusion until now. She has, from step to step, made a great deal of progress, "the path she walked before becoming each time for her the point of departure for a superior reality" and a new "prelude to ascent".[1]

3:6 *What is this coming up from the desert*
like a column of smoke,
breathing of myrrh and frankincense
and every perfume the merchant knows?

As the start of the second poem had been vivacious and joyful like a dance, the beginning of the third one is slow and grave like a solemn march.

This one opens with a striking vision: "What is this?" This is truly a neutral form that we must read together with Dhorme, Joüon and Robert: "What is this?" Coming from the depth of the desert, a long column as yet indistinct shows up on the horizon. But it is not really so much the distance, the remoteness, of the column that causes the chorus of the nations

[1] Saint Gregory of Nyssa, *In Canticum Canticorum*, Homily 6, PG 44, 890–894.

to ask the question; it is rather the very nature of the column and the mystery surrounding it. The chorus of the nations is confronted with the very mystery of Yahweh.

Indeed, everything suggests that this is he; the question itself, always rising from the heart of man when God reveals himself, is already that of the Hebrews in the desert when faced with the mystery of the manna—"What is that?", they too had asked (Ex 16:15)—or of Moses confronted with the mystery of the burning bush (Ex 3:3).[2] Indeed Yahweh himself is coming today, as in the days of Exodus, before his people. He comes from the depth of the wilderness with his people toward the promised land. (In the Bible, people always come up, toward Jerusalem.) He leads them, visible and invisible at the same time in the column of smoke (Ex 13:21). "A column of smoke," the Song says, like the one that rose from the mountain before the covenant was made: "The mountain of Sinai was entirely wrapped in smoke, because Yahweh had descended on it in the form of fire. Like smoke from a furnace the smoke went up" (Ex 19:18). In the same vein, Isaiah, on the day of his vocation, had seen the Temple filled with smoke (Is 6:4), an aromatic smoke yielding the perfumes that are precisely linked to the Temple in the liturgy, myrrh and frankincense, but with them also "every perfume the merchant knows", radiating from the presence of him who is at the same time King of his people, King of all the foreign nations, and "beyond everything".

It is noteworthy however that one does not see him.

---

[2] René Laurentin points out very aptly that during the first apparitions of the Virgin Mary in Lourdes, Bernadette always and spontaneously described with the neutral "that" (*Aquerò* in the Lourdes patois) the strange and mysterious object of her visions. "Thus the mystics, be they cultured or not," comments Laurentin, "at times evoke the light of God in terms of night, his transcendental existence in terms of nothingness. This comes from a concern not to express oneself vulgarly and inadequately about all that is 'other'." "Vie de Bernadette", *Le livre du centenaire* (Paris: Desclée de Brouwer, 1978), 56.

3:7 *See, it is the litter of Solomon,* the chorus proclaims.

It is his litter, and not him, that is seen. Budde and Joüon note quite judiciously that the Hebrew of the Song tells about the noble companions who are "around it" (i.e., the litter) and not "around him": just as the armies of Israel used to advance around the ark (the litter) sheltering the invisible power of Yahweh.

If the name of Solomon is invoked, and it is three times in this passage, this is not really in memory of the most prestigious king of Israel but because he who advances in such a way, sovereign and brother at the same time to his companions, as Lord but also as one among us, is the true son of David, the prince of peace, according to the etymology itself of Solomon's name. "Do you really believe", asks Gregory of Nyssa, "that I want to talk about that Solomon born of Bathsheba? . . . No, but of another Solomon signified by the first one. He too was born of the race of David, according to the flesh (Rm 1:3); his name is 'peace' (Heb 7:2); he is the true King of Israel (Jn 1:49; 12:13); he is the builder of God's Temple (Mt 16:18; 26:61; 27:40); he is the one whose wisdom is unlimited or rather whose very being is wisdom (1 Co 1:24) and truth (Jn 14:6)."[3] He is the king of whom Isaiah had rightly prophesied that he would one day take the lead of his people to bring them back victoriously to their land, he "who heralds peace, brings happiness, proclaims salvation, and tells Zion, 'Your God is king!'" (Is 52:7). He is the genuine Solomon, "the king of peace and glory", and the gates of his city are too low to let him pass when he arrives: "Gates, raise your arches, rise, you ancient doors," the psalmist orders, "let the king of glory in! Who is this king of glory? He is Yahweh Sabaoth, King of glory, he!" (Ps 24:9–10).

---

[3] Saint Gregory of Nyssa, *In Canticum Canticorum,* Homily 1, 766CD.

He is, in absolute truth, by both his divine and human features, absolutely unique while intimately united to his people—the messiah-King—and the heroes of his people surround
the litter (the ark) of his presence:

3:7 *Around it are sixty champions,*
    the flower of the warriors of Israel;

3:8 *all of them skilled swordsmen,*
    veterans of battle.
    Each man has his sword at his side,
    against alarms by night.

These fearless men do not represent a threatening force. They
are the impressive guard of the King. The sixty heroes show
above all the valor of their commander. In the service of the
son of David and in his company, they have served "for a long
and patient time". They have become veterans, dexterous and
knowledgeable. They are discerning men. And each one of
them is armed against the powers of the night—above all
against the prince of darkness, whose surprises are always
threatening—with his sword at his side, with which Saint Paul
also tells the Ephesians to arm themselves so as to face "the
darkness in this world" (Ep 6:10–17).

The Song calls them the "champions" of Solomon, the very
word used in the Second Book of Samuel to describe the thirty
brave men guarding David (2 S 23:8–39). But the guard of the
son of David, the new Solomon, is twice as large as that of
David: there are "sixty champions".

He whom we saw arriving at the beginning from the desert,
hidden in the column of smoke and perfume, whose litter then
enters the gates of the city under the guard of his champions, is
now entering his palace and ascending to his throne; his title of
King is at last given to him. After having suffered for a long
time on the road among his people, he now appears among
them in all his glory:

3:9   *King Solomon*
      has made himself a throne
      of wood from Lebanon.

3:10 *The posts he has made of silver,*
      the canopy of gold,
      the seat of purple,
      the back is inlaid with ebony.

We use the word *throne* as did André Robert, a word that many exegetes translate as "litter". It is, as the description suggests, a piece of furniture that has a purple seat, silver posts, and a gold canopy and on which King Solomon will sit. These are the very features of a throne; the word *appiryon,* which we encounter only in this passage of the Bible, indicates, however, that this throne is something wholly unique: "Your throne, God, shall last for ever and ever", as is said in Psalm 45 to the messianic King (Ps 45:6). Thus there is most likely a desired contrast between the litter surrounded by the champions, the humble tabernacle of Yahweh's presence in the desert marches when he "led a wanderer's life in a tent" (2 S 7:6), and the royal seat that he is taking today.

This throne captures the attention of the Song's poet. Of the entire palace of the King, nothing is described except this symbol of infinite grandeur and majesty. "I saw the Lord Yahweh seated on a high throne." It was all that Isaiah could perceive when he "looked at the King" (Is 6:1, 5) in this same Temple of Jerusalem, where gold, silver, Lebanon's precious woods, the purple of the veil for the Holy of Holies were composed like here for the throne of the King of the Song, a sort of hymn to both the power and the splendor of the royal Bridegroom of Israel. The Book of Kings says: "The king also made a great ivory throne, and plated it with refined gold. . . . No throne like this was ever made in any other kingdom" (1 K 10:18, 20). The King of the Song has a throne that can well compare with that of the historical Solomon. Was it not promised to the true son of David, on the day of the Annunciation, that "the Lord God will give him the throne of his ancestor David" (Lk 1:32)? It is even the only detail associated with sovereignty in the entire narrative of Luke.

This throne is received by the new Solomon from God, from himself, as it is written: "Yahweh's oracle to you, my Lord, 'Sit at my right' " (Ps 110:1); and "Your throne, God, shall last for ever and ever" (Ps 45:6—JB). This is why the Song stresses that he "made himself a throne". No one gives it to him. And yet a whole people, in fact all of mankind, worked at it humbly and courageously.

And it is all of mankind that we hear in the voices of the daughters of Jerusalem, pressing the people of Zion to get out of the city, to recognize the universal sovereignty of the coming King:

3:11 *Daughters of Zion,*
come and see
King Solomon,
wearing the diadem with which his mother crowned him
on his wedding day,
on the day of his heart's joy.

It is only in this third poem, at the very core of the Song, that the Bridegroom is thus revealed in the fullness of his majesty. In the Prologue and the first poem, he could appear as King only through his hold over the heart of his beloved—"The King has brought me into his rooms" (1:4); "while the King rests in his own room" (1:12). But here, in the third poem, he is the acknowledged King, acclaimed and crowned by the holy city of Jerusalem, city of God and city of men, called here and exclusively in the Song, Zion, in the context of a royal advent wholly similar to the one described by Isaiah: "Say to the daughter of Zion, 'Look, your savior comes' " (Is 62:11); and more directly yet in Zechariah: "Rejoice heart and soul, daughter of Zion! Shout with gladness, daughter of Jerusalem!

See now, your king comes to you; he is victorious, he is triumphant" (Zc 9:9).

How could we not draw a parallel between the acclamations of the crowd at the arrival of the Song's King in his city with these prophetic words of Zechariah, which Saint John sees quite explicitly as accomplished in the welcome given to Jesus on Palm Sunday? "The crowds who had come up for the festival heard that Jesus was on his way to Jerusalem", and Jesus, at the end of a long ascent, also has a solemn entry into this very city of Jerusalem, the only time in his life when he is acclaimed as a king: *"Blessings on the King of Israel, who comes in the name of the Lord. . . . Do not be afraid, daughter of Zion; see, your king is coming"* (Jn 12:12–15).

And the author of the Song is not incoherent when he writes that "King Solomon [is] wearing the diadem with which his mother crowned him on his wedding day" just because "he was not crowned by his mother, and the ceremony of crowning has nothing to do with the wedding day."[4] Because the new Solomon, the true son of David, will indeed be the child of our race. "If there is", Saint Ambrose says, "only one mother of Christ according to the flesh, all are begetting Christ according to the faith."[5] He is "a child born for us, a son given to us" (Is 9:5), and at the same time, through the new covenant, he will be the Bridegroom of our humanity, which recognizes him as its head, the head of the whole body (cf. Ep 1:22), and crowns him as King. Psalm 45, whose messianic character is acknowledged, celebrates in the same way the crowning of a King issued from our race "and the fairest of the children of men" at the same time as the wedding is taking place (Ps 45:3, 7–8, 13–16).

King Solomon has entered the city. He has come into his palace. He sits on his throne, wearing the royal diadem. He abandons himself to "his heart's joy", his joy as acknowledged

<hr />

[4] Émile Osty, "Introduction au Cantique des Cantiques", *La Bible* (Paris: Seuil, 1973), 1366n.

[5] Saint Ambrose, *Sur saint Luc* (cf. SC 45) (Paris: Cerf, 1971), 84.

King and beloved Bridegroom. We are now awaiting the en-
throning speech. The King will most likely confirm his absolute power over his people. But to our great astonishment, all
his discourse is far from being an act of government: it is a love
declaration, an endless praise of his dearly beloved Bride, a
song of passionate admiration for her who is always present to
his heart:

4:1 *How beautiful you are, my love,*
     how beautiful you are!
     Your eyes, behind your veil,
     are doves;
     your hair is like a flock of goats
     frisking down the slopes of Gilead.

4:2 *Your teeth are like a flock of shorn ewes*
     as they come up from the washing.
     Each one has its twin,
     not one unpaired with another.

4:3 *Your lips are a scarlet thread*
     and your words enchanting.
     Your cheeks, behind your veil,
     are halves of pomegranate.

4:4 *Your neck is the tower of David*
     built as a fortress,
     hung around with a thousand bucklers,
     and each the shield of a hero.
     Your two breasts are two fawns,
     twins of a gazelle,
     that feed among the lilies.

The King of the Song does not claim any sovereignty except
that of his love. And as King of love, he has nothing to speak
of but love. He has no thoughts, no words, this most wonderful of Kings, except to praise the beauty of her whom he loves.

His admiration does not attach itself at the start to any particular feature since everything in her seems miraculous to him. He contemplates at length this perfect beauty in its simple unity: "How beautiful you are, my love, how beautiful you are!" He cannot but repeat this cry. The Bridegroom always starts in such a way; it is always his reaction when he sees his love: "how beautiful you are!" This exclamation arises nine times from his lips in the Song (1:15; 2:10, 13; 4:1, 7; 6:4; 7:7). Had not Yahweh already said in Isaiah, "as the bridegroom rejoices in his bride, so will your God rejoice in you" (Is 62:5), and in Psalm 45, "the king will fall in love with your beauty" (Ps 45:11)? We know that she holds that beauty solely from him, as is recalled in Ezekiel: "The fame of your beauty spread through the nations, since it was perfect, because I had clothed you with my own splendor" (Ezk 16:14). This is also why the Bride would be quite wrong in worrying whether she is truly lovable or not and worthy or not of love since all her beauty is made of her resemblance to her Bridegroom, whose holy face was engraved in her since the very first day and wants to be more and more deeply engraved in her. Thérèse of Lisieux understands this very well when she reads this verse of the Song: "Adorable face of Jesus, only beauty ravishing my heart, deign to imprint on me your divine resemblance so that you may not be able to look into my soul without seeing yourself."[6]

Transported at the outset by a global and unique vision of perfect beauty, the Bridegroom does not tire then in detailing each feature. Starting with the top of her face, he sees all the Holy Land rushing in multiple colors on his palette: white and fluttering doves, black goats on the mountains, ewes at the trough, red fruits of the pomegranate, high images of the city.

And again, the *eyes*, which are not dimmed by the veil covering the face, draw the attention of the Bridegroom. We already know that these eyes, through their mobility, vi-

---

[6] Saint Thérèse of the Child Jesus, *Histoire d'une âme,* Édition du Carmel de Lisieux (Lisieux, 1953), 258.

vaciousness, innocence and grace are living doves. The jet black hair, on the other hand, seems rather untamed. It flows freely down the shoulders in long wavy curls like the black goats of the desert frisking down the slopes of Gilead.

Another contrast: the sparkling white *teeth*. The Bride of the Song must be smiling very brightly for all her teeth are showing, and the Bridegroom, who is also a Shepherd, and, as we know, full of humor (there is so much of it in the Bible), smiles too. Could not one see in these regular teeth white ewes coming back from the river, still wet and huddling one against the other? The teeth of the Bride are thus perfect, as we are poetically advised!

In spite of the first impression, this hyperbolic portrait should not be seen as a mere refinement of humor or affectation. For the contemporary Jew, many references that escape us today must have been clear. An old Jewish tradition, partially followed by Gregory of Nyssa, sees for instance in the black goats frisking down the mountain of Gilead, with which is compared the *black* and freely cascading *hair* of the beloved, the nations that are foreign to Israel.[7] The Jacob-Israel shepherd had not yet brought them back from the mountains of Gilead in the foreign land of Syria to the land God had promised in Canaan (cf. Gn 31:21–23). On the contrary, the ewes coming back from their bath in the river (the goats go down frisking while the ewes go up in orderly fashion!), to which the teeth of the Bride are compared, represent a gathered and fully united Israel (each has its twin and none remains unpaired) under the watch of her good shepherd, who leads her to the water of rest (Ps 23).

If we accept a version that would perhaps be more faithful to the original Hebrew, verse 2 might read as follows: "Her teeth [those of the Bride] are like ewes coming back from the trough; none of them aborts, and each gives birth to twins." In the context of the Song, in which the theme of unity is so dom-

[7] Cf. Matthew, 25:31, note g in TOB.

inant, one could then understand why the Bride is called to be the ever-fecund mother of the ewes that are now separated; the schism but will one day be fraternally united since they were born from the same mother, namely, Israel.

With the *lips,* a new color is introduced in the symphony of the face—lips "like a scarlet thread"! The Bride had, at the beginning of the Prologue, yearned for the kiss of the Bridegroom: "Let him kiss me with the kisses of his mouth"! Should we say with Gregory of Nyssa that, having now been rewarded, her lips became red with the blood of her Bridegroom,[8] and obey ourselves the pressing invitation of Catherine of Siena: "Put then your lips on the side of the Son of God; his wound is a mouth breathing out a fire of charity and pouring blood to wash our iniquities"?[9]

The lips draw a delightful mouth or, more precisely, a mouth uttering delightful words. In the same vein, the inspired author of Psalm 45, whose "heart is stirred by a noble theme", writes that the Bride whispers a continuous "poem to the King" (Ps 45:2). Her cheeks blush near this fire and appear then, under the light veil that covers them until the wedding day, like the two halves, round and scarlet, of a cut pomegranate. If the apple is the fruit of the Bridegroom, the pomegranate is that of his love (4:3, 13; 6:7; 8:2), two love fruits, two fruits whose round form—there are so many images of the Bridegroom and his love in the Song that evoke the spherical shape of fullness—expresses fully how the Bridegroom and his Bride are symmetrical in their beauty.

Holding now the admirable face that is mobile and slim (doves, goats, ewes), here is the *neck,* which, on the contrary, is strong, stable, powerful and straight like a proud watchtower: the tower of David, yes indeed, a royal tower! For as beautiful as she is, the Bride is also strong, and her Bridegroom is rightly proud of this fact. "That day", he told Isaiah, "this

---

[8] Saint Gregory of Nyssa, *In Canticum Canticorum,* Homily 7, 927CD.
[9] "Catherine de Sienne", vol. 2, DSp, c. 329.

song will be sung in the land of Judah: 'We have a strong city' "
(Is 26:1). Would it not seem then that the shiny necklace joyfully tinkling around her neck has an almost military look? All
these medals evoke indeed, in the exalted imagination of the
Bridegroom, the shields of the valiant warriors of Israel, which
are hung around the walls of the city and put down, of course,
during peacetime but which can still impose respect when seen
from afar. The powerful and beautiful tower challenging the
attacks of the enemy also challenges the wear and tear of the
centuries. "You rise like a powerful tower outside the wear
and tear of the centuries", as is sung in a hymn from Gertrude
von Le Fort. [10] Thus the Fathers of the Church saw in the tower
of David, the glory of Jerusalem, to which the Bride is compared, the Virgin Mary herself *(turris davidica)*, true neck of the
mystical body, connecting the head (Christ) to all the other
members.'[11]

However this slight military air, as Saint Francis de Sales
stresses, must not prevent us from hearing the fundamental
note of peace. For, "though she is belligerent and warring, she
is altogether so peaceful that, among the armies and the battles,
she goes on singing songs of unsurpassed melody."[12]

Moreover, the portrait of the Bride concludes with an image
of grace and peace since her breasts evoke the "two fawns,
twins of a gazelle, that feed among the lilies." One thinks at
first that this refers to the fecundity of the bride: "Your
mother", Saint Augustine writes about this verse, "is the
Church, whose breasts are the two testaments of Holy Scripture. Such therefore the milk of all its mysteries."[13] But even
though the idea of fecundity is not to be excluded, it seems that
here the image evokes unity. The equal and twin breasts seem

[10] Gertrude von Le Fort, *Hymnes à l'Église*, tran. André Duzan, 1982, 55.

[11] Henri de Lubac, *Méditation sur l'Église* (Paris: Aubier, 1953), 291.

[12] Saint Francis de Sales, *Traité de l'amour de Dieu, Oeuvres*, Bibliothèque de
la Pléiade (Paris: (NRF–Gallimard, 1969), VIII:12, 749.

[13] Saint Augustine, *Commentaire de la Première épître de saint Jean* (Paris: Cerf,
1966), 187.

to suggest the two brotherly kingdoms of Israel and Judah, born at the same time from the same mother, but now living apart, divided since the schism of Rehoboam in 931. Now they are united again in one sole kingdom with the advent of the messiah-King. Two twin fawns of the same mother gazelle, feeding together, reconciled among the lilies, i.e., in the Holy Land, where they were born at the same time, as could already be understood in the parable of Ezekiel: " 'Son of man, take a stick,' Yahweh said, 'and write on it: "Judah". . . . Take another stick and write on it: "Joseph". . . . Join one to the other to make a single piece of wood and say: "The Lord Yahweh says this: 'I am going to take the sons of Israel from the nations where they have gone. . . . I shall gather them together from everywhere. . . . I shall make them into one nation. . . . One king is to be their king. They will no longer form two nations nor be two separate kingdoms. . . . My servant David will reign over them, one shepherd for all.' " ' "[14]

Let us go back for one moment to this first portrait of the Bride: it is strikingly similar to what Olivier Clement points out about icons. Here, as with icons, priority is given to the eyes, "places of the greatest transparency, foci of light", eyes always so big and enlarged in all icons. On the other hand, the mouth is "without thickness" ("scarlet thread", says the Song). The ears are "very reduced" in icons because the whole face is listening to silence. Only the soul listens. (The Song does not even allude to the ears of the Bride.)

In any case, the Bridegroom sees only perfection in the one he loves:

4:7 *You are wholly beautiful, my love,*
and without a blemish.

It seems that here we should read verse 7 before verse 6. It is in fact a repetition, an inclusion of sorts of 4:1 (as we had already

[14] Ezekiel, 37:15–27, TOB.

noted in the second poem: 2:10 and 2:13). After having itemized every feature of his love, the Bridegroom lets himself be captured again by the global vision of a unique beauty. In the end, he can only say of her whom he loves that she is beautiful, wholly beautiful and without any reservation: "immaculate in the infinity of love".[15] It is understandable that the Church traditionally applied this verse to the Virgin Mary, the only beloved of God, the one who is absolutely worthy of him. We must always keep in mind when we talk about the Bride of the Song the very felicitous comment of Isaac of Stella: "The same thing is said *universally* of the Church; *especially* (i.e., in an absolutely privileged way) of Mary; *particularly* (i.e. applicable to each one of us) of the human soul."[16] Paul Claudel is inspired to say: "The soul and the Church are the twin aspects of a same lover, whose faces endlessly mingling and renewed are colored by the rays of the Immaculate."[17]

In his enchantment, the Bridegroom yearns only for one thing: union. Let the hour of the wedding come!

4:6 *Before the dawn wind rises,*
   before the shadows flee,
   I will go to the mountain of myrrh,
   to the hill of frankincense.

How could anyone resist any longer such an accomplished beauty? The Bridegroom will not accept any delay in his impatient desire. It will be "before the dawn wind rises, before the shadows flee," yes, tonight, tonight! Thus he is now the one who is tormented by haste and who uses the very words of his love in the second poem (2:17).

[15] André Chouraqui, *Le Cantique des Cantiques* (Paris: Presses Universitaires de France, 1970), 58.

[16] Quoted by de Lubac, *Méditation*, 301.

[17] Paul Claudel, *Paul Claudel interroge le Cantique des Cantiques* (Paris: NRF-Gallimard, 1948), 213.

He must, without delay, settle in the very heart of her whom he loves, unite with her on "the mountain" of Zion, "on the hill" of the Temple, their common dwelling, where rise endlessly from the midst of the beloved city the smells of myrrh and frankincense, always connected with the presence of the Bridegroom (3:6). "I will go", he says, "to the mountain of myrrh, to the hill of frankincense"—what a determination in these words, what haste of the Bridegroom toward Jerusalem! (cf. Lk 9:51)—to go back to that mountain that the Bride herself had called the mountain "of the covenant" (2:17). The mountain of myrrh is indeed that of the Temple, as is obvious in the Hebrew pun on "myrrh" and "Moriah". Moriah was the mountain where Abraham had to sacrifice Isaac, and, according to tradition, it was also that on which the Temple had been built (2 Ch 3:1), from which rise myrrh and frankincense.

Some Fathers of the Church, including Origen and Gregory of Nyssa, also thought that they had already heard in these words—"I will go to the mountain of myrrh, to the hill of frankincense"—the call of the Lord to join him first in death (symbolized by myrrh; cf. Jn 19:39), to take part in his divinity (symbolized by frankincense): "for it is impossible to live with me without having been changed by the myrrh of death into the divinity of frankincense."[18]

"I will go", the Bridegroom says. Let his love hasten to be there. Let her tear herself away from all that could still hold her back.

4:8 *Come from Lebanon, my promised bride,*
come from Lebanon, come on your way.
Lower your gaze, from the heights of Amana,
from the crests of Senir and Hermon,
the haunts of lions,
the mountains of leopards.

[18] Saint Gregory of Nyssa, *In Canticum Canticorum*, Homily 8, 940B.

But how can we understand that the Bride, whose beauty brought the Bridegroom to ecstasy and to whom he just spoke so ardently, has to come all the way from Lebanon?

This is because his love, even though she is totally present to his eyes and heart, is still far from her beloved. In spite of what she had said, "My Beloved is mine and I am his" (2:16), she is, in fact, not with him as he is with her. He never leaves her with his heart and eyes; he is always present to her. But, on the other hand, how difficult it still is for her to be with him! Thus, in the parable of the prodigal son, it is said of the father that he saw his son "when he was still very far". And he happened to be just there at the moment of return, for in fact he had never left his prodigal son, even though the latter was in a distant country (Lk 15). "You were with me," Augustine confesses, "but I was not with you."[19] With the patience and concern of the father in the parable, the Bridegroom of the Song is unceasingly waiting for the true return of her whom he loves; and unceasingly also he must recall to himself the one that nothing should separate from him: "Come from Lebanon, my promised bride, come from Lebanon, come on your way"![20]

The beautiful betrothed is kept back in Lebanon. Lebanon, which is always associated with beauty in the Bible, is also a foreign land for Israel, and this suggests that even though she has the beauty of the most beautiful land, the Bride is still in a foreign country and thus threatened. She is still separated from her Bridegroom by high mountains, haunted by her enemies,

---

[19] Saint Augustine, *Confessions*, Book X, 27(38); PL 32, 795; CCL 27, 175.

[20] Faithful to this thought, which is at the core of his mystical theology, i.e., that "to find God is to look for him unceasingly", Gregory of Nyssa understands in the following way the invitation extended to the Bride to come back: "As it progresses, the soul is under the impression that it is only at the beginning of its ascent toward God, which is why the Lord repeats 'come' to her who has already come, and 'come, my love' to her who has already done so. For the one who ascends never ceases to do so, going from beginning to beginning through beginnings that have no ends." *Vie de Moïse* (cf. SC 1) (Paris: Cerf, 1968), 271ff.

the northern invaders, lions and leopards (cf. Jr 5:6), far more dangerous than the "little foxes" (2:15), the hated Canaanite neighbors. "I lie surrounded by lions greedy for human prey", the exiled psalmist sighs (Ps 57:4). And in the Song as in the psalm we can see under the ferocious mask of the enemies the frightening face of the beast: "I saw that the beast", Saint John says in Revelation, *"was like a leopard,* with paws like *a bear* and a mouth like *a lion"* (Rv 13:2).

But how could she, with nothing but her strength, join the one she loves? Does he not recall her former cry: "Draw me" (1:4)? However, the Bridegroom knows her weakness better than she does, and he also knows that without him she can do nothing (Jn 15:5). Then he tells her, "Come"! "Come from Lebanon, my promised bride, come from Lebanon, come on your way"! How encouraging he becomes! In Psalm 45, which is, after all, according to Father Tournay, thirty to forty years older than the Song and whose references to this third poem are numerous,[21] the Bride is also about to leave her country, the city of Tyre (in Lebanon): "Listen, daughter, . . . forget your nation and your ancestral home, then the king will fall in love with your beauty, . . . daughter of Tyre" (Ps 45:10–12), says the royal psalmist. It is noteworthy that, in Psalm 45 as well as in the Song, the Bride is at the same time present with the King ("daughters of kings are among your maids of honor; on your right stands the queen, in gold from Ophir") and far from him since it is said later that she is "led in to the king . . . and enter[s] the king's palace to general rejoicing" (Is 45: 9, 14–15).[22] Same situation, same intention. But here, in the Song, it is not the minister of the King who presses the Bride

<hr/>

[21] Raymond Tournay, "Les affinités du Psaume XLV avec *le Cantique des Cantiques* et leur interprétation messianique", *Supplements to Vetus Testamentum IX,* Congress Volume (Bonn, 1962), 168–212 (cf. Introduction, note 12).

[22] Marina Mannati, for one, noted many parallels between Psalm 45 and the third poem of the Song of Songs: Sg 3:6 and Ps 45:8; Sg 3:7 and Ps 45:3–5; Sg 3:9–10 and Ps 45: 6a, 8b; Sg 3:11 and Ps 45:9–15; see *Les Psaumes,* Cahiers de la Pierre-qui-vire, vol. 2 (Paris: Desclée de Brouwer, 1957), 106 n.

to leave her nation and join her Bridegroom; the Bridegroom himself presses on: not only does he invite her to join him, but he goes out to meet her and to triumph, together with her, over all her enemies.

She should therefore not fear: "Lower your gaze" (JB), i.e., "be without timidity or complexes". See at your feet the Assyrian lions and the Chaldean leopards, your oppressors. What can they do to you when I am with you?" ("With me, with me, come!"—Joüon and Chouraqui translate literally.) What insistence, imploring and stimulating at the same time, in this repetition! "With me!" is also used unceasingly in Scripture by Yahweh to reassure his servants: Moses, Joshua, Gideon, Isaiah, Jeremiah. "I will be with you." Jesus also says: "I am with you always" (Mt 28:20). "It is I! Do not be afraid" (Mt 14:27). "Immanuel", God with us, is in fact the name that God himself gave to the messiah in Isaiah (Is 7:14). "With me, with me, come!" the Bridegroom says in the Song. Come! How could I still suffer the slightest hesitation on your part? And, overcoming all the obstacles that still held her in fear of her enemies, the Bride joins her all-powerful lover.

The joyful hymn starts again on the lips of the Bridegroom, but instead of being, as before, one only of admiration, the song, now that she is here—now that she is with him as he is with her—becomes a song of intoxication and passion:

4:9 *You ravish my heart,*
   my sister, my promised bride,
   you ravish my heart
   with a single one of your glances,
   with one single pearl of your necklace.

There is quite a contrast between the vivaciousness, even the humor, of the first celebration of the Bride (4:1–7) and the muted passion expressed here. The eyes, not anymore such as described previously, but "a single one of your glances," a single pearl of your necklace,"[23] of her whom he now calls his promised bride; everything in her, everything about her, deeply moves the Bridegroom.

"Promised bride" is, in fact, surprising at first. It is a new word in the Song, used six times in this passage and nowhere else, a phrase that is all the more surprising since the Bride is already far beyond the betrothal promises. But indisuptably the word we read here is *promised bride (kallah)*.[24]

A promised bride she is, for a twofold reason it seems: first, even though she is so wonderfully loved and admired, the Bride has not yet reached the stage that will be hers when she attains perfect union. Thus, however dazzling it is, her face is still veiled as that of a promised bride (4:1, 3). And Paul explains that "this veil remains and is not lifted because it is in Christ that it vanishes."[25] Thus the Bride is still sighing with John of the Cross: "Cease if you want! Break the veil of this happy encounter!"[26] And then will come the wedding.

But we must also be aware above all of the very special tenderness that the Bridegroom puts in this expression "promised bride". Often in Scripture, God delights to call Israel by this same name since he gave her the covenant: "Like a young man marrying a virgin, so will the one who made you wed you, and as a bridegroom rejoices in his bride, so will your God", in Isaiah.[27] And did he not say several times in the Book of Hosea: "I will betroth you to myself for ever, betroth you with integrity and justice, with tenderness and love; I will betroth you to myself in faithfulness, and you will come to know Yahweh"

---

[23] Paul Joüon, *Le Cantique des Cantiques* (Paris: Beauchesne, 1909); André Robert, *Bible de Jérusalem* (Paris: Cerf, 1951).

[24] Édouard Dhorme, *La Bible*, Bibliothèque de la Pléiade (Paris: NRF-Gallimard, 1959); JB; TOB.

[25] 2 Corinthians, 3:14 (TOB).

[26] Saint John of the Cross, *Vive Flamme d'amour*, Stanza I, *Oeuvres complètes*, Bibliothèque européenne (Paris: Desclée de Brouwer, 1958), 717.

[27] Isaiah, 62:5 (TOB).

(Ho 2:21–22)? To Gomer, the adulterous, the prostitute, her husband Yahweh-Hosea had said: "Betrothed is used only for a virgin and not for a woman who was already married."[28] But there is no infidelity that can resist such a merciful love, for which to forgive is to re-create.

Thus the Lord is revealing the ever absolutely new and incredible nature of his love, independently of the past, for her who never ceases to be betrothed while being bride, as we will hear again at the end of the Scriptures in the Revelation of John: "Come here and I will show you the bride that the Lamb has married" (Rv 21:9). The love of Yahweh for his bride is always a betrothal love, young, ardent and pure as he is. "I will betroth you to myself for ever."

And we must be daring enough to add: a wonderful love, but a passionate one. Does not the Bridegroom say, "You make me lose my reason"?[29,30] Is it really he, the Word of Wisdom, who speaks in such a way? The phrase had been used in the Book of Hosea to describe the intoxication of Israel: "Wine, new wine makes one lose one's reason" (Ho 4:11, French version of JB). But here the Bridegroom himself says that he has lost his reason. Indeed, he is not only "in love" with his friend, as is the king in Psalm 45 (Ps 45:11); he is, he says so himself, completely led astray by the violence of his passion: as indeed is Jesus, whose kin think that he is "out of his mind" (Mk 3:21). Herod proclaims him "mad". Saint Thérèse of Lisieux writes: "And I agree with him. Our beloved was mad."[31] "He is mad love", Nicolas Cabasilas says.

And so little is required from the promised bride to provoke such a madness. One of her glances is enough, not even a glance, but a single pearl from her necklace, the slightest sign,

---

[28] Hosea, 2:22 (TOB).

[29] JB (French version); TOB; Bible du centenaire.

[30] The Hebrew Levavtani means literally: you fascinate me, you overwhelm me. — Trans.

[31] Saint Thérèse of the Child Jesus, Lettres (Paris: Cerf/Desclée de Brouwer, 1977), Letter 169, 298.

the least object and gift of love, the smallest of all pearls when its radiance has captured a unique and priceless love.

By calling his love "promised bride", the Bridegroom is not showing a lesser attachment, just as when he calls her "sister" or rather "my sister, my promised bride", a sort of composite phrase attempting to signify the absolutely unique nature of this extraordinary love, as Chouraqui discerns it so well. The love of betrothal and wedding with the Bridegroom is "based", he says, "on an essential fraternity with him".[32] To put it more clearly, let us say that the phrase "my sister, my promised bride" will reach the fullness of its meaning in the Incarnation. The Bride "will then truly become his sister", explains Saint Bernard, "since they now have the same Father as does his Bride since they are one in the Spirit."[33]

The Bridegroom can therefore say in the intoxication of such a presence:

4:10 *What spells lie in your love,*
      my sister, my promised bride!
      How delicious is your love, more delicious than wine!
      How fragrant your perfumes,
      more fragrant than all other spices!

The Bride herself, at the beginning of the poem, had said, "Your love is more delightful than wine" (1:2). She is not alone in saying so; the Bridegroom is also inebriated with love and with the maddest love yet. Caresses and tokens of tenderness from his sister-promised bride are a heady wine for him. And just as she had added, "delicate is the fragrance of your perfume" (1:3), he too is haunted by the multiple scents, the fragrances from all over the earth, that she breathes out: "more fragrant than all other spices!"

---

[32] André Chouraqui, *Le Cantique des Cantiques,* 59.

[33] Saint Bernard, *Sermons sur le Cantique des Cantiques, Oeuvres mystiques,* Sermon 8 (Paris: Seuil, 1953), 139.

In the Song, when the perfumes are associated with the Bride, they express, as it were, the nature of her whole being. They first tell of her seduction: perfumes from her simple robes—"the scent of your garments is like the scent of Lebanon", of the infinitely aromatic essences, her Bridegroom will say in a moment, reiterating the words already uttered in the Book of Hosea (Ho 14:7); perfumes that, on a deeper level, emanate from the very person of the Bride and in which all the fragrances of the universe are intermingled. But the perfumes also mean the spiritual nature of the attraction since, being through their subtlety a sort of intermediary between matter and spirit, the perfumes lead us to understand that the beauty of the Bride, however intoxicating it may be, does not awake carnal echoes in the heart of her friend. Lastly, whether one talks about him or her, perfumes always have in the Song a liturgical and sacral value: perfume of aloe, myrrh and frankincense, which are generally associated in the Bible, and even exclusively so in the case of frankincense, with the rituals; like those that were rising in the Temple from an altar called the altar of incense and that Saint John will see: "another angel, who had a gold censer, came and stood at the altar. . . . The smoke of the incense went up in the presence of God and with it the prayers of the saints" (Rv 8:3–4). From this viewpoint, the perfumes of the Bride are those of a soul slowly consumed by her love, offered to her Bridegroom as a sacrifice of pleasant odor, having infinitely more price in his eyes than all the sacrifices of the Temple: "more . . . than all other spices!"

The words then uttered by the Bridegroom confirm again this interpretation of the spiritual and liturgical—rather than carnal—effect that the Bride has on him:

4:11 *Your lips, my promised one,*
      distill wild honey.
      Honey and milk
      are under your tongue;
      and the scent of your garments
      is like the scent of Lebanon.

Honey and milk—the sweetness of honey strengthened by that of milk—bear witness indeed to the fact that the intoxication of wine and perfumes coming from the Bride is not of a kind that excites and causes fever. It is a very strong intoxication but one given in peace and sweetness by the person as well as by all the words of the Bride, for "honey and milk are under your tongue". Therefore, the Word of God must have become her own word, and she must have assimilated it perfectly for the Bridegroom to find in it the same taste of honey that Ezekiel found when swallowing the Scriptures (Ezk 3:3) and that made the psalmist exclaim in jubilation, "Your promise, how sweet to my palate! Sweeter than honey to my mouth!" (Ps 119:103). Today, the Bridegroom himself is using the same words and addressing them to his sister-promised bride. "Honey and milk", he says, "are under your tongue". The honey of wisdom with the milk of childhood, so much childlike innocence and so much maturity at the same time—this is what I find in all your discourses. In the end, are you not for me, even silently, the true promised land, "where milk and honey flow" (Ex 3:8)?

And more yet! For above all the joy, all the sweetness and intoxication that she brings to him at any moment, the Bridegroom puts this rare privilege: she whom he loves is exclusively his, she is all his, only his; she is exclusively vowed, dedicated, consecrated to him.

4:12 *She is a garden enclosed,*
    my sister, my promised bride;
    a garden enclosed,
    a sealed fountain.

Garden and fountain seem always to be connected in Scripture. One does not go without the other. The fountain brings beauty to the garden. It is the source of the living water of love in the heart of the Bride, which brings extraordinary riches and beauty to the garden of her life, just as the Bridegroom of Israel himself had made her hope: "their soul will be like a watered garden" (Jr 31:12). And, more directly: "you shall be like a watered garden, like a spring of water whose waters never run dry."[34]

It can be said that the theme of the garden runs through the entire Scriptures: the garden of creation in the first chapter of Genesis; the garden where the prince of life will be buried and where Mary Magdalen will come on Easter Sunday; the garden of the new world in the last chapter of Revelation; the garden of the Bride at the center of the third poem of the Song, of the whole Song itself, and of all the Scriptures. Five times, the Bride is admired here as the garden from which life draws its source and triumphs (4:12–5:1).

With this essential qualification that the master of the garden, the owner of the fountain, is the one and only! Only the Bridegroom has access to the garden. The time is thus gone when he was complaining that his Bride has "abandoned [him], the fountain of living water, only to dig cisterns for [herself], leaky cisterns that hold no water" (Jr 2:13). The time has come for the garden to open up to the Bridegroom only. Only he will have the key, and only he will walk about as Ezekiel had announced: "This gate will be kept shut. No one will open it or go through it. . . . And so it must be kept shut" (Ezk 44:2); "I place the key of the House of David on his shoulder; should he open, no one shall close; should he close, no one shall open" (Is 22:22). Neither will anyone but he drink from the fountain at the center of the garden because it is sealed. "For fear its leaves shall fall," Yahweh had said, "night and day I will watch over it."[35]

In these two verses of the Song, the words "enclosed" and "sealed" are repeated three times to express how exclusive love is, exclusively belonging to God, a radical and absolute consecration to the Bridegroom of the one who is "enclosed, closed, sealed", writes Chouraqui, "like the most secret and authentic document, revealing its message only to the lover";[36] of her who is united to her Bridegroom because, as Saint Paul reminds the Christians of Corinth: "I arranged for you to marry Christ so that I might give you away as a chaste virgin to this one husband" (2 Co 11:2).

How then can we explain that, as soon as we have read these words, the Bridegroom utters what appears to be a complete contradiction to them:

4:13 *Your shoots form an orchard of pomegranate trees,*
      the rarest essences are yours:

4:14 *nard and saffron,*
      calamus and cinnamon,
      with all the incense-bearing trees;
      myrrh and aloes,
      with the subtlest odors.

4:15 *Fountain that makes the garden fertile,*
      well of living water,
      streams flowing down from Lebanon.

Paradox is one of the overwhelming features of the Song: in each poem we find a Bride who is totally dedicated to her Bridegroom—a "garden enclosed", a "sealed fountain"—and who, at the same time, is open to all the inhabitants of the universe. Such are in fact the meaning and the import of these verses. The enclosed garden grows shoots way beyond its limits, all the way to the ends of the world. They grow over the whole earth, as God has predicted to Isaiah: "In days to come, Jacob will put out shoots, Israel will bud and blossom and fill the whole world with fruit."[37] And we also read in the Book of Hosea: "his shoots will spread far" (Ho 14:7). Not only will they make of the land of Israel a paradise of pomegranate trees with the most exquisite of all fruits, but the rarest exotic es-

[36] Chouraqui, *Le Cantique des Cantiques,* 60.
[37] Isaiah, 27:6 (TOB).

sences of all the foreign nations (India, Arabia, Yemen)—the perfect number of seven is given!—are the fragrant fecundity of the secret and wonderful garden of the Bridegroom. The closed garden with essences unknown in the Holy Land thus becomes the entire world, whose countless perfumes it seizes and brings back only to return them, improved, to the very ends of the world, perfuming the whole creation of God, which will be filled with the scent of nard (the name is heard again in the house of Bethany—Jn 12:3). Thus the soul that is consecrated to God collects in itself all the yearnings of the earth to turn them into praises, vivifying and renewing the universe.

And, in the same vein, we see the "sealed fountain" becoming the spring of gardens, not anymore the sole interior garden of the Bride but all the gardens of the world; becoming "a well of living water" and "streams flowing from Lebanon", with all the depth of a well and the free outpouring of running waters![38] Just as the river in the paradise of Genesis "flowed from Eden to water the garden, and from there it divided to make four streams" that watered all of creation (Gn 2:10), the fountain reserved exclusively to quench the thirst of the Bridegroom goes on to be poured out throughout the world, while not ceasing to be sealed.

The very structure of 4:12–15 is quite expressive. After insisting on a "garden enclosed", then on a "sealed fountain" (4:12), the author introduces now an indefinite extension of the garden, as it were (4:13–14), an uninhibited outpouring of the fountain (4:15). The Song could not be more openly opposed to the maxim mentioned in the Book of Proverbs: "Do not let your fountains flow to waste elsewhere, nor your streams in the public streets. But let them be for yourself alone, not for strangers at the same time" (Pr 5:16–17).

---

[38] "This is the most paradoxical of all: while all wells contain stagnant water, the Bride is the only one to have in her running waters, so that she is at the same time the depth of the well and the perpetual mobility of the river." Saint Gregory of Nyssa, *In Canticum Canticorum*, Homily 9, 978C.

Such is not, in any event, the feeling of the Bridegroom of the Song. The more his Bride is exclusively consecrated to him, the more universal also is his opening to the world and its fecundity. The sealed fountain will therefore, freely and impetuously, water the universe with its living water, as Jesus promises to the Samaritan woman: "the water that I shall give will turn into a spring inside him, welling up to eternal life" (Jn 4:14). Thus the most hidden soul, the most unknown, living only for God, finds that "from his breast too, shall flow fountains of living water" (Jn 7:38).

Meditating on these verses—the garden and the fountain— Saint Amadeus of Lausanne does not find it difficult to apply them to the Virgin Mary: "Source of spiritual gardens, well of living waters bubbling as torrents from the divine Lebanon, she pours, from Mount Zion to all the nations surrounding her or to be found in distant parts, rivers of peace and streams of grace cascading from the heavens."[39]

To be at the same time so many flowers and perfumes and fruits, a fountain and a stream of living water for the growth and beauty of the entire universe, while existing only for the sole joy of the Bridegroom, such is also the one joy of the Bride. She says it now, raising her voice for the first time in this third poem, in which her Bridegroom sang so wildly. Unique beauty, she also wants, as he does, to be uniquely dedicated to him, consumed by him, consummated in him:

4:16 *Awake, north wind,*
come, wind of the south!
Breathe over my garden,
to spread its sweet smell around.
Let my Beloved come into his garden,
let him taste its rarest fruits.

---

[39] Saint Amadeus of Lausanne, *Huit homélies mariales* (cf. SC 72) (Paris: Cerf, 1960), 193.

The Bride can say at the same time "my garden" and "his garden", for it is the same. She belongs to herself because she belongs completely to him. The more she is his, the more she is herself. All her desire from then on is to yield to his presence in total self-surrender.

For this purpose, she calls on all the winds from north to south. Let them come, let them rush rather, and let them blow over her garden—be it cold or warm, no matter—so that the beautiful garden can breathe its fragrances and carry them to the heart of her friend. But let them rather blow cold and hot, as Chouraqui understands it: "The loving Bride wishes her beauty to be caressed at the same time by the icy wind coming from the northern mountains and by the burning wind of the Arabian desert. They must breathe, sweep her garden, take her fragrances, tear her away from her solitude and open the way of communication with her lover. . . . Like the wind, the latter must breathe in her beauty and, as is done in a sacrifice, eat her delicious fruit, which is that of the knowledge of love."[40] Icy wind, we say of suffering and trial, or burning wind of the joys and consolations of love, the Spirit of God, breath of life; everything works for the beautiful garden to yield all the perfumes that the Bridegroom expects from it.

As for Saint John of the Cross, he seems to have retained mostly the beneficent effect of the hot southern wind, which he calls "Auster" in a magnificent passage: "Come Auster, you who awaken love, come breathe over my garden. . . . Auster is a wind vulgarly called the African wind. It is a pleasant and rainy wind that causes herbs and plants to germinate, flowers to blossom and yield their perfumes. . . . The soul means by this wind the Holy Spirit and says that it awakens love because when the divine wind breathes over it, it sets it afire, re-creates it and animates it. . . . Breathing with its Divine Spirit over her flowery garden, it thus opens all the buds of virtue, discov-

---

[40] Chouraqui, *Le Cantique des Cantiques*, 61.

ers the perfumes of the gifts, the perfections and riches of the soul; and opening this treasure and this inner domain, it unveils all its beauty."[41]

But it is not enough for the garden to distill, drop by drop, under the combined action of all the winds, its secret perfumes, letting their fragrance rise to the heart of the Bridegroom, as the Bride had once been contented in doing. "While the King rests in his own room [his enclosure]", she had whispered as if to herself, "my nard yields its perfume" (1:12). The Bridegroom himself must go down to the garden; let him enter and take possession. And let him not only breathe in the perfumes, but let him pick, let him taste, the delightful fruits.

4:16 *Let my Beloved come into his garden,*
let him taste its rarest fruits.

"Daring words," Saint Gregory of Nyssa points out; ". . . To whom is she offering her fruits? For whom is she preparing a repast of her goods? . . . For him from whom, through whom, from whom and in whom are all the goods! . . . At first, she was the one who enjoyed the fruit of the apple tree, when she said, 'His fruit is sweet to my palate.' But here she becomes in her turn a beautiful and delightful fruit, offered to the gardener for his joy."[42] In truth, how well we already see the Holy Spirit revealing his presence in the soul of the Bride in these verses of the Song! She truly is the garden of the Spirit: in which the living water of the Spirit flows, in which the strong and sweet wind of the Spirit blows; in which are wafting the perfumes of the Spirit's countless gifts, as Saint Paul tells the Galatians, the first of them being the fruit of love (Ga 5:22).

"Let [him] come into his garden", the Bride had said. "I

---

[41] Saint John of the Cross, *Cantique spirituel,* Stanza XXVII, *Oeuvres complètes,* Bibliothèque européenne (Paris: Desclée de Brouwer, 1958), 641.
[42] Saint Gregory of Nyssa, *In Canticum Canticorum,* Homily 10, 985D.

come into my garden", the Beloved goes on immediately. He did not wait long. To the surrendering soul, he surrenders all of himself. "He cannot suffer", Saint Teresa of Avila notes, "to refuse himself to the one who gives herself totally."[43] "If anyone loves me," Jesus says, ". . . my Father will love him, and we shall come to him and make our home with him" (Jn 14:23).

5:1 *I come into my garden,*
my sister, my promised bride,
I gather my myrrh and balsam,
I eat my honey and my honeycomb,
I drink my wine and my milk.

The Bridegroom does recognize the full value of the rich offering of the one who loves him and gives her life to him, as we sense in the solemn and emphatic repetition in his declaration: "I gather, . . . I eat, . . . I drink". "I gather my myrrh and balsam, I eat my honey and my honeycomb, I drink my wine and my milk." In six words, paired two by two, the Bridegroom signifies that, together with the life of the Bride, he has been given all that the world can offer of its penetrating perfumes, all that is sweet and pleasant to the taste, all that can be refreshing to drink, all that can be strengthening and intoxicating at the same time. The Bride fulfills all his desires. She is myrrh and balsam, honey, wine and milk; she is perfume, sweetness and intoxication.

And what fullness of joy in the total possession of these "my's": my garden, my promised bride, my myrrh, my balsam, my honey, my honeycomb, my wine, my milk! This is the hour of the wedding banquet and of consummated love. Origen attempts—not without a certain humor—to transpose

---

[43] Saint Teresa of Avila, *Pensées sur l'amour de Dieu*, *Oeuvres complètes*, Bibliothèque européenne (Paris: Desclée de Brouwer, 1964), 6:9, 598.

in terms of evangelical virtues this prestigious menu: "Tell me", he asks, "what princely dishes will be served to the guests. Well, first will come peace; then and all together humility, patience, meekness and sweetness; for a dessert of exquisite sweetness, purity of heart. But the main course of the banquet will be love."[44]

This banquet, different from what we have seen so far in the Bible, is offered by the Bride to her Bridegroom. We had indeed read in Isaiah: "On this mountain, Yahweh Sabaoth will prepare for all peoples a banquet of rich food, a banquet of fine wines, of food rich and juicy, of fine strained wines" (Is 25:6). The psalmist had also said: "They feast on the bounty of your house, you give them drink from your river of pleasure" (Ps 36:8). But this is totally new. The Bridegroom knows the joy of the banquet that has been prepared and already can tell his love: "I was hungry and you gave me food; I was thirsty and you gave me drink" (Mt 25:35).

Though why does it seem now that he is getting up from the table? That he is opening wide the doors to the wedding hall where his Bride was offering him such a feast? And that he shouts to the outside, aloud and as it were to all the winds, this incredible invitation:

5:1 *Eat, friends, and drink,*
   drink deep, my dearest friends.

It is true that we had already heard such an invitation coming from the depths of Scripture: "Come"—Wisdom was crying on the squares—"and eat my bread, drink the wine I have prepared!" (Pr 9:5). And also: "Oh, come to the water all you who are thirsty; though you have no money, come! Buy corn without money, and eat, and, at no cost, wine and milk" (Is 55:1). It is the same invitation that the Bridegroom extends to-

---

[44] Origen, *In Canticum Canticorum*, PG 13, 139C–D.

day. But here the table of his love becomes his table; the feast to which his love had invited him becomes the feast to which he invites all his friends; the repast she offered him—and she was the honey, the milk, the wine and all the fruits—is changed, "transubstantiated" into a meal that he himself offers to all; as one day five barley loaves and two fish offered by a small child will be made into bread to satisfy the crowds (Jn 6:9), and as on the last evening, sitting at table with his friends, he will say of the bread and the wine of our earth: "Take it and eat, . . . Drink all of you" (Mt 26:26–27).

For all are invited by him to the wedding feast without any restrictions or distinctions, all the friends, i.e., all men. And she who was his exclusive beloved, all closed and sealed, and whose fruits were so jealously his, is now seated at the common table, sharing everything like him, with all; sharing herself with him among all. And he who constantly said until now "my friend, my beloved", says now—and this is the last word of the poem—"my dearest friends." All have become his dearest in the only beloved. Is this not a foreshadowing of the Church, bride of Christ and gathering of all mankind?

At the wedding feast enlarged to receive the whole world, the bread will not fail, neither the wine, which is poured superabundantly. For the desire of the Bridegroom is not only that one drink but that all drink to the point of intoxication. One must be daring! Saint Francis de Sales laments the fact that one still sees too many who are content only with eating at the feast of love. A few dare to drink "with pleasure and abundantly", but so few go the extent of getting drunk![45]

---

[45] Here is the full text of this excerpt from the *Traité de l'amour de Dieu:* "To drink is to contemplate, and this is done without pain or resistance, with pleasure and easily; but to get drunk is to contemplate so often and so ardently that one is out of oneself to be all in God. Holy and sacred intoxication, which contrary to the bodily one does not alienate us from the spiritual senses but from the carnal ones. It does not stupefy us or make us dull but turns us into angels and, as it were, divinizes us." VI:6, 627.

On this true anticipated banquet of the Kingdom, banquet of the wedding of the Bridegroom and the Bride, to which all are invited, the third poem of the Song ends very significantly. "The kingdom of heaven may be compared to a king who gave a feast for his son's wedding", Jesus says (Mt 22:2). "And men from east and west, from north and south, will come to take their places at the feast in the kingdom of God" (Lk 13:29). Is this not what we have already seen here in adumbration: "Eat, friends, and drink, drink deep, my dearest friends"?

And mankind responds through the mouth of John, in the last book of Scripture: "Happy are those who are invited to the wedding feast of the Lamb" (Rv 19:9).

The Storm of Summer

Fourth Poem

Chapters 5:2–6:3

The Bride

I sleep, but my heart is awake.
I hear my Beloved knocking.
"Open to me, my sister, my love,
my dove, my perfect one,
for my head is covered with dew,
my locks with the drops of night."
— "I have taken off my tunic,
am I to put it on again?
I have washed my feet,
am I to dirty them again?"
My Beloved thrust his hand
through the hole in the door;
I trembled to the core of my being.
Then I rose
to open to my Beloved,
myrrh ran off my hands,
pure myrrh off my fingers,
on to the handle of the bolt.

I opened to my Beloved,
but he had turned his back and gone!
My soul failed at his flight.
I sought him but did not find him,
I called to him but he did not answer.
The watchmen came upon me
as they made their rounds in the City.

They beat me, they wounded me,
they took away my cloak,
they who guard the ramparts.

I charge you,
daughters of Jerusalem,
if you should find my Beloved,
what must you tell him . . . ?
That I am sick with love.

THE CHORUS

What makes your Beloved better than other lovers,
O loveliest of women?
What makes your Beloved better than other lovers,
to give us a charge like this?

THE BRIDE

My Beloved is fresh and ruddy,
to be known among ten thousand.
His head is golden, purest gold,
his locks are palm fronds
and black as the raven.
His eyes are doves
at a pool of water,
bathed in milk,
at rest on a pool.
His cheeks are beds of spices,
banks sweetly scented.
His lips are lilies,
distilling pure myrrh.
His hands are golden, rounded,
set with jewels of Tarshish.
His belly a block of ivory
covered with sapphires.
His legs are alabaster columns

set in sockets of pure gold.
His appearance is that of Lebanon,
unrivaled as the cedars.
His conversation is sweetness itself,
he is altogether lovable.
Such is my Beloved, such is my friend,
O daughters of Jerusalem!

The Chorus

Where did your Beloved go,
O loveliest of women?
Which way did your Beloved turn
so that we can help you look for him?

The Bride

My Beloved went down to his garden,
to the beds of spices,
to pasture his flock in the gardens
and gather lilies.
I am my Beloved's, and my Beloved is mine.
He pastures his flock among the lilies.

The Storm of Summer

If the Song of Songs were only an ordinary love poem or novel, it should end with the third poem. It seems that it has reached a summit, and, this time, it would not be possible to come down again. The Bride has given herself totally, irrevocably. The Bridegroom recognizes this and, in a way, announces it to the whole world, asking it to witness his wedding. Lastly, the third poem ends—in contrast to the first two poems—without the Bridegroom's having to charge the daughters of Jerusalem not to awake his love.

The latter, at the beginning of the fourth poem, happens to be asleep or rather half asleep, as she herself tells it:

5:2 *I sleep, but my heart is awake.*[1]

The total sincerity of her love is not in question, and she truly surrendered without reservation at her wedding. However, until the end of life, the most sublime love remains exposed, threatened, as we already pointed out at the end of the first two poems, even if the Bride has already progressed much since then. Let us say that on the affective level, without her being aware of it, she is not yet fully integrated in love. The desire and drive of her heart are tremendous; but the decision remains fragile. As Chouraqui points out: "The diamond is pure and beautiful, but there is a flaw."[2] Isaiah had said, more roughly: "Your wine is watered."[3]

---

[1] "I was sleeping, but my heart is awakening." (Cf. TOB, Sg 5:2 and note.)
[2] André Chouraqui, *Le Cantique des Cantiques* (Paris: Presses Universitaires de France, 1970), 63.
[3] Isaiah, 1:22 (TOB).

Hence the incomprehensible fall from the highest summit of love: "I sleep," the Bride says, "but my heart is awake." "At night my soul longs for you", says Isaiah, "and my spirit in me seeks for you" (Is 26:9). The context of the fourth poem, unfortunately, does not allow us to interpret the Bride's words in the same way. No, in spite of contrary interpretations,[4] her heart is not yet fully awake, fully watchful. It is still torn between watchfulness and sleep. In adumbration, she is like the three disciples in the transfiguration scene, of whom Saint Luke tells us they "were heavy with sleep, but they kept awake" (Lk 9:32). And that is no compliment!

In this state of drowsiness, the Bride hears a knock on the door of her room. Her heart is immediately alerted:

5:2 *I hear my Beloved knocking.*

In fact, this is no longer his rapid step, his joyful leap over the hills, but a discreet knock on her door. It is enough. Only he arrives so suddenly; only he knocks in such a way, so discreetly and so personally at the same time.

But here he is now, calling from the outside, in the night:

5:2 *"Open to me, my sister, my love,*
my dove, my perfect one,

One should hear this verse in Hebrew with the four stresses at the end of the four three-syllabic words, each ending with a very soft "i" (six times "i").[5] "Open"! Let her hasten to open,

---

[4] "For whoever simply reads the text of this sacred poem, it is impossible to discern the least trace of allusion to any infidelity of the Bride. It is not possible to interpret in this way the delay—if there is a delay—in her opening the door for him at the beginning of the fourth poem." Lucien-Marie de Saint-Joseph, *Le Cantique des Cantiques* (Paris: Desclée de Brouwer, 1953), 22.

[5] The Hebrew text reads: *"P'takhili, Akhoti, Ra'yati, Yonati, Tamati"* (the letter *i* having the same pronunciation as in Latin or Italian and denoting *a*), the feminine form of the imperative b), c), d), e), f), the first person in an indirect complement—"to me"—and then as a possessive: *my* sister, *my* friend, etcetera. — *Trans.*

as Saint Bernard adjures her to do: "Here is the desired of all the nations knocking at your door. Ah, if while you delay, he were to pass by, compelling you to look again for him in tears, for him whom your heart loves."[6] And to make her open without delay, he multiplies the sweetest names, the dearest to his heart, names that truly belong to her as they do to him, with this possessive tenderness repeated four times: "my sister, my love, my dove, my perfect one." There is a sense of deepening from one name to the other, for you are my sister by nature, I made you so through the Incarnation; and by choice you are my love because "I have loved you with an everlasting love" (Jr 31:3); and I call you my dove because you have the same glance, the same heart, the same Spirit as I do; and lastly you are my perfect one, my immaculate one whom I washed and sanctified in my blood.

"My perfect one", said the Bridegroom. Did we hear rightly? Yes, and he says so without irony, as if without delusion about the real weakness of her whom he loves. Is she not all for him? But will she finally hear? Finally understand? "These names," says Claudel, "we hear them one after the other, full of tenderness, but we cannot move as we slowly realize with astonishment: my sister, my love, my dove, my immaculate. What? Is he really talking to us? To us?"[7]

But as if the light knock on the door and the sole sound of his voice were not enough, the Bridegroom seeks her compassion by pointing out his pathetic state:

5:2 *for my head is covered with dew,*
   my locks with the drops of night."

He is a miserable love, waiting in the cold night on her doorstep. He does not come in an imposing manner, but he implores; he is not a lord and master; he does not rush in with

---

[6] *Louange de la Vierge Marie,* Abbaye N.D. D'Orval, microfiche of lecture M21.

[7] Paul Claudel, *Paul Claudel interroge le Cantique des Cantiques* (Paris: NRF-Gallimard, 1948), 192.

strength and splendor—and she would only be able to kneel lovingly before him. But this time he comes in dressed as the poorest and most pitiful of all. With this face of a humiliated servant, which should also be hers! And he is begging, he is asking for compassion even though he is the richest and happiest of all. Of course, he is rich, he fulfills her so totally; but he is also poor because he is never fulfilled. In truth, he is the greatest, the highest but also the smallest because "the characteristic of love is always to lower oneself."[8] And he is also the living water, the inexhaustible fountain, and whosoever brings his lips to him experiences the fact that from him "flow fountains of living water" (Jn 7:38); but at the same time he is a thirsty beggar, on the side of the road, imploring, "Give me a drink" (Jn 4:7); he is the "thirsty fountain".[9] As Saint Augustine puts it in one of his magnificent sentences: "He is in need as the one who is about to receive; and he is in abundance as the one who is going to fulfill."[10]

Such is the paradox of love. "Love is the son of Poros and Plenia, of abundance and famine", Plato says in a parable of the *Banquet*.[11] The paradox is well expressed here in the dual symbolism of dew and drops of the night: "my head is covered with dew, my locks with the drops of night." In the Bible, dew is always associated with blessing, fecundity, as for instance in Psalm 133: "copious as Hermon dew falling on the heights of Zion, where Yahweh confers his blessing, everlasting life" (Ps 133:3). In the desert, the manna fell like dew in the morning (Ex 16:13). And the messiah is expected like the dew of the earth: *Rorate caeli desuper*. "Send victory like a dew, you heavens" (Is 45:8). Did not God himself say through the

---

[8] Saint Thérèse of the Child Jesus, *Histoire d'une âme* (Paris: Cerf/Desclée de Brouwer, 1972), 21.

[9] Marie-Nöel, *Notes intimes* (Paris: Stock, 1959), 311.

[10] Saint Augustine, *Commentary on the Gospel of John*, XV:12, 1514.

[11] Plato, *Le banquet*, pt. 2, *Oeuvres complètes*, vol. 4 (Paris:Les Belles Lettres, 1929), 55, 203C.

prophet Hosea: "I will fall like dew on Israel. He shall bloom like the lily" (Ho 14:6)? Thus the head of the Bridegroom is covered with dew.

But together with the dew, there are those drops on his locks: "my locks with the drops of night." Drops of rain in the night, drops of distress seeming to foreshadow those drops of sweat and blood covering Jesus' brow in the night of Gethsemane while his friends are also sleeping. Thus the Bridegroom of the Song stands as a pitiful beggar at the door: "He wanted to convince us that he loves us with a delirious love; thus he invented this abasement."[12]

Alas! If the Bridegroom is truly here, in person, she whom he loves and who was being called his perfect one is also here in her own poor truth. What a pathetic and disappointing response to him who was calling her so tenderly:

5:3 — *"I have taken off my tunic,*
am I to put it on again?
I have washed my feet,
am I to dirty them again?"

Would not one think that she is called to a superhuman effort, an impossible feat? To get dressed again, to run the risk of dirtying her feet? This is too much for me! It does not make sense! One must pay attention to this repetition: "Am I . . . ? Am I . . . ?"

There may not be in the entire Bible a more stunning representation of sin. To say this might seem quite exaggerated, excessive, so insignificant does the infidelity of the Bride appear at first sight: some laziness, some exasperation. (Why does he always come so late, without warning? Never at my time, always at his?) Some desire, undoubtedly, to be begged, a hint of vanity; indeed, nothing too serious. Thus we are ac-

[12] Nicolas Cabasilas, *La vie en Jésus-Christ*, tran. S. Broussaleux (Chevetogne, 1960), quoted by Paul Evdokimov in *L'amour fou de Dieu* (Paris: Seuil, 1973).

customed to measure our sins according to our psychological
and moral criteria, according to our categories and catalogues
and current opinion. But not in reference to God. Not as a re-
fusal of offered love. Not as a delay and tardiness imposed on
a love that, without any calculation, gives itself. Truly, the
more insignificant and futile are the motives given by the bride
not to get up and open, the more they truly show the real se-
riousness and nature of sin: infidelity to love. For if God is
love, there can only be in the final analysis a single sin: not to
love, to refuse to open oneself to the waiting love.

"Late have I loved you, beauty, even conceit, ever new; late
have I loved you", Saint Augustine writes in the *Confessions* to
explain his inner past of infidelity.[13] The closer the beauty reveals itself, the more radiant the face of love is, the more serious it is also to turn away, even for one moment. It is easy to
see that through this sort of psychodrama played by the Bride,
the author of the Song means this: it is after the extraordinary
celebration of the wedding in the third poem and also in the
continuity of the whole biblical story of this infidelity of
love—its true name is adultery—that the Bride is exposed,
even after she has received the greatest favors. Even though she
was awakened, she prefers to remain in the night. At a signal
from her Brid groom, she did not run toward him, she did not
leap to meet him. She remained motionless on her bed. When
he called her, she refused to listen. Then she looked for futile
excuses to justify herself—"I have taken off my tunic, am I to
put it on again?" In this she truly shows herself to be the
daughter of her first parents, who after the first sin also at-
tempted to justify themselves though their eyes were opened
and immediately "they realized that they were naked" (Gn
3:7). Preferring her own self to the one who chose her above all
others, the Bride shuts the door on him. "He came to his own
domain and his own people did not accept him", says Saint

[13] Saint Augustine, *Confessions*, Book X, 27(38); PL 32, 795; CCL 27, 175.

John (Jn 1:11). To be sure, "without beauty, without majesty [we saw him], no looks to attract our eyes" (Is 53:2).

Even though rejected, the Bridegroom does not give up. But he who earlier was knocking, then called and implored, and to soften the heart of his love was multiplying the sweetest words, now without saying another word, and in the violence of his passion, puts his hand in the hole of the door, in the lock:

5:4 *My Beloved thrust his hand*
through the hole in the door;

In his impatience, it seems that he would want to force the door. But he does not enter. He respects too much, infinitely so, the freedom, the free decision of the one he loves. "Even though he is able to enter," Saint Ambrose says, "he does not want to go in by force. He does not want to constrain those who refuse him. . . . Happy thus is the one at whose door Christ is knocking. But listen to the one who knocks, listen to him who wants to go in, . . . lest the Bridegroom, when he comes, go away because the house will be closed to him."[14]

The house remains closed; he passes on and goes away. And Saint John of the Cross has, as it were, perceived the echo of his pain, in the very moving poem of the Shepherd:[15]

> A lonely shepherd goes in pain.
> No pleasure or joy for him,
> For always he thinks about his shepherdess,
> And his heart is heavy with love.
>
> He does not weep because of love's wound
> For this is not his pain
> Though pain is gripping his heart,
> He weeps, thinking himself forgotten.

[14] Saint Ambrose, *Expositio Psalmi CXVIII*, 12, 13–14; CSEL vol. 62 (Vienna, 1913), 258–259.
[15] Saint John of the Cross, *Poèmes, Oeuvres complètes,* Bibliothèque européenne (Paris: Desclée de Brouwer, 1964), 925.

This very thought of being forgotten
By his shepherdess, is his great pain.
He is so outraged in a remote land
And heartbroken with love.

Alas, says the shepherd, how unhappy the one
Whose love chases him away so far from her heart.
She did not want to enjoy my presence,
And left my heart so crushed with love.

Then, after a long time, slowly,
He climbed on a tree, stretched his beautiful arms,
And died, held fast by those arms,
Heartbroken with love.

The knock on the door, the voice of her lover, the dear and
sweet names he gave her, did not succeed in tearing the Bride
from her torpor, while now she is struck by the sight of the
hand briefly attempting to open the door, the hand that was
trying in vain to enter into her life. Yet, how is it that this so
powerful and creative hand never knows how to force but only
to offer itself?

5:4 *My Beloved thrust his hand*
through the hole in the door;
I trembled to the core of my being.

The Bride is overwhelmed. This is a knock on her heart, her
belly, if the word must be translated in all its strength. Victim,
among his people, of the same infidelity, Jeremiah voices the
same complaint: "I am in anguish, I writhe with pain!" (JB); "I
am doubled up with pain" (Jr 4:19, TOB).

5:5 *Then I rose*
to open to my Beloved,
myrrh ran off my hands,
pure myrrh off my fingers,
on to the handle of the bolt.

Indelible mark of the Bridegroom! Permanent sign of the Bridegroom! The hands of the Bridegroom could not have touched a life even so slightly without its being forever penetrated and made fragrant. Myrrh, being a liquid perfume, always accompanies the presence of the Bridegroom in the soul; it alone can express to what extent the contact of the Bridegroom, no matter how humble, discreet and rapid, penetrates to the deepest recesses of life, as only the most liquid, penetrating and subtle of all perfumes can do. And she knew it so well, this perfume of myrrh! "My Beloved", she had said, "is a sachet of myrrh lying between my breasts"—perfume identified with the Bridegroom, "perfume of God", writes Saint Gregory of Nyssa, "that creation, like a perfume vase, holds in itself through the wonders we see in it."[16] For the Bride, this perfume was always the symbol of his presence; but now it becomes, on the handle of the door bolt, the heartbreaking sign of his absence, for she is abruptly aware that the Bridegroom himself has vanished. She only has a memory, the fragrant trace of his passage. He is gone:

5:6 *I opened to my Beloved,*
   but he had turned his back and gone!
   My soul failed at his flight.

"Look, I am standing at the door, knocking", the negligent church of Laodicea is told; "if one of you hears me calling and opens the door, I will come in to share his meal . . . with him" (Rv 3:20). He came. He humbly stood by the door. He knocked patiently. He waited patiently. The beautiful betrothed heard his voice. But she did not open (the word is now on her lips for the second time), and he did not come in.

It is impressive to hear an Indian mystic of the fourteenth century, in his still obscure soul, lending his voice to the pain of the beloved:

[16] Saint Gregory of Nyssa, *In Canticum Canticorum*, Homily 1, PG 44, 784A.

> He came to seek me.
> The night was dark.
> Heavy clouds ran in the sky.
> He came on this solitary path,
> Soaked with rain.
> I was here with my friends,
> And I played with their childish toys.
> I did not go to greet him.
> He came, he stayed under the trees,
> Soaked with rain.[17]

How different, as Saint Bernard points out, is the other Bride on whose door the Bridegroom will also knock one day and who will so promptly and totally open up to him: "Blessed Virgin," Saint Bernard says, "in this solemn moment, open your heart to faith, your lips to consent, your womb to the Creator. He is the desired of all the nations knocking at the door. And Mary rose immediately: 'I am your servant, the handmaiden of the Lord', she says; 'let it be done according to your word'."[18]

The Bridegroom—we must stress this again and again since it is so unbelievable—left without any complaint, any reproach, any protest. Silently. Can one imagine such a reaction in an ordinary lover? What noble anger, what cries, what curses would the passion of the rejected lover provoke! It is clear that one stanza is missing here: the one in which the cry of a rejected love is heard! But the Song is no ordinary poem; the Bridegroom of the Song is no ordinary lover. Just like Jesus with the Samaritan woman or with the sinful woman at Simon's house or the adulterous woman or Zaccheus or with his disciples after the Resurrection, like the father in the parable of the prodigal son, the Bridegroom never utters the slightest reproach to the one he loves throughout the entire Song. To be

---

[17] A poem by Chandidas, quoted by George Morel, *Question d'homme, l'autre,* vol. 2 (Paris: Aubier-Montaigne, 1977), 239.
[18] Saint Bernard, *In Laudibus Virginis Matris,* IV:8 (Paris: Éd. cist., 1966), 54.

sure, he has no illusions about her fragility, her weakness. He suffers from her infidelity. But never does he criticize or utter harsh words. All he can say when he sees her sleeping is: "[Do] not . . . stir my love, nor rouse it, before it please to awake" — words of infinite patience and tenderness.

We can ask ourselves, however, why after having shown so much desire and haste, the Bridegroom withdrew so quickly. Would he be playing a game in reaction to the pitiful comedy of his Bride? In fact, after having spoken to the heart of his love to tear her away from her nonchalance and languor, he now wants by his very absence and the suffering it will cause to purify her completely and thus take her to the real perfection of love and union. This is quite in keeping with the normal pedagogy of the Bridegroom: we already saw it in the second poem, when he runs away in such a fashion.

From now on, her soul failing, she becomes aware, with his flight, that he was her only good and the very life of her life. "In the measure and in the direction of God", Nicolas Cabasilas reminds us, "human desire was prepared since the beginning, like a huge jewel case, large enough to contain God himself. This is why nothing in this world will ever satisfy us, nothing will fulfill our desires."[19] How can one live without him?

5:6 *My soul failed at his flight.*

Madly, she runs after him without taking into account the cold, the night, her pain, in a halting race. And this does indeed bear witness, in her very weakness, to the greatness of her love. But all her efforts are futile.

5:6 *I sought him but I did not find him,*
I called to him but he did not answer.

She who before had not responded to the voice calling her is apparently condemned to cry in the wilderness. Silence of God. Absence of God. Not as a reprisal! But God is silent and

[19] Nicolas Cabasilas, *La vie en Jésus-Christ,* II; PG 150, 559ff.

hidden so that the heart, thus pierced and hurt by desire, may finally open up to him, with a greater capacity for receiving him.

This is noted by Saint Gregory the Great in an essential text: "The Bridegroom hides when he is sought, so that, not finding him, the Bride may seek him with a renewed ardor; and the Bride is hampered in her search so that this delay may increase the capacity for God, and that she may find one day more fully what she was seeking."[20]

In a similar vein, Saint Augustine says in his beautiful commentary on the first Epistle of John: "God, by making us wait, stretches desire. Stretching desire, he stretches the soul. Stretching the soul, he makes it capable of receiving. . . . Such is our life: we must endeavor to desire."[21]

And likewise, Saint Gregory of Nyssa: "God wants the delay in pleasure to set afire the desire [of the soul] so that together with this ardor his joy may also increase, . . . [so that one can go so far as to say that] finding God means to seek him continually. . . . This is truly seeing God when one is not sated in desiring him. . . . God is eternally sought."[22]

It may be that, in the long mystical tradition in which these texts are written, Saint Bernard is the one who has best expressed this theme in the most personal and human way, when he confides for instance to his brothers: "As soon as the Word appears after many vigils and endless prayers, long works and torrents of tears, he escapes all of a sudden, just when you thought that you could securely possess him. At another time, he will come close to the one who weeps and runs after him; he lets himself be possessed for a while, but not to be kept forever; for just a moment later, he flees and escapes."[23]

Poem of union, the Song is also the poem of search and thirst

---

[20] Saint Gregory the Great, *Moralium*, V:6; PL 76, 683A.

[21] Saint Augustine, *Commentaire de la première épître de Saint Jean* (Paris: Cerf, 1966), 231–233.

[22] Saint Gregory of Nyssa, *In Canticum Canticorum*, Homily 2, 801D.

[23] Saint Bernard, *Sermons sur le Cantique des Cantiques, Oeuvres mystiques*, Sermon 74 (Paris: Seuil, 1953), 761ff.

for God. It is, as it were, totally contained, as we already observed for the second poem, in these two paired words that are so important for prophets and evangelists: "seek-find". But how many are they who seek God with this patience and passion? Martin Buber tells the following anecdote: One day, the grandson of Rabbi Baruch was playing hide-and-seek with another little boy. He hid, but the other refused to seek him and left. The child went to complain to his grandfather. Then, his own eyes full of tears, Rabbi Baruch cried: "God says the same thing. I hide, but no one comes to seek me."[24]

The complaint of the Bride is now that of the abandoned psalmist: "As a doe longs for running streams, so longs my soul for you, my God" (Ps 42:1); it is the complaint in the first verse of the Spiritual Canticle of Saint John of the Cross:

> Where did you hide, friend,
> Who left me in mourning?
> Like a hind you fled,
> Leaving me desolate,
> Crying, I went out after you,
> And you were gone![25]

Thus the Bride goes off in the streets of Jerusalem during the night. She does not collapse under sterile regrets or guilt feelings. We do not hear her sigh: What did I do? How mad I was! For her, to bemoan her fall is to rush once again after the one who could not have ceased to love her. This trait is quite in keeping with the ardent Bride we met in the first two poems. And once again, she meets the watchmen of the city.

5:7 *The watchmen came upon me*
   as they made their rounds in the City.

---

[24] Martin Buber, *Les récits hassidiques* (Paris: Plon, 1963), 145–158, quoted by Evdokimov in *L'amour Fou*, 36.
[25] Saint John of the Cross, *Cantique spirituel, Oeuvres complètes*, Bibliothèque européenne (Paris: Desclée de Brouwer, 1958), 537.

> *They beat me, they wounded me,*
> *they took away my cloak,*
> *they who guard the ramparts.*

The very same guards she had met before but who then had
not paid any attention to her and had not even answered her
when she questioned them (3:2–3) are those who today approach her before she even has the chance to utter a word but
not in order to help her or inquire about her too visible pain.
They attack brutally, without any reason. They beat her, they
wound her, they undress her. Thus is revealed in the Song the
city of men as it truly is, the city of violence, as opposed to the
Jerusalem of peace whose King is the Bridegroom. The psalmist observes this sadly: "I can see how Violence and Discord fill
the city; day and night, they stalk together along the city walls.
Sorrow and Misery live inside. . . . Tyranny and Treachery
are never absent from its central square" (Ps 55:9–11).

Thus the harshness and persecution of men are frequently
added to the absence of God, and the soul, wherever it turns,
now finds no consolation. The very people in whom one
thought to find help, counsel, support, comfort, contribute
many times to the pain and aggravate it. It must also be said
that, contrary to the second poem, where the Bride did not go
away from the Bridegroom of her own volition—and then all
the forces of her enemies (the watchmen) could do nothing
against her, against the invisible assistance given by the Bridegroom—this time, having refused herself to her Bridegroom,
she lost his support; and her enemies, as usual, despoil and attack her. She had just said to her husband: "I have taken off my
tunic, am I to put it on again?" (5:3) so that she could not respond to his call; the cruel irony is that the guards now forcefully take her cloak away as a punishment because she did not
want to put it on to greet the Bridegroom (cf. Ezk 16:36–37).

However, one can also see in this encounter the great, the ultimate progress made by the Bride; to what degree, through
trials and even because of the infidelity that cost her the Bride-

groom, her love has risen! She seems insensitive to all out-
rages. She does not voice any complaint. She does not think
about herself, but only about her beloved.It even seems that all
the abuse she is receiving only helps to strengthen her in her
loving search. If she turns again, as before, to her maiden companions, the daughters of Jerusalem, it is not to beg for help or
pity for herself. But only,

5:8 *I charge you,*
daughters of Jerusalem,
if you should find my Beloved,
what must you tell him . . . ?
That I am sick with love.

The very same maiden companions to whom the Bridegroom
said so clearly that they should not stir or rouse the Bride before she pleased (2:7; 3:5) receive now from the Bride herself
words of adjuration like those of her Bridegroom, the assurance that she is quite awake now. Fully repenting her infidelity, she is only seeking her love—to the point of being sick. "I
am sick with love." He who was her life has left her; how then
could she live and keep her health? "If then, by chance,"she
says in Saint John of the Cross, "you see the best-loved, tell
him that I am in pain, suffering and dying."[26]
Her present languor is quite different from that which had
kept her a few hours ago in her rooms. This one is not of weakness but of excessive love. Languor of mourning love throws
her actively in search of the Bridegroom. We have, clearly expressed here, a difference between bad and good spiritual passivity. The bad passivity withdraws within itself; the good
passivity, on the contrary, opens itself to God and neighbor
and brings about attention and charitable initiatives of all
kinds.

[26] Ibid., Stanza II, 544–545.

We must stress the extraordinarily pathetic effects of "what must you tell him?" She would like him to be told, but she can talk only directly to him. She cannot have anything conveyed to him by others. No! If, by chance, the daughters of Jerusalem were to meet him, they could not communicate anything on her behalf. Let them only bear witness to her condition: her face expresses eloquently her distress, and her distress comes from the passion of her love. "Lord, she whom you love is sick, sick for your love."

The reaction of the daughters of Jerusalem is rather disappointing:

5:9 *What makes your Beloved better than other lovers,*
    O loveliest of women?
    What makes your Beloved better than other lovers,
    to give us a charge like this?

Contrary to the watchmen, the daughters of Jerusalem are not hostile. But even though there are no blows, the sharpness of their words is felt just as much, and Gregory of Nyssa thinks that they well deserve here the name of "thorns" that the Bridegroom had given them when he had said that his beloved, among her maiden companions, was like a lily among thorns.[27]

Let us say, at least, that the astonished questions of the daughters of Jerusalem express very well the feelings of those who, not having yet had the grace of meeting the Bridegroom, cannot easily imagine that he is so important in her life and can hurt her so much by his absence. This Bridegroom, can he really be loved with such a love that it makes her sick when he goes away? Is he really this lover to whom no earthly lover can be compared? "What makes your Beloved better than any

[27] Saint Gregory of Nyssa, *In Canticum Canticorum*, Homily 4 and Homily 13, 842 and 1045.

other lovers, O loveliest of women?" The daughters of Jerusalem, in their astonishment, reiterate the same question. We
probably hear one of those questions with which the pagan nations, represented here by the daughters of Jerusalem, were ha-
rassing Israel in exile and of whom the psalmist makes himself
the sad echo: "All day long they ask me, 'Where is your
God?' " (Ps 42:10). But is not the disciple of Christ called today in the same manner?

The daughters of Jerusalem might, however, feel something
of the sovereign loveliness of the Bridegroom if only through
the contemplation of the exceptional radiance of the one whose
love he is—"O loveliest of women", as they say with some
envy, probably. He must really be unique, he who makes his
beloved so uniquely beautiful. He must be supremely existent
and not a myth, he whose love gives life and radiance to such
an extent in a human being.

Thus goaded by the chorus of the daughters of Jerusalem,
the Bride abandons herself, in response, in an effusive praise of
her Bridegroom. In the extreme suffering caused by his absence, she finds relief and calm only by letting her heart endlessly pour out praises for the one she loves. To talk about him,
to sing his praise, to celebrate his beauty, to deliver the innermost soul of all the admiration and love that is in it is now her
only sweetness and is also an absolute necessity. The love for
the Bridegroom cannot remain unproclaimed.

5:10 *My Beloved is fresh and ruddy,* she begins,
       to be known among ten thousand.

Before she itemizes with pleasure all the features of her Bridegroom (as he had done for her), she first lets herself be fascinated by the global contemplation of his person. The
daughters of Jerusalem ask about his superiority over the other
lovers. In truth, no comparison could be possible. He is "to be
known among ten thousand", meaning, among all! Eisenberg

notes in this respect the first meaning of the word *qadosh* (holy), which is: who has no equal. "To be *qadosh*, holy, is to be unique in the world, different, irreducible."[28] The Bridegroom is absolutely unique; he is the only one. And the one you, daughters of Jerusalem, called "loveliest of women" is beautiful indeed, but she is still black. Yes, as she herself admits, she is black, and her complexion is dark, somber and burnt in comparison with the fresh and ruddy face of her Bridegroom. This is perhaps what depicts him best.

5:10 *My Beloved is fresh and ruddy,*

i.e., he has all the signs of health, youth, life and beauty. It is said of David in 1 Samuel, according to an interpretation justified in the TOB, that he had "a fresh complexion". The Bridegroom of the Song, son of David, has the same characteristic (cf. 1 S 16:12 and 17:42). In fact, we have, in his face, the union of *sah* (white) of the light—as is said about the clothing of Jesus during the transfiguration: "his clothing became brilliant as lightning" (Lk 9:29)—with red, crimson *(adom)*, which is the color of love. Light and love, this then is his whole being! This is the radiance of his glory. But with signs, at the same time, that will be those of the Incarnation, as Gregory of Nyssa is able to discern it: the whiteness of his flesh and the red of his blood.[29] All the glory and humility of the incarnate Word, such as Saint John always contemplates them, are thus felt at the beginning of the Bride's hymn.

After this first moment of fascination and ecstasy, the Bride surrenders to the enchantment of a detailed portrait of her beloved, somewhat in the style he had used to describe her in the third poem (5:10–16 is in fact a response to 4:1–15). But still, it was easier to get an idea about the features of the Bride through

---

[28] Josy Eisenberg, *A Bible ouverte* (Paris: Albin Michel, 1980), 183.
[29] Saint Gregory of Nyssa, *In Canticum Canticorum,* Homily 13, 1052D.

the images that her Bridegroom used than to guess now at the features of the Bridegroom through the images given by his love.

Is this because the symbolism is subtle and refined to the point of affectation? The Bride has been described on the model of the Holy Land; all the beauty of the land is, as it were, reflected and reproduced in her body. She has the beauty of all the geography and flora of her country. Should we think with André Robert that the Bridegroom is described by his Bride on the model of the Temple of Jerusalem? Will it not be said about Jesus, in Saint John, that he is the true Temple? "He was speaking about the Temple that was his body" (Jn 2:21). Would the Bride also see the beauty of her Bridegroom represented in the wonders of the Temple? It is certain that gold and ivory, metals, stones, and very precious woods, especially the cedars of Lebanon, which she evokes one after the other to describe him whom she loves, were indeed materials used in the construction and decoration of the Temple.

But we can ask ourselves if there is, in this unique portrait of the Bridegroom, which is made in his absence—a very important point to keep in mind—a real concern for description. The Bride does not truly care to let us see the one she loves. How could she? Clement of Rome says: "The greatness of his beauty, who could express it?"[30] If, in the face of all the wisdom and glory of Solomon, the queen of Sheba, according to 1 Kings, feels that she is fainting and that she is left breathless (1 K 10:5), how could the Bride of the Song, at the sole evocation of the beauty of her King, also not feel faint, for "there is something greater than Solomon here" (Mt 12:42)? She can only sing that he is a priceless treasure and the unique pearl of her life. Gold, ivory, precious stones and metals, priceless woods—she gathers the most beautiful, rare, fabulous, won-

---

[30] Saint Clement of Rome, *Épître aux Corinthiens* (SC 167) (Paris: Cerf, 1971), 181.

derful things that the universe offers to compose a hymn to absolute glory, to praise in a unique way the one who is unique to her heart as he is in the whole world. Thus Saint John will do the same one day in Revelation to describe the one seated on the throne, and the Bride draws from the infinite well of symbolism.

5:11 *His head is golden, purest gold,*

Gold is used four times in this portrait of the Bridegroom. And it is not enough for the Bride that his head be of gold: in her inability to show the face that is above all other faces, she adds, "purest gold". And André Robert concludes that the author of the Song, talking about the head of the Bridegroom, is thinking about the Holy of Holies at the very back of the Temple of Jerusalem, head of the Temple, which was the very locus of Yahweh's presence and where Solomon had in fact put much gold.[31] "The Holy of Holies Solomon covered with fine gold. He made a cedar altar in front of it and covered it with gold" (cf. 1 K 6:20). This is quite possible, but here gold expresses the superabundance of the divinity. And "purest gold", i.e., without any of these mixtures from which the most perfect beauty is never exempt in this life, means the supereminent holiness of him who is three times holy, as the icon painters, so much in love with gold, have always felt.

5:11 *his locks are palm fronds
       and black as the raven.*

The hair of the Bridegroom flutters and quivers around his face as palms do at the top of a palm tree. Long locks, sumptuous and black, like those of the Bride, but neater! Always sensitive to the analogy with the Temple, A. Robert believes that he can

[31] André Robert and Raymond Tournay, *Le Cantique des Cantiques* (Paris: Gabalda, 1963), 214.

see the hair of the Bridegroom in the countless representations of palms decorating the gates of the Holy of Holies itself. This might also be possible. But we must remember above all that black suggests the invisibility of God, as opposed to gold's proclaiming his dazzling glory.

5:12 *His eyes are doves*
at a pool of water,
bathed in milk,
at rest on a pool.

In a more ingenious manner yet, Robert invites us to decipher the specific part of the Bridegroom's face in the most particular details of the Temple's ornamentation. Doves, notably, were one of the important details of decoration. As to the water, it could be that of the pools and the beautiful water basin, which was the bronze sea of the Temple. This might be. But it is also a characteristic of visionaries to metamorphose what they see. *Doves* was the word used by the Bridegroom for the eyes of his love. Eyes like those, like his, are enlightened by the Spirit. Water and milk are again the wonderful clarity and childlike innocence of her eyes. Doves, water and milk — these images that are at the same time airy and limpid, images of inexpressible candor, freshness and sweetness — attempt in vain to depict with what peace and what tenderness the eyes of the loved one are gazing at his love. "I send peace flowing like a river", the Lord had promised (Is 66:12). What must have been in truth the depth, serenity and transparency of his gaze, that of the light of the world! To the extent that Saint Thérèse of the Child Jesus says that even when cast down, the eyes of Jesus are radiating light: "He made me enter in a cave where I see nothing but a half veiled light: the light radiating from the half shut eyes of my beloved's face."[32]

---

[32] Saint Thérèse of the Child Jesus, *Lettres* (Paris: Cerf/Desclée de Brouwer, 1977), Letter 110, 181.

We may notice in passing that the images of the ewes and goats do not follow the doves in the portrait of the Bridegroom. Such images belong especially to the Bride, the flock of the Good Shepherd.

5:13 *His cheeks are beds of spices,*
banks sweetly scented.
His lips are lilies,
distilling pure myrrh.

We must avoid pressing the images in speculation. Claudel, as usual, has no sympathy for commentators who launch into sophisticated and heavy explanations: "It must be said", he writes, "that they are splashing their heavy shoes where angels fear to tread."[33] Long before the surrealistic school of poetry, the psalms had familiarized us with images that are meant for the sole eyes of the soul. Thus are not the cheeks of the Bridegroom—when the cheeks of the loved one touches them—like a double bed bank of rest and delight, two beds of spices? And the lips? Not as was said of hers "a scarlet thread", but one of these red lilies to which she had compared herself. And from the lilies of these lips, half-opened petals distill the same perfume that the Bridegroom had left behind at the door lock after his flight: "His lips are lilies, distilling pure myrrh." Unction and perfume of virgin myrrh, which have the ineffable sweetness of the Holy Spirit, thus enter into the innermost depths of the soul to re-create at any moment the lips of the Bridegroom, as it is said at the moment of man's creation—"he breathed into his nostrils a breath of life" (Gn 2:7)—as he will also do at the birth of his Church—"he breathed on them and said: 'Receive the Holy Spirit' " (Jn 20:22). From the very first note of her song, the Bride aspired to this very sweet kiss of the Spirit received from the lips of her beloved: "Let him kiss me with the kisses of his mouth."

---

[33] Claudel, *Paul Claudel*, 223.

5:14 *His hands are golden, rounded,*
set with jewels of Tarshish. [34]
His belly a block of ivory
covered with sapphires.

Those who pursue in detail the analogy between the Bridegroom and the Temple of Jerusalem see in the two high columns placed at the right and left of the gate to the Holy of Holies, with a large base rounded at the bottom, the arms and the belly of the Bridegroom. This is undoubtedly going a bit far. The gold of the hands and the ivory of the belly are very poor expedients to which the Bride resorts in her inexpressible enchantment, as when Saint John said at a later date in Revelation that "the one who was seated on the throne and the Person sitting there looked like a diamond and a ruby" (Rv 4:3). The Bride talks about the jewels of Tarshish, which might well come from the great theophany at the opening of the Book of Ezekiel: "The wheels [of Yahweh's chariot] glittered as if made of chrysolite or golden jewels of Tarshish."[35]

5:15 *His legs are alabaster columns*
set in sockets of pure gold.
His appearance is that of Lebanon,
unrivaled as the cedars.

The portrait of the Bridegroom starts with the head, detailing the locks of his hair, then going to the eyes, the cheeks, the lips; it goes on with the description of the hands and belly. Now the Bride admires the legs, compared to columns of alabaster. The impression here is one of power as much as of beauty. The Bridegroom has nothing in common with the idols of the nations, of whom the psalmist (Ps 115:7), as does Daniel, mocks

---

[34] Incrusted with "chrysolites" according to Dhorme and Osty.
[35] Ezk 1:16; cf. Paul Joüon, *Le Cantique des Cantiques* (Paris: Beauchesne, 1909), 255; and TOB, 1606, note f.

the feet that do not walk. He could not be shaken by anything. He is the rock: *"His feet"*, Revelation says, *"like burnished bronze"* (Rv 1:15). The Bride therefore knows that she can, in all security, lean on him: on two "alabaster columns set in sockets of pure gold", he will not falter.

Before we go on, we should perhaps open here a parenthesis about the colors used in the "portrait" of the Bridegroom — five colors: white, red, gold, black and sapphire blue. Two colors are dominant: white ("my Beloved is fresh" — (white) — doves of the eyes, milk in which they wash, block of ivory, alabaster columns; and gold. Gold is even named directly five times (with chrysolite, the golden stone). Now these last two colors, white and gold, are properly speaking those of divinity, as the painters of icons still remember in their fidelity to Christ (white garments of the transfigured or resurrected Christ; gold of the King of glory exalting his divinity). Gold is also symbolically associated here in the Song with the head, the hands and the legs (symbolizing thought, power and the immutability of the Bridegroom).

Just as a global impression had introduced the praise of the Bridegroom, the Bride will conclude with a global vision after her detailed description of his beauty. Her Bridegroom is "like Lebanon". What more could she say? He has Lebanon's incomparable splendor, incomparable in the eyes of the Jews, especially because of the high regal cedars covering the mountains, towering above all the other trees. If he is recognizable among ten thousand, as she had said in the beginning, it is because of his stature and absolutely unique majesty, like a cedar. Wisdom says: "grown tall as a cedar on Lebanon" (Si 24:13). The cedar and the apple tree are, in the Song, the two trees of the Bridegroom. But if the apple tree, with the beauty of its flowers and the sweetness of its fruits, symbolizes especially the humanity of the fairest of the children of man, the cedar evokes through its unsurpassed stature his transcendence as divinity. And if, for beauty, the Bridegroom is among men "as an apple tree among the trees of the orchard", he cannot, like the cedar, be compared to any other on the level of divinity: he is unrivaled.

Once the portrait is finished, the Bride adds what is perhaps even more precious to her and more delightful than the beauty of her lover: the words she hears from his mouth.

5:16 *His conversation is sweetness itself,*

"How beautiful you are . . . how delightful!", she had exclaimed at the first encounter (1:16). And together with her, the psalmist: "Your promise, how sweet to my palate! Sweeter than honey to my mouth" (Ps 119:103). The reason is that the beauty of the one she loves, even though she thinks she has seen it at times, even if she attempts to describe it in her song, is essentially a hidden one. "Truly, God is hidden with you" (Is 45:15). On the other hand, his discourses, spoken in her inner life, are like his perfumes: something that she experiences; this Word, in particular, that speaks to her secret heart, so sweetly and tenderly at times. Yes, "his conversation is sweetness itself" and "there has never been anybody who has spoken like him" (Jn 7:46).

5:16 *he is altogether lovable.*

"The maiden companions of the sacred bride", notes Saint Francis de Sales, "had asked her who was her beloved and she answers by an admirable description of all the details of his perfect beauty: his complexion is white and crimson, his head golden. . . . There she goes, meditating in detail on this sovereign beauty until she finally concludes in a kind of contemplation, putting all the beauties into a unique one: 'he is altogether lovable.' "[36] What indeed could she add? There is

[36] Saint Francis de Sales, *Traité de l'amour de Dieu, Oeuvres,* Bibliothèque de la Pléiade (Paris: NRF-Gallimard, 1969), VI:5, 622.

no better proof, it seems, that the Bridegroom of the Song is God himself than the way, both dazzling and obscure, in which the Bride speaks at the only time she attempts to represent him. This language is purely symbolic; it is the language of mystery, through which the soul attempts to tell about God, what he is for her, but gives up trying to describe him as she would a man. Because we do not "see" the Bridegroom at all at the conclusion of the Bride's description.

And how could she describe him? "She is in love with the inaccessible", writes Gregory of Nyssa; "she yearns for the unseizable."[37] "Nothing that we know reveals him; neither shape nor color nor outline nor eye nor face nor comparison nor analogy. . . . Beyond any representation, he escapes totally the grasp of those who attempt to seize him. . . . The Bride imagines indeed a whole variety of apt words to express the inexpressibly good, but the whole impressive capacity of language is left behind. Which is why the Bride says: 'I named him as I could, imagining words to describe him who is inexpressible beatitude, but he was beyond any designation.' . . . In like manner, the great David calls the divinity many times with an infinity of names and confesses that the truth is beyond him. He confesses that on earth the name of God is not an object of knowledge but of admiration: 'O Lord our God, how admirable is your Name on all the earth!' "[38]

Quite sensitive to the inner music of the Bride's song, Saint Augustine also grasps its feature of desperation: "It is", he says, "a vision going beyond all the beauties of the earth: of gold, silver, woods, landscapes, the beauty of the sea and of the air, the beauty of the sun and of the moon, the beauty of the stars, the beauty of the angels, . . . a beauty above all, for it is from it that all things draw their own beauty. . . . The tongue says what it can; the heart has to understand the rest! . . . We cannot give its true name to this reality; we call it gold, we call it wine; whatever name we give to what cannot be named,

[37] Saint Gregory of Nyssa, *In Canticum Canticorum*, Homily 12, 1028BCD.
[38] Ibid., 1028BCD.

it wine; whatever name we give to what cannot be named, whatever name we claim to give it, its name is God."[39] "Besides, this very name of God is not his name", Saint Justin the Apologist had dared to say two centuries before Saint Augustine, "for if anyone dares to claim that God has a name, he is mad. These words of Father, God, Creator, Lord and Master, are not names but words to call him because of his goodness and works. The word God is not a name but an approximation, which is natural to man when he attempts to describe the unexplainable."[40]

This is why the Bride of the Song, in the last analysis, does not make us see anything and does not even tell us anything about him whom she loves! We only experience a deep feeling of loving adoration with her while she is talking. This adoration was described by Elizabeth of the Trinity as "the ecstasy of love crushed by beauty, the extreme force and greatness of the beloved object",[41] of him about whom Hedwig of Antwerp had dared to write that "the unfathomable abyss is his most beautiful shape, . . . and his most sublime state sinks us to the bottom."[42]

The Bride can therefore conclude now, with the very last of her strength:

5:16 *Such is my Beloved, such is my friend,*
O daughters of Jerusalem!

More than a conclusion, this is a victorious note that she sings very loudly, holding it at the end of her song. In truth, we fail to see how the daughters of Jerusalem, to whom she just gave such a description of her Bridegroom, could be of any practical use to her in finding the one she lost. But she spoke far less for

[39] Saint Augustine, *Commentaire*, 231–233.
[40] Saint Justin, *Apologies: Première apologie*, LXI, 131; *Deuxième apologie*, VI:2–3, 161 (Paris: Alphonse Picard, 1904).
[41] Elizabeth of the Trinity, *Oeuvres*, vol. 1 (Paris: Cerf, 1980), 170.
[42] Elisabeth de Miribel, *La liberté souffre violence* (Paris: Plon, 1981), 241, quoting Hedwig of Antwerp.

the daughters of Jerusalem than for herself, gazing at an invisible horizon. And then, as if she found her maiden companions again, she cries: "Such is my Beloved, such is my Friend". This is the only time in the Song, as Father Joüon points out and as the latest edition of the Jerusalem Bible also notes, that the Bride calls the one she loves her "friend", while she calls him "Beloved" more than twenty-five times.[43] There is some triumphalism in this last cry, and almost a challenge in that, having been challenged herself by the daughters of Jerusalem — "What makes your Beloved better than other lovers"? — the Bride, after a most delirious celebration, retorts proudly: Now you really want to know? Well, he is my friend! And I can add nothing else. "When that day comes", the Lord had announced in the Book of Hosea, "she will call me 'my husband' " (Ho 2:18); and in the Book of Isaiah: "For now your creator will be your husband" (Is 54:5). The Bride could not express more clearly the covenant that makes for her, out of the most wonderful of the earth's beloveds, the absolutely unique Bridegroom: "Such is my Beloved, such is my friend".[44]

It seems that no modern interpreter other than Chouraqui has been able to enter so profoundly into the song of the Bride, into what he himself calls "the Song of the absent one", and which is indeed so much in keeping with the prayer of Israel, to whom God says that no one can see him and that one should not even attempt to represent his face, as idol makers were trying to do (cf. Is 40:18; 46:5). "The Bride, broken-hearted, broken in body, sings her song to the absent one, to the one who dwells in her and whom she cannot reach anymore. Verses 10 to 16 of Chapter 5 are an offering of love to the inaccessible prince, the song of Israel to her absent King. Instead of a dirge,

[43] Joüon, *Le Cantique des Cantiques*, 76–77.
[44] *Ra'ayi* means "friend", "special one", not husband, which would be *Ba'ali*. The Bridegroom calls his love *Ra'yati*, which is the feminine equivalent and is translated both in French and in English as "my friend" or "my love" and never as "my wife". — *Trans.*

here is a song of glory that enables her to achieve the miracle of renounced love. Even when he is absent, she belongs totally to him; even absent, he is the only one, the most handsome; the face she has seen and kissed remains forever in her the incarnation of absolute beauty. . . . This is not only a man but the absent and present Person whom she adores. Twenty terms of comparison are used: colors, metals, stones, birds, elements, the earth, water, trees, perfumes, flowers—all this constitutes a man, and this is how the daughter of Israel sees her lover. Not only does this surrealism embarrass the commentators, but it poses an enigma to them, an unfathomable truth. For her, man is described as the measure of the universe, and love is without boundaries: she is the crucified Bride of the absent prince, whom she praises, whose absence makes her the widow of all creation. But faith, through its miracle, transforms her pain. She has only praise in the ecstasy that enables her to describe for the daughters of Jerusalem her absent prince."[45]

Did Chouraqui, when he wrote these lines, know the admirable poem credited to Saint Gregory Nazianzen (fourth century)?

> O you, who are beyond anything, are not these words all
> that can be sung about you? . . .
> What hymn could tell about you, what language?
> No word can express you. . . .
> Only you are unutterable.
> Only you are unknowable. . . .
> You are all beings and you are none of them. . . .
> Yours are all the names, and how will I call you,
> The only one who cannot be named? . . .
> O you, who are beyond everything,
> Is this not all that can be sung about you?[46]

Is it not characteristic that the unutterable beauty of the Bridegroom is celebrated in the Song as an invariable and im-

---

[45] Chouraqui, Le Cantique des Cantiques, 66–67.

[46] Saint Gregory Nazianzen, Poème, quoted by Henri de Lubac, De la connaissance de Dieu (Paris: Éditions du Témoignage chrétien, 1948), 173.

mutable beauty? This is different for the Bride, whose beauty
is essentially mobile and changing like that of the doves, the
ewes and the goats of her country; whose beauty borrows especially from the tender but ephemeral splendor of the flowers
and plants of the Holy Land, while, on the contrary, the beauty
of the Bridegroom, in this unique passage of the Song, when
the Bride attempts desperately to evoke it, appears to be a still
beauty, an absolute one, as it were. Significant in this hymn to
the Bridegroom is the preference of the Bride for gold, metals,
stones, cedar wood, all that which seems to be immutable in
this world. Saint Augustine says in a luminous passage: "The
one you yearn for is not moving. The one who is called 'I am',
because he truly is, is immutable. He reigns forever; he could
not change; there is nothing corruptible in him. He does not
progress because he is perfect. He does not decline because he
is eternal."[47]

Unlike profane love songs, the Song of Songs does not give
to the beauty of the woman a privileged and exalted place.
Thus I fail to see how one could agree with one of André
Chouraqui's most recent opinions, according to which, "in the
couple [of the Song] the woman is predominant."[48]

The daughters of Jerusalem listen in deep silence without
ever interrupting "the Song of the absent one". Now they
speak again, not with a surprised or even ironical and sceptical
tone of voice, as had been the case before ("What makes your
Beloved better than other lovers"). They are overwhelmed by
the hymn to the Bridegroom. They ask no more about him,
but offer themselves promptly to the Bride in order to seek
him with her:

6:1 *Where did your Beloved go,*
O loveliest of women?
Which way did your Beloved turn
so that we can help you look for him?

[47] Saint Augustine, *Commentaire*, 229.
[48] André Chouraqui, *Retour aux racines* (Paris: Le Centurion, 1981), 216.

Here again is a passage of the Song in which we perceive the radiance, the contagious nature of the love of the Bridegroom for those who are in contact with the Bride. These women, who were almost insolent before, are caught now. They perceive, through the beauty, voice and praise of the one they recognize as the "loveliest of women", that they too might be called to love this Bridegroom and be loved by him. For now, they passionately ask questions about the departure of the Bridegroom, the direction that he followed when he left: thus they convey very well their double question and double evocation of the Bridegroom's name: Where? Where did he go? Where did he turn? And they themselves give him this name of "Beloved", which they learned from the Bride. Their ardor, as we can see, does not come only from a charitable desire to help their sister. It is a desire for the Bridegroom himself that carries them: "so that we can help you look for him". "Draw me in your footsteps," the Bride had said at the beginning of the poem, "let us run" (1:4). Now, her maiden companions, drawn by her song, are ready to follow her.

Did not Zechariah prophesy: "In those days, ten men of nations of every language will take a Jew by the sleeve and say, 'We want to go with you, since we have learned that God is with you' " (Zc 8:23)? The love of Israel, people of the covenant, is contagious. It is the catching love of the Bride–Church: "If it is not too daring to say so," writes Gregory of Nyssa, "it might be that seeing the beauty of the Bridegroom through the Bride, [her maiden companions] can admire what is invisible and incomprehensible to any human being, for 'no one has ever seen God' (Jn 1:18). [He] 'whom no man is able to see', as Paul testifies (1 Tm 6:16), made the Church into his own body. . . . He shapes the face of the Church by imprinting on it his own features (cf. Ep 5:27). The maiden friends of the Bride might see in this Church, when contemplating the Bride in a more penetrating way, the one who is invisible: like all those who are unable to look directly at the sun itself contemplate its reflection in the water. Thus in this mirror of the

Church, they see the sun of justice."[49] May it please God that all those who receive from him the gift of knowing him always be for those who have not yet discovered him pure mirrors of his face!

To those who now question her passionately about the direction the Bridegroom might have taken in his flight, the Bride says, as if unexplainably quieted after her long exaltation:

6:2 *My Beloved went down to his garden,*
    to the beds of spices,
    to pasture his flock in the gardens
    and gather lilies.

One could think that the questions of the daughters of Jerusalem—the questions of the nations—made the Bride aware that the one she was looking for was nowhere else but in her own heart. So often do others reveal to us the presence by which we secretly live. The Bridegroom, during all the time that his friend was calling him and running after him in desolation, had not run away to the end of the world. He silently retreated to the heart of his love. The Bridegroom, as we know, has no other garden than the soul of his love (cf. 5:1) It is there that she must always look for him, as we are told in the beautiful verses of Claudel: "You must know, my sweet little girl, my poor child, that he simply pretended to go away. . . . Now he is present in some obscure corner of this ivory tower, where you made him so happy. Listen, . . . this happy thing, which makes you blush and shiver like childish lips touching your heart, it is he!" "It is enough for me to withdraw within my heart to find him again and to cease being where he is not."[50]

---

[49] Saint Gregory of Nyssa, *In Canticum Canticorum*, Homily 8, 949AB.

[50] Paul Claudel, "Cantate à trois voix", *Oeuvre poètique* (Paris: Gallimard, 1957), 352.

6:2 *My Beloved went down to his garden,*

This is what the Bride knows now. He went down. The verb *to go down* is frequently used in Israel to mean that from Jerusalem and the Temple one goes down to the Holy Land. But more deeply, this is the bowing of the royal Bridegroom to the heart of his very poor and very small beloved, who had been unfaithful to him but came back with her whole heart; he bows down to her whom he had called "a garden enclosed", which is expressed in these words: "My Beloved went down to his garden". Immediately after the dazzling hymn to the transcendence of the Bridegroom, this is the wonderfully peaceful song of his no less ineffable interiority. How could she have imagined that the one she had celebrated as inaccessible could thus be held in her very life? That he could be at the same time, as Saint Augustine puts it in an extraordinary way, "inside the deepest and above the highest of his being"? *(Tu autem eras interior intimo meo et superior summo meo.)*[51]

No matter how poor and tiny is the garden of her life in which the Bridegroom has retreated, it still remains a "garden [with] beds of spices". In itself it does not yield such powerful perfumes, even though the Bridegroom did find some rare ones in it (4:12–15). But they are due to the Bridegroom, who took it as his dwelling, for "it is God", Ruysbroeck says, "who in the depths of our being receives God. And God contemplates God."[52]

While he is dwelling in perfect repose at the core of the soul, the Bridegroom is not inactive, for he went down in it "to pasture his flock in the gardens and gather lilies." This is rich in significance. But first we must note that there are some peculiar things in this last stanza of the fourth poem. First, the word

---

[51] Saint Augustine, *Confessions,* Book III, 6(2); PL 32, 63, 688; and CCL 27, 33.

[52] Jan van Ruysbroeck the Admirable, *Ornement des noces spirituelles,* Book II, XX, *Oeuvres* (Brussels: Vromant, 1920), 187.

garden and then the word *lily* are both used twice. Moreover, in the original Hebrew, garden is at first singular and then plural.

Such kinds of anomalies disappear if one pays attention once more to the missionary and universalist dimension of the experience of the Bride, in itself so personal and unusual. God indeed cannot communicate very intimately to the one he loves, "go down" in her soul, without achieving in her and through her, in the innermost part of her garden, his essential work, which is—as Jesus puts it clearly in Saint John—to unite all men: "to gather together in unity the scattered children of God" (Jn 11:52).

Here we can already perceive this. Gardener and shepherd at the same time, in the Song as in the Gospel of John, in which the Magdalen very significantly mistakes the risen Jesus for "the gardener" (Jn 10:11 and 20:15), the Bridegroom, hidden in the innermost depths of the garden of the one he loves, does not cease to work through her in the immense garden of the universe. Thus the plural "in the gardens", i.e., in all men, after the singular of "his garden". Thus already in the third poem, she whom the Bridegroom called "a garden enclosed" became the source of gardens (4:15). And to Mary Magdalen, who wants to hold him back in the closeness of the garden, the risen Jesus says: "Do not cling to me. . . . But go and find the brothers" (Jn 20:17).

Moreover, just as in his role of shepherd the Bridegroom gathers and unites in himself all the thoughts and feelings of her in whom he dwells ("he pastures his flock among the lilies", he unites interiorly in himself the one he loves) in the same way he works in her and through her to gather all the lilies, i.e., to gather all the peoples into one. For "there are other sheep I have [Jesus says] that are not of this fold, and these I have to lead as well. . . . There will be only one flock, and one shepherd" (Jn 10:16).

The very structure of the stanza seems to confirm this interpretation; the first two verses concern only the Bride (6:2a and b), and the last two, again, only the Bride. So that the two verses about mankind (6:2c and d) are very expressively included between the verses of the Bride. In the same way, in the last stanza of the third poem, the Bride's friends were already included, as it were, in the Bride: "I come into my garden, my sister, my promised bride. . . . Drink deep, my dearest friends" (5:1).

To her Bridegroom, found again in the depth of her heart and in such openness and communion with all, the Bride can only whisper lovingly:

6:3 *I am my Beloved's, and my Beloved is mine.*
   He pastures his flock among the lilies.

This is her "refrain". But does not the insistence of the Bride in saying again and again that she fully belongs to her Bridegroom, according to the very terms of the covenant, also aim at destroying forever a very ancient past of unfaithfulness, of which her recent fall was a sad reminder? One day—how could she dare lose the memory?—her Bridegroom wanted to call himself Hosea: and she was called Gomer, an adulterous and prostitute wife. Her Bridegroom told her: "For she is not my wife nor am I her husband" (Ho 2:4); and, more explicitly yet, "You are not my people and I am not your God" (Ho 1:9).

But all this belongs now to the remote past. Today she wants to be totally his, as he is hers. "I am my Beloved's, and my Beloved is mine" can therefore appear as the exact and fervent response, in the terms of the renewed covenant, to the horrible formula of divorce that had once been uttered. Thus the pair of the Song formed by the Bridegroom and his love seems, in many respects, in the mind of the inspired author, an antitype of the unhappy couple of Hosea and Gomer.

We must also note that this time the Bride does not say, as she had done before, "My Beloved is mine and I am his" (2:16). She reverses the order of the propositions to stress the perfect reciprocity of their love at this point in time. As he is hers, so she is his. As he always had the initiative to love her first, she in turn claims to love him first, so as not to love him less than she is loved by him. ("Of us two, tell me, who is the lover?" asks the betrothed in an English poem). Yet, as Saint Bernard points out delicately, the Bride would not be able to love as much as the Bridegroom, "for the waters do not gush with the same force from her who loves and from love, from the soul and from the Word, from the Bride and from the Bridegroom, from the creature and the Creator. The difference is no less great than that which exists between a thirsty being and the fountain. . . . But even if the creature loves less because of its limitations, as long as it loves with all its being, nothing is missing from this love."[53]

In placing in the mouth of the Virgin Mary, the so constant and perfectly faithful Bride, this sentence, which concludes so peacefully the fourth poem, which had started so dramatically, Paul Claudel feels very clearly its both personal and cosmic dimension: "I am indeed a garden, the Bride says, Mary says. From Eden to Nazareth, I do not cease to work at this garden that he asks me to be. . . . I am all these gathered lilies that are united in one single stem and a supreme corolla, where the Holy Spirit will not cease to gather pollen. My beloved is mine, and I am his. I am somebody in his arms, giving him all of mankind to breathe so that he can feed on it."[54] We needed a poet to gather together the various themes sung by the Bride, grown from the poor sleepyhead she was at the beginning of the poem to the Immaculate Virgin offering all of mankind to God in her womb.

However, it is not only for the Bride that the difference is great between the beginning and the end of the poem. It is also true for the Bridegroom, even if, in his deepest being, he does not change. At the start of the fourth poem, he was a beggar, pitifully imploring in the cold of the night. At the end, he is the prince whom no image in the world, no matter how beautiful

[53] Saint Bernard, *Sermons*, Sermon 83, 851.
[54] Claudel, *Paul Claudel*, 265.

and precious it be, could evoke. We had already come across this stunning antinomy in the third poem: between the chief surrounded by his companions arriving from the desert in a long march ("What is this?" the Chorus had asked) and the King seated at his wedding feast. This is the same. And we start, it can be said, to perceive the features that are so contradictory in the one face: the holy face of the suffering servant, such as we contemplate it in the fourth song of the servant in Isaiah, and the radiant face of the glorious resurrected One at Easter.

The Autumn of the Fruits

FIFTH POEM

Chapters 6:4–8:4

THE BRIDEGROOM

You are beautiful as Tirzah, my love,
fair as Jerusalem,
terrible as an army with banners.
Turn your eyes away,
for they hold me captive.
Your hair is like a flock of goats
frisking down the slopes of Gilead.
Your teeth are like a flock of sheep
as they come up from the washing.
Each one has its twin,
not one unpaired with another.
Your cheeks, behind your veil,
are halves of pomegranate.

There are sixty queens
and eighty concubines
(and countless maidens).
But my dove is unique,
mine, unique and perfect.
She is the darling of her mother,
the favorite of the one who bore her.
The maidens saw her, and proclaimed her blessed,
queens and concubines sing her praises:

THE CHORUS

> *"Who is this arising like the dawn,*
> *fair as the moon,*
> *resplendent as the sun,*
> *terrible as an army with banners?"*

THE BRIDEGROOM

> *I went down to the nut orchard*
> *to see what was sprouting in the valley,*
> *to see if the vines were budding*
> *and the pomegranate trees in flower.*
> *Before I knew . . . my desire had hurled me*
> *on the chariots of my people, as their prince.*

THE CHORUS

> *Return, return, O maid of Shulam,*
> *return, return, that we may gaze on you!*

THE BRIDEGROOM

> *Why do you gaze on the maid of Shulam*
> *dancing as though between two rows of dancers?*

THE CHORUS

> *How beautiful are your feet in their sandals,*
> *O prince's daughter!*
> *The curve of your thighs is like the curve of a necklace,*
> *work of a master hand.*
> *Your navel is a bowl well rounded*
> *with no lack of wine,*
> *your belly a heap of wheat*
> *surrounded with lilies.*
> *Your two breasts are two fawns,*
> *twins of a gazelle.*
> *Your neck is an ivory tower.*
> *Your eyes, the pools of Heshbon,*

by the gate of Bath-rabbim.
Your nose, the Tower of Lebanon,
sentinel facing Damascus.
Your head is held high like Carmel,
and its plaits are as dark as purple;
a king is held captive in your tresses.

THE BRIDEGROOM

How beautiful you are, how charming,
my love, my delight!
In stature like the palm tree,
its fruit clusters—your breasts.
"I will climb the palm tree," I resolved,
"I will seize its clusters of dates."
May your breasts be clusters of grapes,
your breath sweet-scented as apples,
your speaking, superlative wine.

THE BRIDE

Wine flowing straight to my Beloved,
as it runs on the lips of those who sleep.
I am my Beloved's,
and his desire is for me.
Come, my Beloved,
Let us go to the fields.
We will spend the night in the villages,
and in the morning we will go to the vineyards.
We will see if the vines are budding,
if their blossoms are opening,
if the pomegranate trees are in flower.
Then I shall give you
the gift of my love.
The mandrakes yield their fragrance,
the rarest fruits are at our doors;
the new as well as the old,
I have stored them for you, my Beloved.

Ah, why are you not my brother,
nursed at my mother's breast!
Then if I met you out of doors, I could kiss you
without people thinking ill of me.
I should lead you, I should take you
into my mother's house, and you would teach me!
I should give you spiced wine to drink,
juice of my pomegranates.

His left arm is under my head
and his right embraces me.

THE BRIDEGROOM

I charge you,
daughters of Jerusalem,
not to stir my love, nor rouse it,
until it please to awake.

The Autumn of the Fruits

At the start of this, the last poem of the Song, we have to say with Chouraqui that the beloved reveals herself at the same time as "identical and other."[1] Here is how, it seems, we may understand this. She is "identical" in that she expresses the same passionate admiration for her beloved; the same ardor in loving him; the same extraordinary generosity in overcoming anything to join him. But at the same time, she is "different, other", because the trial of search and suffering, even the trial of her infidelity and her fall, have matured her. Now she knows her weakness and understands that her love has no other assurance than in her beloved.

Lastly, we do not see in her, in this fifth poem, any sign of fragility, faintness or even indolence. Quite to the contrary, she is strengthened, deepened, integrated and has become capable of offering herself as she had never been able to before.

6:4 *You are beautiful as Tirzah, my love,*
  fair as Jerusalem,
  terrible as an army with banners.

The Bridegroom at the start of the fifth poem appears mysteriously, as he is wont to do, without any preparation or introduction. "Without rhyme or reason, such is his poetry", Hedwig of Antwerp says very simply.[2] And as usual, he speaks only to rave about the beauty of his love. Thus, nine times we hear in the Song, as we have already noted, praise of

---

[1] André Chouraqui, *Le Cantique des Cantiques* (Paris: Presses Universitaires de France, 1970), 68.

[2] Quoted by Elisabeth de Miribel, *La liberté souffre violence* (Paris: Plon, 1981), 241.

the Bride's beauty from the lips of the Bridegroom (1:15a; 1:15b; 2:10; 2:13; 4:1a; 4:1b; 4:7; 6:4; 7:7).

"How beautiful you are"! But how much stronger the beauty of the Bride has become! This is not anymore the beauty of the Holy Land in the spring but that of the two strong cities of Tirzah and Jerusalem, i.e., the capital cities of the northern and southern kingdoms at the time of the schism of 931. It is also a promise for Israel, for the Bride, that the full return to her Bridegroom will cause the return of the brothers. They will be reunited as are now in her name the two previously hostile cities of Tirzah and Jerusalem. Tirzah and Jerusalem, Israel and Judah, North and South, will be reconciled. After the division experienced today will come the time of unity, which is the great yearning of Israel after the exile, as it remains today the great aspiration of the Church. This idea, which always underlies the Song, is that the union found again with God is linked with the reunion of the brothers. "For he is the peace between us," Saint Paul says, "and has made the two into one" (Ep 2:14).

But why Tirzah, when we rather expected Samaria as the capital of the North? First because Tirzah had in fact been the first capital of Israel before Samaria (1 K 14:17). And then because Samaria was hated by Israel; it was not thinkable to compare the Bride with it! Lastly, the name Tirzah means "my pleasure" and "pleasant". And did not God promise: "No longer are you to be named 'Forsaken', nor your land 'Abandoned', but you shall be called 'my delight', and your land 'the wedded' "?[3]

With Tirzah, Jerusalem. The Bride, "beautiful as Tirzah", is "as fair as Jerusalem". "And fairness is still greater than beauty", as La Fontaine wrote. In her grace, her beauty, the Bride can only be compared with Jerusalem. The latter is always tremendously admired. Almost all the psalms bear witness to this: "The holy mountain, beautiful where it rises, joy

[3] Isaiah, 62:4 (TOB).

of the whole world" (Ps 48). "How I love your palace, Yahweh Sabaoth" (Ps 84). "He prefers the gates of Zion to any town in Jacob" (Ps 87).

It is therefore not surprising that, comparing the Bride with the two most "beautiful" and "fair" cities of Tirzah and Jerusalem, the Bridegroom adds these words (they should not be deleted simply because they are repeated later on): "terrible as an army with banners." If indeed this Bride is all beauty and fairness, she is all the same "terrible". In admiration for the beauty of the city, the psalmist does not forget either that she could resist anyone foolish enough to attack her: "Go through Zion, walk around her, counting her towers, admiring her walls, reviewing her palaces" (Ps 48:12–14). The Bridegroom had already said in the third poem: "Your neck is the tower of David, built as a fortress, hung around with a thousand bucklers, and each the shield of a hero" (4:4). To attack her would be quite foolhardy, for this admired beauty is also an invincible one. Does it not seem when we read what follows that the Bridegroom himself is impressed?

6:5 *Turn your eyes away,*
   for they hold me captive.

It could not, of course, be fear of his dearly beloved that would make him exclaim thus. His beloved is terrible to him only through the unbearable ardor of his love. Didn't she herself say about her Bridegroom, in the first poem, "the banner he raises over me is love" (2:4)?

This time the Bridegroom is the one who feels too weak, as it were, in the face of his excessively powerful love. In fact, in the game of love, he is infinitely more vulnerable and wounded than we are. "Turn your eyes away, for they hold me captive"—literally translated, "they assault me."[4]

---

[4] André Robert, *La Sainte Bible,* 864, note e.

The Bridegroom feels that he is disarmed in the face of a love whose eyes are not only those of a sweet and peaceful dove— "your eyes are doves", as he told her—but also those of a victorious beauty whom he cannot resist. Loving revenge of the Bride! "O Love," Marie of the Incarnation dares to say, "you enjoyed tormenting me; I must have my revenge by inflicting on you the same wounds you gave me. . . . Oh yes, I must have my revenge!"[5]

The praise that follows is deeply marked by this dominant impression of strength in the bride. It seems that the portrait is the same as in the third poem, which is echoed here (4:1ff.). But as Chouraqui points out, "under the invariable aspect of love, a much more imposing and serious beauty is celebrated."[6]

6:5 *Your hair is like a flock of goats*
     frisking down the slopes of Gilead.

6:6 *Your teeth are like a flock of sheep*
     as they come up from the washing.
     Each one has its twin,
     not one unpaired with another.

6:7 *Your cheeks, behind your veil,*
     are halves of pomegranate.

Those were already the images of the third poem. There are some color contrasts: the hair is jet black like the goats of the country; the teeth are white like white sheep, and, of course, they are regular and well aligned. It must be said, in passing, that this stress in the Song on the comparison of the Bride's teeth with innocent sheep (cf. 4:2) is rather surprising; it is not in conformity with biblical tradition, especially that of the psalms, in which the teeth are always those of wild beasts tear-

---

[5] Guy-Marie Oury, *Marie de l'Incarnation,* vol. 1 (Québec/Abbaye de Saint-Pierre, Solesmes: Presses de l'Université Laval,) 129.

[6] Chouraqui, *Le Cantique des Cantiques,* 68.

ing and devouring without pity.[7] The teeth of the Bride, on the contrary, evoke only the peaceful sheep of the Good Shepherd that come back purified and clean from the washing. While, under the veil, the cheeks lose nothing of their splendor: as was already described in the third poem, they are the scarlet red halves of a pomegranate. Black, white, red—such then are the colors of the Bride. It is noteworthy that gold is absent. In the Song, gold is reserved for the Bridegroom.

In the praise the latter sings about the beauty of his love, he seems to be rather repetitious! The same images, with a few nuances, that are used in the third poem. There is not much novelty in his declarations! This tune has already been heard.

But it is sung in another register. Undoubtedly we have the same themes, but the tempo is quite different. Far from giving us repetition, he offers us wonderful inventions. Since he had to withdraw because of a door shut in his face, he remained silent. Since then, he has not uttered the slightest reproach or the least complaint. His Bride was left alone to discover by herself the magnitude of her folly. She had in fact wept terribly, sought and questioned endlessly. And since she could not talk to him anymore, she had launched into the most extraordinary celebration of the Bridegroom. Again, she was all his with all her soul, more in love than ever. She now has found him again, always present in the deepest core of her garden. She had whispered, "I am my Beloved's, and my Beloved is mine." But will his words be the same as before when they exchange their love again? To be sure, the Bridegroom will not blame or reproach her. She knows it. But will he sing the same song again?

And here it is: the joyful song of the Bridegroom rising up to her as it did before, his wedding song. Without the slightest reference to the past, without asking for any explanation, the Bridegroom sings again the song of the third poem in the intoxication of his love. It is his way of showing her that nothing

[7] Paul Beauchamp, *Psaumes nuit et jour* (Paris: Seuil, 1981), 70ff.

has changed. He even manages to show here, without irony, that he sees her as being much stronger, beautiful like the fortified cities of Tirzah and Jerusalem. He had never said this before. And it is true, she has become much stronger since she overcame her fall, so much so that she gives the impression, as the Bridegroom says, of being terrible as an army with her banners.

Wonderful Bridegroom! For him, to pardon is always to sing higher and more clearly the song of love. He even has to tell his love that she is the only one, the one he prefers among all others, not only, as he once laughingly hummed to her, "as a lily among the thistles" (2:2), that is in comparison with other women. She is the only one who matters to him, the only one in his heart, independently even of her obvious superiority in beauty over all other women.

Indeed she is more beautiful than they, the most renowned, the noblest, the queens, and all the more so than the others; this is clear:

6:8 *There are sixty queens*
    and eighty concubines
    (and countless maidens)[almoth].

6:9 *But my dove is unique,*
    mine, unique and perfect.
    She is the darling of her mother,
    the favorite of the one who bore her.

The author of the Song might have remembered here Solomon's fantastic harem, which bore witness, as always in ancient times, to the greatness and vastness of the sovereign's power. Thus there is a mention in the Book of Kings of the "seven hundred wives of royal rank, and three hundred concubines" (1 K 11:3ff.). However, what the Bridegroom of the Song wants to stress here is that even if we suppose that in his oriental opulence he had in his court "sixty queens, . . . eighty concubines (and countless maidens)"—as those who in the Book of Esther wait to be introduced one day to the King (Est 2:12–17)—his love for her is unique, absolutely unique. "But my dove is unique, mine, unique and perfect!" Gregory of Nyssa says. "He who has exchanged the condition of slave and concubine for that of royalty has become, through freedom and purity, capable of receiving the Spirit; he is the perfect dove that the Bridegroom contemplates when he says, "My dove is unique, . . . unique and perfect.""[8]

Contrary thus to old Solomon, who lets himself be ensnared by the charms of countless women, the Bridegroom is constantly faithful and loves with an exclusive heart that does not share his Bride, today more than ever. She had said of him, when she imagined that he was lost forever, "[He is one] among ten thousand. . . . [He is] unrivaled" (5:10, 15), undoubtedly as an echo to the famous *Shema Israel,* which she knew by heart: "Listen, Israel: Yahweh our God is the one Yahweh. You shall love Yahweh your God with all your heart, with all your soul, with all your strength" (Dt 6:4–5). Well then, for him too, his beloved, his perfect one, is also unique, as he had already told her, though in a less ardent manner in the same Book of Deuteronomy: "For you are a people consecrated to Yahweh your God; it is you that Yahweh our God has chosen to be his very own people out of all the peoples on the earth" (Dt 7:6).

All the nations of the earth happen to be there, her younger sisters: queens, concubines, countless maidens—depending on their distance from the Bridegroom—they are present. But the Bridegroom may look at them, and he can only repeat to his Bride that she is unique. Of mother-mankind, she is, among all her sisters, an only daughter as it were, the favorite one. What can then be said about what she is in the heart of her Bridegroom? Unique by birth, she is even more so through

[8] Saint Gregory of Nyssa, *In Canticum Canticorum,* Homily 15, PG 44, 1118B.

the choice he made. Unique by her creation, she is even more
so through election. And if she wins over all the daughters of
her mother, over all the other women of the world, it is, in the
last analysis, far less because of her beauty than because of the
wholly unique love that the Bridegroom has for her; as Isaiah
puts it: "you are precious in my eyes, . . . and I love you" (Is
43:4).

Never did Israel, in all her history, lose the memory of these
verses of the Bridegroom in the Song. And never will she cease
thanking him, as we hear in this later hymn, sounding so much
like the Song:

> Of all the forests of the earth and its trees
> You chose a unique vineyard.
> Of all the flowers of the universe,
> You chose only one lily.
> Of all the birds among the creatures,
> You called only one for yourself: "my dove". [9]

With Israel, it is also the Church and all of mankind and every one of us who can recognize in this stanza his hymn of
praise to the one who loves us with an ever-preferential love,
as Elizabeth of the Trinity feels she has to remind us all: "Let
yourself be loved more than those."[10]

However, this unique love must also be requited with a
unique love, not with such feelings as those of the maiden
companions of the Song, at least as Saint Francis de Sales
thinks he can understand them: they certainly love the Bridegroom with all their heart—among other things. He writes,
"While the great King Solomon was still blessed with the Holy
Spirit and composed the sacred Song of Songs, he had, in the
way of those days, a great variety of ladies and maidens dedicated to his love under various conditions and with diverse
qualities. But there was one who was the unique love, the all

[9] Origen, *Homélies sur le Cantique des Cantiques* (Paris: Cerf, 1966), 13, quoting the fourth book of Esdras.
[10] Elizabeth of the Trinity, *Oeuvres*, vol. 1 (Paris: Cerf, 1980), 196.

perfect, the all rare, like a particular dove, with whom the others could never be compared, and this is why he called her by her name: Shulamith. And after that one, there were sixty who held first rank in his esteem and honor and were called queens; in addition there were eighty ladies who were not really queens but shared the royal bed as honorable and legitimate friends; and lastly there were young maidens, countless, waiting in reserve, as in a kind of nursery, to take the place of the former ones, should they falter. . . . Now these souls, called maidens in the Song, having perceived the scent of the Bridegroom's name breathing out only salvation and love, love him with a true love but a love that like them is in its very youth. All the more so that these young maidens do love their bridegroom if they have one, but do not give up loving very much rings and ornaments and the companions with whom they amuse themselves, playing, dancing, romping about with little birds, puppies, squirrels, and other such toys, these young and novice souls do truly love the sacred Bridegroom but with a multitude of distractions and voluntary diversions, so that loving him above all things, they still do not quit entertaining themselves with things that they do not love with him, but outside of him and without him."[11]

Fortunately nothing of the kind is said about the young maidens of the Song! All are in fact very generous. They first listened in total silence to the song of praise sung by the Bridegroom, commenting in passing how, having addressed his Bride directly — "your eyes, . . . your hair, . . . your teeth" — he suddenly interrupts the flow of his loving discourse and, turning toward the group, seeks their testimony, exclaiming: "There are sixty queens and eighty concubines (and countless maidens). But my dove is unique, mine, unique and perfect." Yet, they are not offended.[12] The youngest do not become jeal-

---

[11] Saint Francis de Sales, *Traité de l'amour de Dieu, Oeuvres,* Bibliothèque de la Pléiade (Paris: NRF-Gallimard, 1969), X:4, 820–821.

[12] "One must not say that because of her [the Blessed Mother's] prerogatives, she eclipses the glory of all the saints like the sun, which, when it rises,

ous. All these women, all the nations of the world, rejoice very much because of the unique happiness of the eldest, in whom they perceive their own achievement and the justification of their hope:

6:9 *The maidens saw her, and proclaimed her blessed,*[13]
  queens and concubines sang her praises:

The Bride, while being praised by her Bridegroom, receives the unanimous praise of the whole world, like Judith, who, on the day of her victory, received the homage of her people: "You are the glory of Jerusalem! You are the great pride of Israel! You are the highest honor of our race!" (Judith 15:9). It is not only the people of Jerusalem who greet the Bride of the Song and praise her. It is, in fact, the chorus of all the nations of the earth that we hear in these verses, as a fulfillment of Yahweh's promise to Ezekiel—"The fame of your beauty spread through the nations" (Ezk 16:14)—and also in the prelude to the Magnificat of her who is full of grace: "All generations will call me blessed."

Saint Francis de Sales perceives that the words of the Song apply fully to the Virgin Mary only, to her of whom Max Thurian said that her Son led her "from the state of mother to that of bride." "There is indeed only the very Holy Virgin Mary", Saint Francis de Sales writes, "who reached perfectly this degree of excellence in love of her dearly beloved: for she is a dove so uniquely unique in her love that all the others, when compared with her, deserve the name of crows rather than that of doves."[14] We can think of the response of Bernadette,

---

makes the stars disappear. *Mon Dieu!* How strange this is. A mother who would hide the glory of her children! I think, on the contrary, that she will greatly increase the glory of the elect." Saint Thérèse of the Child Jesus, *Derniers entretiens,* vol. 2 (Paris: Cerf/Desclée de Brouwer, 1972), 314.

[13] TOB; Émile Osty, "Introduction au Cantique des Cantiques", *La Bible* (Paris: Seuil, 1973).

[14] Saint Francis de Sales, *Traité,* X:5, 825.

whom people asked in Nevers: "Was the Virgin Mary very beautiful?" "Oh," Bernadette replied, "she is so beautiful that if you have seen her once you would want to die just to see her again."[15]

The theme of universal praise addressed by the chorus of the nations to the unique one, blessed among women, continues in the following verses:

6:10 *"Who is this arising like the dawn,*
fair as the moon,
resplendent as the sun,
terrible as an army with banners?"

The Bride, when going back to her Bridegroom, always seems to "arise". On the one hand, indeed like the prodigal son of the parable, she is coming from very far and rising from very low. But more precisely yet, she arises in the eyes of her companions, as one would say about the dawn or a star appearing on the horizon. She arises and then ascends little by little, grows, and imposes herself irresistibly in the end. New and surprising, at first like the dawn, her splendor becomes radiant like that of the moon in the night sky, and in the end like the sun at noon. Queen of the night and queen of the day. The various moments of light will be used to describe the progress of her radiance—at first timid like the dawn, then dazzling like the moon and finally triumphant like the sun through the sole reflection on the face of the Bride of him who is the only lamp in the city (Rv 21:23).

The victorious splendor of the sun brings back the image of a beauty "terrible as an army with banners" *(acies ordinata)*. It seems to have been inspired by a very ancient biblical tradition, seeing in the constellations the armies of Yahweh Sabaoth, God of hosts. The author of Genesis talks about the creation of

[15] René Laurentin and Sister Bourgeade, *Logia de Bernadette,* vol. 3 (Paris: Letheilleux, 1957), 41–47.

"heaven and earth . . . with all their array" (Gn 2:1). Thus, in the eyes of the pious Jews, the stars appear as the legions of the Almighty, always marching and advancing in good order at his command, of whom Deborah sings that she received his assistance on the day of battle: "From high in heaven fought the stars" (Jg 5:20). While being very beautiful and radiant, more than all other stars, the Bride of the Song has therefore also the power to scatter enemy powers like the sun victorious over the shadows of the night. The very radiance of her beauty makes her terrible, like an army to the world of darkness, as is said in Revelation of the woman conquering the dragon (Rv 12).[16]

Robed in the sun, the moon under her feet, crowned with the stars, as the woman appears in Revelation (12:1), the Bride of the Song therefore cannot feel—contrary to the psalmist—that she is crushed by the sight of creation and exclaim with him: "I look up at your heavens, made by your fingers, at the moon and stars you set in place—ah, what is man that you should spare a thought for him?" (Ps 8). On the contrary, she sees the whole universe, and not only the Holy Land, composing her beauty, serving it and magnifying it. Or rather, she is, of the celestial and terrestrial universe at once, the apotheosis and the crowning. As Father Teilhard de Chardin says about the Virgin Mary: "She is the pearl of the cosmos."[17] Like a pearl she concentrates and condenses the water, the light and all the wonders of the world. One would like to sing, in the face of this exalted vision of the Son's beloved, the verses that Dante puts on the lips of Saint Bernard when our Lady is revealed to him in the thirty-second canto of *Paradise*: "Look

---

[16] "Spiritual beauty seems to have what makes it attractive and in itself cause fear. Thus it seems to be the opposite of bodily beauty. In fact, to attract desire, the latter has to have something sweet to the eyes, charming, remote from anything that could cause fear or anger. But pure beauty, spiritual beauty, will be accompanied by the virtue of strength, which inspires fright and fear . . . and chases away the armies of concupiscence." Saint Gregory of Nyssa, *In Canticum Canticorum*, Homily 6, 899.

[17] Pierre Teilhard de Chardin, "La vie cosmique", *Écrits du temps de guerre* (Paris: Seuil, 1976), 68.

now at the face which is closest to that of Christ because only its light can prepare you to perceive Christ. I found it, that face, shining with such a happiness that nothing I had seen thus far had filled me with so great an enchantment and offered me an image so similar to that of God. . . . O Virgin, mother and daughter of your Son, humble and higher than all other creatures, . . . you are the one who ennobles our human nature. . . . In your womb the fire of love was relit. . . . You are for us the torch of love's high noon."[18]

And who speaks in the following verses? Who echoes the chorus of admiration of the daughters of Jerusalem and all the nations of the world? It seems quite obvious that it is the Bridegroom himself. No other than he could say:

6:11 *I went down to the nut orchard*
to see what was sprouting in the valley,
to see if the vines were budding
and the pomegranate trees in flower.

To the Bride, who, in the motion of the constellations, rises up to him, corresponds antithetically the motion of the Bridegroom, who goes down to her who is also his garden. He "went down to his garden," she has already said (6:2). She rose that high only because he came down that low. Chouraqui observes this: "The apparition of the loving Bride in the sky of glory corresponds to the descent of the lover to the earth he has found again."[19] There can be no divinization of man except through the humanization of God.

This might perhaps be why, in the face of the enthusiastic words of the nations' chorus, the Bridegroom, who knows the human condition of his incomparable Bride, seems at first to hesitate before letting himself become intoxicated: "I went down to the nut orchard". The nut tree, growing in humid

---

[18] Dante, *Divine comédie: Paradis,* Cantos 32 and 33, *Oeuvres complètes* (Tours: Mame, 1963), 445–447.

[19] Chouraqui, *Le Cantique des Cantiques,* 70.

soil, belongs to the complex of associations of garden and water characterizing the Bride (cf. 4:12). The Bridegroom goes down to his garden, as if he were anxious to see ("to see" is repeated) whether the signs of spring are well-confirmed this time; if this new spring has definitely triumphed over winter; if the Bride is now awakened for good, fully ready for him, if in "the nut orchard", under the shell that was so hard to crack for a while, the tender fruit of the nut is now present and ripe. One perceives in this stanza of the Song—and even more than at the time of the "little foxes that make havoc of the vineyards" (2:15)—an extreme attention to and almost anxiety on the part of the Bridegroom about the complete strengthening of his love. He watches jealously all the signs: the young shoots that are sprouting, the budding vines, "the pomegranate trees in flower."

It is written in the third chapter of Genesis, immediately after man committed his first sin, that God was "walking in the garden in the cool of the day". Would it not seem that coming down once again to his garden, the Bridegroom is watching for the flowers of renewal? And since it seems to him that the *élan* of the flowers in the beloved and beautiful garden cannot be reversed now, he gives in to an impulse that he had never dared express while the chorus of the nations was praising the Bride and that is now invincibly strong:

6:12 *Before I knew . . . my desire had hurled me*
     on the chariots of my people, as their prince.[20]

This verse is a thorn in the side of the Song's exegetes. All commentators are unanimous in declaring it almost incomprehensible. "It challenges any interpretation" (JB). Thus people multiplied conjectures and corrections. We must give up, even though it did bring about a beautiful commentary by Saint

[20] André Robert, "Le Cantique des Cantiques", *La Bible de Jérusalem* (Paris: Cerf, 1958).

John of the Cross, the reading of "the chariots of Aminadab" adopted by the Septuagint and the Vulgate, and quite recently and brilliantly by Father Tournay.[21] But should we give up all interpretation? Should we not recall here what Gregory of Nyssa writes: "For those who are determined to learn the Hebrew language, there is nothing [in the Song] that seems to lack coherence"?[22] The justified conjecture of André Robert, in the first edition of *La Bible de Jérusalem,* has at least the merit of agreeing with the context of the passage and the entire poem. It can be understood as follows:

The image of his Bride has kept all its charms in the eyes of the Bridegroom; it has been praised before him magnificently by the chorus of the nations; he has seen for himself in his garden that the irreversible spring has come; this image acts so powerfully on his heart that he hurls himself, irresistibly as it were, in his extreme impatience on the chariot[23] that will draw him victoriously into the heart of his people, into the heart of his Bride, to settle there forever. "When love carries you away," says Saint John of the Cross, "don't ask where it is taking you." And so it is with the Bridegroom. The "before I knew" introducing the stanza does express the kind of sudden and uncontrollable impulse against which he cannot struggle anymore, having already said twice to his Bride: "You ravish my heart" (4:9).

Didn't it happen for the first time during the course of the third poem that he interrupted his praise of his love because he could not bear to wait for her? Because though she is always present to his heart, she was too slow in uniting herself with him? Did he not run impetuously to meet her? "Come from

[21] Saint John of the Cross, *Cantique spirituel,* Stanza XI, *Oeuvres complètes,* Bibliothèque européenne (Paris: Desclée de Brouwer, 1964), 686ff. Cf. Raymond Tournay, *Quand Dieu parle aux hommes le langage de l'amour* (Paris: Gabalda, 1982), 73–82.

[22] Saint Gregory of Nyssa, *In Canticum Canticorum,* Homily 2, 796B.

[23] To justify the fact that "chariot" is in the singular form, cf. Paul Joüon, *Le Cantique des Cantiques* (Paris: Beauchesne, 1909), 273.

Lebanon, my promised bride, come from Lebanon, come on your way", he had cried in his impatience (4:8). This is the same motion, more dramatic yet, and more impetuous, carrying him today toward his Bride. The latter had come back to him very fast—her infidelity belonging to the past—running to him with all the strength of her poor broken self. But in spite of all her efforts, her weakness in taking the last steps toward union does not enable her to succeed. There is a certain way to reach the summit, and it cannot be achieved without him. "Bring me back, let me come back", she had said once (Jr 31:18). Without waiting for her to ask again, the Bridegroom hurls himself on his chariot to meet her. He cannot be content with walking or even running to meet her. He has to rush on his chariot. "As a prince", André Robert added in his first translation of the JB. (Crampon: "as a chief".[24]) Did not Ezekiel say: "my servant David shall be their ruler" (Ezk 34:24)?

For its part, the chorus of the nations, entering as it were into the feelings of the Bridegroom, presses her who is now called Shulamith to respond with haste to the haste of the Bridegroom, somehow as if, foreshadowing the words of Paul to the Philippians, she were told: "try . . . to capture the prize for which Christ captured me" (Ph 3:12). Yes, let your twofold drive unite and become only a single one!

7:1 *Return, return, O maid of Shulam,*
   return, return, that we may gaze on you!

This "return", addressed four times with such insistence by the chorus to the Bride, is again one of these words used by the prophets to talk about the return to God and about conversion *(shuv)*. Unlike the other passages where it is used, this one must not be understood as an adjuration to the unfaithful Bride to abandon her adultery and return to her Bridegroom. Rather, the Bride is invited in an imploring tone by the chorus

---

[24] Canon Crampon, *La Sainte Bible* (Paris: Desclée de Brouwer, 1960).

of the nations, who are expecting so much themselves from the conclusion of her wedding, to respond eagerly to the incredible eagerness of her Bridegroom. One can still talk about a movement of conversion, though it would have to be in the sense given to this word by Teresa of Avila: up to the last step of the mystical ascent.

What confirms the interpretation of this repeated "return" is the very aim assigned by the chorus of the nations to the return of the Bride: "Return," they sing, "return, that we may gaze on you!" Yes, so that we can contemplate you, admire you in the full fire of your love, no matter what proper perspective you must always retain about your total insufficiency. Return, for the joy and wonder of our eyes! Thérèse of the Child Jesus understands this when, talking about these verses of the Song, she writes to her sister: "What a call that of the Bridegroom! So we did not dare look at ourselves since we saw ourselves as plain and devoid of adornment! But Jesus is calling us, and he wants to look at us at his leisure!"[25]

Even the new name given here to the Bride bears witness to the meaning and unity we now find in the whole passage. Twice, and only in this part of the Song, the chorus calls her "maid of Shulam", i.e., the "pacified one", the one who, being the bride of Solomon the peaceful (*Shalom*, cf. the third poem, 3:7ff.), bears his name as a matter of course and enjoys his peace. "As the Savior is called peaceful and pacific," Saint Francis de Sales points out, "his bride is called maid of Shulam, tranquil daughter of peace."[26]

Thus if the Bride, as long as this life will go on, must continue to get closer to her Bridegroom, to "return" to him, it is in order to be more open to him. André Chouraqui feels this very deeply as he comments on this passage of the Song: "Up until now, the Bride was black, beautiful, veiled and, more, the lily of Sharon, the rose of the depths, the dove, the immac-

---

[25] Saint Thérèse of the Child Jesus, *Lettres* (Paris: Cerf/Desclée de Brouwer, 1977), Letter 165, 286.
[26] Saint Francis de Sales, *Traité*, VIII:12, 749.

ulate, the closed garden, the sealed fountain, the source of gardens, the well of living water, the promised Bride, the sister, the perfect, the wonderful, the terrible, identical to dawn, to the moon and to the sun; more than twenty images describe her in her fiery beauty, in the torments of her love. And here she finds at last, after the drama of exile is over, her true name. In her new wedding, in the eternity of her mystical wedding, she is the maid of Shulam. . . . Love transforms the Bride into a living figure of plenitude and peace. . . . She is the image of triumphant peace"[27] that the chorus of the nations is impatient to admire endlessly as "she runs, to win the crown", as Saint Paul puts it (1 Co 9:24).

But more than a race, this is the enchanted spectacle of a dance that the Bride, in her renewed dynamism, is offering to the admiration of all, as we hear in the words of the coryphaeus, or one of the maidens composing the group, inviting all her companions to celebrate thus:

7:1 *Why do you gaze on the Maid of Shulam*
     dancing as though between two rows of dancers?

It might rather well be, as in the Jerusalem Bible, that the Bridegroom himself utters these words as if to give himself the incredible joy of hearing again and again all the women of the world, the immense chorus of the nations on earth, celebrating the unique beauty of his unique love. It might only appear strange that he then sees her "dancing as though between two rows of dancers".

But this is strange only for those who lose sight of the fact that the Bride is above all called Israel and that Israel, since the schism, is divided into two groups of tribes, into two camps: Israel and Judah. The word that we translate here as "two rows of dancers [or choruses]", *mahanayim,* could in fact be better translated as "camps". ("Why do you see the maid of Shulam as in a dance between two camps?"[28]) The author of the Song,

---

[27] Chouraqui, *Le Cantique des Cantiques,* 71.
[28] Osty, "Introduction au Cantique des Cantiques".

haunted again by the desire to see Israel reunified, sees Israel rediscover her unity and two peoples becoming one, thus changing the two hostile camps into a double row of dancers. The name itself "maid of Shulam", peaceful one, given here by the Bridegroom to his love, confirms this interpretation: the passage from war (two enemy camps) to peace and reconcilation (two rows of dancers). Chouraqui, as also Father Joüon, expresses it very well: "The chorus contemplates in the Bride the dance, i.e., the dynamic harmony of reconciled opposites. The two camps that were enemies yesterday—with the hardships of separation and exile—are now reconciled in the reflection of triumphant love. . . . Love reconciles the opposites, resolves them in its cosmic dance, reflected by the maid of Shulam returning from exile and being wed again. . . . She must appear in the eyes of creation so that the latter might be fulfilled in the contemplation of a reconciled universe, re-created to the image of the couple who is triumphant in the unity of love. Yes, a dance and no more a war of the two camps. . . . The maid of Shulam continues to bear in her womb two camps that are now pacified in the new rhythm of their cosmic dance."[29]

Such is the miraculous transformation of the two camps: so recently enemies who were warring and now a pair of dancing lovers! A deep dream of ecumenism in the heart of the divided Christians; an old dream of mankind hoping for the gathering of all peoples into a single one, with the assurance of being fulfilled one day. Did Ignatius of Antioch, the great martyr and bishop of the second century, remember these verses of the Song when, in his own passion for unity, he wrote to the Ephesians: "Let every one of you become a chorus of song, so that in the harmony of your concord, adopting the melody of God in unity, you will sing for the Father with one voice, in Christ Jesus"?[30] Alas, the chorus of dance and that of war must coexist for a long time: "What do you see in the Bride", Saint Thérèse

---

[29] Chouraqui, *Le Cantique des Cantiques*, 72.
[30] Saint Ignatius of Antioch, *Lettre aux Éphésiens*, IV:1 and 2 (cf. SC 10) (Paris: Cerf, 1945), 51.

of the Child Jesus writes, "if not choirs of music in an armed camp?"[31]

In the Bride of the Song, we see only dance. And in this long stanza, quite likely modulated with song, hand clapping and tambourines, the chorus of the nations falls into ecstasy at the sight of her beautiful steps:

7:2 *How beautiful are your feet in their sandals,*
     O prince's daughter!
     The curve of your thighs is like the curve of a necklace,
     work of a master hand.

7:3 *Your navel is a bowl well rounded*
     with no lack of wine,
     your belly a heap of wheat
     surrounded with lilies.

Here the images seem to be daring, even carnal at first sight. But there is no reason to be shocked or even to be scandalized by seeing in them a meaning they do not have. They are as neat and pure in their realism as those used by the Lord in the first chapters of Hosea and Nehemiah, for instance, or also in chapters 16 and 23 of Ezekiel, not to mention some chapters of Genesis. The Word of God is not ashamed of what God has created. Gregory of Nyssa writes: "Let us listen thus to the divine words with which the Word describes the beauty of his immaculate Bride, in the way of people who are already beyond the things of flesh and blood and have been transformed into spiritual men."[32]

Offered as a dance, this new celebration of the Bride starts quite naturally, this time with the *feet,* and rises progressively to the full light and royalty of the face. Thus is revealed little by little the beauty of a woman in an entire land—rather, in the entire cosmos—working progressively to build the whole

[31] Saint Thérèse of the Child Jesus, *Lettres,* Letter 149, 261.
[32] Saint Gregory of Nyssa, *In Canticum Canticorum,* Homily 9, 953B.

body until the latter finds its perfect accomplishment and achievement in the head. We cannot but think spontaneously, before the body of this Bride evolving, as it were, all along the stanza, "this building up the body of Christ", of whom Saint Paul tells the Ephesians:" In this way we are all come to unity . . . until we become the perfect Man fully mature with the fullness of Christ himself. We shall grow in all ways into Christ, . . . by whom the whole body is fitted and joined together" (Ep 4:13, 15–16). The Bride of the Song, in her harmonious development, foreshadows the very growth of the Church.

7:2 *How beautiful are your feet in their sandals,*
   O prince's daughter!

The beauty of the Song's Bride is not that of a statue but of a living being whose motions are those of a dance. And one hears the clapping of her princess' sandals. "Prince's daughter": this title is not given here only because of the unique grace of her dance but because the prince who rushed toward her on his chariot, her Bridegroom and King, is also her Creator, whose daughter she is, as he tells her in Isaiah: "For now your creator will be your husband" (Is 54:5). We already know that there is no feminine counterpart to King or Beloved in the original language of the Song!

After the feet, the *legs* (in the French version)[33] attract the attention of the poet, with their perfect curve, like that of a vase or cup, or yet a wonderfully chiseled necklace that could have been made only by a master goldsmith. It might also be, as André Robert suggests, that, with a delicate concern for describing the Bride in harmony with the landscape of the Holy Land, the author of the Song thought here about the graceful curve of Jaffa's coastline.[34]

[33] Joüon, *Le Cantique des Cantiques,* 257.
[34] Robert, *La Sainte Bible,* prefers to translate this as "side" or "hips" rather than "legs", a word which generally speaking evokes a curve.

The description of the Bride goes on, without any offense to biblical delicacy and simplicity, with an evocation of the *navel* and the *belly:*

7:3 *Your navel is a bowl well rounded*
with no lack of wine,
your belly a heap of wheat
surrounded with lilies.

We agree with Dhorme, Osty, the JB[35] on the word *navel,* for "any other meaning would not be even remotely probable", points out Joüon, who also notes like Osty that the Hebrew word is already used in describing the Bride of Ezekiel to indicate the umbilical cord (Ezk 16:4). The author of the Song sees in the navel of the Bride a crater or a cup, running over with wine, while the rounded belly is transformed in his imagination into a powerful heap of wheat.

It seems that he wishes to convey the fecundity of the Bride. The Holy Land is a country of wine and wheat, "a land of corn and good wine, land of bread and of vineyards" (2 K 18:32). Now the "wedded" a land (to use the words of Isaiah—Is 62:4–5) will know on the day of the messiah an extraordinary fecundity of wheat and wine, as Joel in particular announced (Jl 2:24). Likewise Zechariah: "Yahweh their God will give them victory when that day comes. . . . Corn will make the young men flourish, and sweet wine the maidens" (Zc 9:16–17). And this will be attested to at the advent of the messiah by the two miracles of the wine streaming at the wedding feast of Cana and the multiplication of the loaves of bread on the mountain (Jn 2 and 6). Wonderful fecundity of the Bride-earth-Israel, wonderful fecundity of the love union between the Bride and the Bridegroom also symbolized by these images of the bowl

---

[35] Édouard Dhorme, *La Bible,* Bibliothèque de la Pléiade (Paris: NRF-Gallimard, 1959); Osty, "Introduction au Cantique des Cantiques"; JB.

of wine and the heap of wheat, expressively associated with the navel and belly of the Bride. Cup "not lacking in wine" (at Cana wine was lacking, and Jesus gave a wine that will not lack) and "heap of wheat", these two expressions of superabundance indicate the inexhaustible nature of that fecundity.

Thus, as the Song stresses immediately, such a fecundity is not carnal in the least, as suggested by the belt or crown of lilies surrounding the belly-heap of wheat. Never, in fact, is there in the entire Song the slightest reference to the fecundity of the Bride according to the flesh. No reference, for instance, is made—and this is quite remarkable in a love poem full of evocations that are so realistic and multiple—to the children that the Bride could humanly conceive from her Bridegroom. Never do we hear the Bridegroom and the Bride say anything about the presence of children that would incarnate their love.

This could be explained as Gerleman explains it by saying that "in the Song, love has no other object than itself; there is no other aim but love. There are no children because the couple of the Song does not have procreation as its goal. It is absolute love, in which the man contemplates the woman in order to become in her a human being. . . . [In this way] the Song is the revolutionary manifesto of liberating love."[36] But quite to the contrary, we have seen throughout the Song what an essential place the others have in the relationship between the Bridegroom and his love. Contrary to Tristam and Isolde, who indeed love each other in total solitude, as if the world around them were abolished, the Bride can at no time go away and dissociate herself from her maiden companions, from the presence of all her people, whom she wants to draw after her (cf. 1:3–4); while he, on his part, at the banquet of love offered by his Bride, wants to see all men "eat, friends, . . . drink deep, my dearest friends" (5:1). It cannot be said therefore that in the Song "eros vibrates in itself without any other purpose

[36] Quoted by André Chouraqui, *Retour aux racines* (Paris: Le Centurion, 1981), 217.

than mutual love . . . and that eros is self-sufficient"[37] or that
the others, and especially children, would have no room here.

We should add that this would be in total opposition to the
commandment given by God to man and woman when he created them: "Be fruitful, multiply" (Gn 1:28). "To have children", Josy Eisenberg reminds us, "is the first of the
commandments of the Bible. . . . This commandment is considered by the rabbis as absolutely fundamental."[38]

The love of the Bridegroom and his beloved is in fact not
only open to the whole world and to everybody, but, while
not being carnal, the fecundity of this love remains quite real
for them. This fecundity is symbolized quite aptly, in connection with the belly of the Bride, by fertility in wheat and wine.
However, though very real, it appears essentially as a spiritual
fecundity, announced and foreshadowed throughout the history of Israel by the sterility of many women to whom God is
granting the miraculous grace of conception. It was this fecundity of grace that the psalmist had in mind when he sings in
praise, "He enthrones the barren woman, . . . making her the
happy mother of sons" (Ps 113) and that was acclaimed by Isaiah when he dared to tell the bride Jerusalem: "Shout for joy,
you barren women who bore no children! Break into cries of
joy and gladness, you who were never in labor! For the sons of
the forsaken one are more in number than the sons of the wedded wife, says Yahweh" (Is 54:1); and Saint Paul takes up these
words again in the Epistle to the Galatians, applying them to
the Church of Christ (Ga 4:26–27).[39]

[37] Hans Urs von Balthasar, *La gloire et la croix,* vol. 3 (Paris: Aubier, 1974),
115–116.

[38] Josy Eisenberg, *A Bible ouverte* (Paris: Albin Michel, 1980), 131.

[39] It is important to stress that, as in the fifty-fourth chapter of Isaiah, it was
to the barren wife who had no husband and who nonetheless sees her children
multiply that Yahweh said: "For now your Creator will be your husband" (Is
54:1–5). It is therefore impossible to understand how Josy Eisenberg, who is so
familiar with Scripture, could adopt the words of Rabbi Kook, i.e., "he who
has not known a woman, he who has not been married, cannot understand the
Song of Songs . . . because a celibate cannot have an exact knowledge of

The love of virginity, in spite of its apparent barrenness, is a love of fecundity, which knows no limits to generation. And in this respect, it is infinitely suggestive for us that in this passage of the Song this fecundity is associated with the two symbols of wheat and wine, which are the two eucharistic symbols, those of the love union between Jesus and his communion with the Church, his bride. "Make your home in me, as I make mine in you", Jesus says in his last talk, which is, as it were, his Song of Songs. And immediately after giving us to understand, in this incredible formula, the intimacy of his union with his community, and the community with him, he adds: "Whoever remains in me, with me in him, bears fruit in plenty" (Jn 15:5). The fruits of a union are the children. In the mouth of Jesus they are all mankind, given in truth as children to whoever lives in communion with him. Fecundity of the soul, fecundity of the Bride-Church, is essentially realized in and through the Eucharist, whose symbols we see in the wheat and wine associated with the belly of the Bride, as John of the Cross sees it in the Living Flame of Love: "The heap of wheat [is made of] the grains that will make up the bread of life."[40]

And is it not remarkable that in this same eucharistic and ecclesial perspective, we read immediately after these two verses:

7:4 *Your two breasts are two fawns,*
  twins of a gazelle.

The image has already been encountered, and we have seen there the great dream of unity between the separate brethren, Israel and Judah, returning to their common mother and becoming again one sole people (cf. 2:16; 4:5; 6:2–3). Thus the theme of unity is linked here to the symbols of bread and wine in the eucharistic mystery, sacrament of our unity. Indefi-

---

man's love for God." Ibid., 125.

[40] Saint John of the Cross, *Vive Flamme d'amour*, Stanza III, *Oeuvres complètes*, Bibliothèque européenne (Paris: Desclée de Brouwer, 1958), 763.

nitely, on the evening of Holy Thursday, Jesus among his disciples will take this song up again (Jn 13:31; 17:26).

Following the very beautiful commentary of Saint Augustine on Psalm 92, Father de Lubac brought to light this treble link between fecundity, virginity and unity, which is found in the Church, as in the Virgin Mary, and also in the Bride of the Song: "The theme becomes a frequent one in St. Augustine: 'for the Church also is both mother and virgin'—and in both he marvels at the same fertile virginity. . . . He underlines and delineates more clearly this likeness between the two Virgins by pointing out that though the Church bears multitudes, she makes of all her children the members of one body, and that similarly, just as Our Lady became the mother of many through the birth of One, so also the Church, by bringing to birth many, becomes the 'mother of unity'."[41]

The ascent of the Bride, begun with the steps of the dance, progresses gradually toward the *head:*

7:5 *Your neck is an ivory tower.*

The thrust, the whiteness and also the vigor of the neck make the poet think, as in the first celebration of the beloved (4:4), about a powerful and graceful tower of ivory. This is barely hyperbole for those who have seen women carrying high and heavy loads on their heads in Africa or the East. What strength there is in their necks, and what dignity in the women! Now, the *eyes:*

7:5 *Your eyes, the pools of Heshbon,*
    by the gate of Bath-rabbim.

We are again invited to fix our gaze on those eyes, extraordinarily enlarged like those of the icons, pools or lakes ("my

[41] Henri de Lubac, *The Splendor of the Church* (San Francisco: Ignatius Press, 1986), 324–326.

eyes, my large eyes, with their eternal clarities", Beauty says in
the poem by Baudelaire[42]), so clear and limpid that we can see
at the bottom of them, as in a transparent lake, the soul of the
Bride. Purity of the dove's eyes, transparency and depth of water in which the whole sky is reflected. It seems that in this
third and ultimate description, the Bride has lost the veil that
until now, no matter how fine it was, was covering her face
(4:1; 4:3; 6:7) and that her eyes, like the water of a peaceful lake,
are now reflecting directly, to use the words of Paul to the
Corinthians, the face of glory of her beloved Lord (cf. 2 Co
3:18).

Would the names of Heshbon and Bath-rabbim be here to
increase by their poetry the impression of purity? But Heshbon
and Bath-rabbim are reminiscent of the Ammonites and Mo-
abites, those detested neighbors (cf. Nb 21:26; Jr 49:3), and is it
not offensive for the Bride to read them in her eyes? We are
thus increasingly reminded in the Song that Israel and the pagan nations are all called to the love that the Bridegroom bears
for his unique beloved. Yahweh says at about the same time to
the prophet Zechariah (9:7) "I intend to destroy the arrogance
of the Philistine. . . . He too will become a remnant for our
God and be like a family in Judah: Ekron shall be like the Je-
busite" (incorporated into Israel, cf. Jg 1:21).

Between the eyes, the *nose*. This is the only time it appears in
the three descriptions of the Bride. Like the neck, it leads the
poet to think about a tower, but a more vigilant, more threatening one than the beautiful ivory tower.

7:5 *Your nose, the Tower of Lebanon,*
    sentinel facing Damascus.

The image of the tower was called up by the thrust of the nose
in the middle of the face (rather, as we are permitted to hope

---

[42] Charles Baudelaire, "La Beauté", *Oeuvres complètes* (Lausanne: La Guilde
du Livre, 1967), 37.

for the sake of the Bride, than by the shape of her nose). The exegetes are numerous enough in agreeing about the geographical significance of this detail. The Great Hermon range in Israel is a promontory rising 8,900 feet above the basin of Damascus. The nose in the middle of the Bride's face is thus thrusting forward as a challenge to the Syrian enemy, who might become too daring. But it is "the Tower of Lebanon" because in the Bride strength never parts from beauty.

While the portrait of the Bridegroom had started in the fourth poem with the head (5:11), the portrait of the Bride started in the fifth poem with the feet and ends significantly with the head.

At the summit of the body, the *head* of the Bride is uncovered now as a splendid crowning:

7:6 *Your head is held high like Carmel,*
    and its plaits are as dark as purple;
    a king is held captive by your tresses.

She is like Carmel above the Holy Land, imposing and graceful. And if the jet black of her hair (similar, as has been said, to the goats of Gilead) seems to have purple highlights, it is because the sun's rays are playing in her tresses. She has been described as "resplendent as the sun". The sun makes her head truly regal. Claudel saw this fire of the sun on the face of the Bride: "The time has finally come, in glory, to let the sun breathe."[43]

For the King, the beautiful black tresses become a net in which he lets himself be caught (and also perhaps because a king lets himself be caught in them, the black tresses acquire purple highlights!).

---

[43] Paul Claudel, *Paul Claudel interroge le Cantique des Cantiques* (Paris: NRF-Gallimard, 1948), 376.

7:6 *a King is held captive in your tresses,* exclaims the chorus.

In the first poem, we had seen the Bride as a captive, a mare attached to the chariot of Pharaoh. And here is the King now, captive of his beloved. To hold him, there is no need of strong chains or iron collars. The light tresses of her hair are enough. So little is needed to hold him! Saint John of the Cross is overwhelmed: "Only one strand, which you saw fluttering on my neck. . . . You looked at it on my neck, and you remained caught by it . . . . Oh, how worthy of all admiration and gladness, that God be caught by one strand. . . . If in his great mercy, he looked at us and loved us first, as Saint John said, he would not be caught by a fluttering strand of our own love because our love does not fly as high as it ought to in order to catch this divine bird who is so high up. But because his love came down to look at us, urging and elevating our flight, giving its value to our love, he let himself be caught in this fluttering strand. He himself was content and let himself be caught. . . . How is it possible to believe that a low-flying bird can capture the high royal eagle, if the latter does not come down, wishing to be caught?"[44]

Saint John of the Cross, chaplain of the Convent of the Incarnation in 1572, certainly knew the poem that Teresa of Avila had composed the year before:

> This divine prison
> of the love with whom I live
> made of God my captive
> and freed my heart.
> To see God as my prisoner
> causes such passion in me
> that I am dying of not dying.[45]

---

[44] Saint John of the Cross, *Cantique spirituel,* Stanza XXIII, 631.

[45] Saint Teresa of Avila, *Poésies, Oeuvres complètes,* Bibliothèque européenne (Paris: Desclée de Brouwer, 1964), 1067.

Thérèse of the Child Jesus, who so loved the image of the eagle, simply says, putting in these words all her absolute confidence in a merciful Love: "How can we fear the one who lets himself be chained by a single strand of hair fluttering on our neck?"[46] "Let yourself be so chained, Almighty of heaven . . . ; be a prisoner of your eternal prisoner."[47] Such also is the prayer of the Church to her Lord.

The King is really caught, he recognizes it and cannot remain quiet. Taking the part of the chorus, he goes on praising his love:

7:7 *How beautiful you are, how charming,*
      my love, my delight!

7:8 *In stature like the palm tree,*
      its fruit clusters your breasts.

The Bridegroom can only stammer in admiration when he sees his love so beautiful because she loves, so beautiful because she is loved. He always starts in the same way: "How beautiful you are"! Is it not remarkable that in the whole Song not only does he never have any reproach, any criticism, any comment against the one he loves, but he does not even give her the slightest advice, does not have the least exhortation or recommendation; he never even suggests a task, a project on which to work together because he knows full well that she will give herself to it without reservation. He speaks to her only to love and admire her. And what names does he give her in his tenderness. One word is never enough for him: she is beautiful, she is charming, she is love itself, she is his delight! He had already made such an unreserved avowal in Jeremiah: "Is Ephraim then so dear a son to me, a child so favored, that after each threat of mine, I must still remember him, still be

---

[46] Saint Thérèse of the Child Jesus, *Lettres,* Letter 191, 347.
[47] Gertrude von Le Fort, *Hymnes à l'Église,* tran. André Duzan, 1982, 61.

deeply moved for him, and let my tenderness yearn for him?"[48]

"My love, my delight!" When we think that the Bridegroom himself gives this name of love, his proper name, to the one he loves, and that he is eternally happy to be "delighted" by his beloved—as he also confesses in the Book of Proverbs, "delighting to be with the sons of men" (Pr 8:31), and in the Book of Isaiah, "You shall be called my delight" (Is 62:4)—we remain astonished. And we can only mumble with Claudel: "You are my delight, and I too become in your arms someone who is your delight."[49]

7:7 *my love, my delight!*

7:8 *In stature like the palm tree,*
   its fruit clusters your breasts.

Tall, erect and slim like an arrow pointing to the sky, the Bride resembles the palm tree by her stature. The image is quite common in oriental poetry. Three women in the Bible bear the name of palm tree, *Tamar*. Tree of beauty and fecundity at the same time, it is a good symbol for woman, while the clusters she carries high are like her breasts.

As soon as the Bridegroom has named the palm tree, a sudden desire awakens his heart; he wants to rush at it:

7:9 *"I will climb the palm tree," I resolved,*
   "I will seize its clusters of dates."

One perceives in these words—"I resolved", "I will climb", "I will seize"—the determination of the Bridegroom. Nothing can stop his impetuosity, his ardent pursuit. He will attempt anything to possess fully his love. And while he is the all great, the all-high, he who always had to come down to her, to his

---

[48] Jeremiah, 31:20 (TOB).
[49] Claudel, *Paul Claudel*, 386.

316 THE CANTATA OF LOVE

garden, now he is the one who must go up to his beloved: "I will climb the palm tree"! His love made him so small that he sees his beloved high above him: "Here I am," the Lord says, "among you as one who serves you." Master and Lord, to be sure, but at the feet of his people. It is truly poignant that he who was described by his beloved in the fourth poem as being inaccessible must now gather and concentrate all his strength to reach his beloved. The ascent of love is, in the last analysis, accomplished by him.

It is understandable that, meditating on this passage of the Song, certain mystical authors thought they could perceive in it the excess of love that would push Jesus to climb on the Cross to embrace the Church and mankind, his bride. "There is a baptism I must still receive," he says in his love for her, "and how great is my distress till it is over" (Lk 12:50).[50] And also: "And when I am lifted up from the earth, I shall draw all men to myself."[51]

Saint Mechtilde of Magdeburg, a German Cistercian mystic of the thirteenth century, looking at the same time at these texts of the Gospel and of the Song, writes that "his noble nuptial bed was the very hard Cross on which he leaped with more joy and ardor than a delighted bridegroom."[52] And Saint Teresa of Avila has this stanza in her Poetry: "From the Cross, the Bride tells the beloved that she is a precious palm tree on which he climbed."[53] The same drive thus pushed the Bridegroom to rush on his chariot to join his Bride and now to climb the palm tree with which she identifies herself (the very hard and very sweet tree of the Cross) in order to embrace her. With what intoxication:

[50] Osty, "Introduction au Cantique des Cantiques".

[51] John, 12:32 (TOB).

[52] Mechtilde of Magdeburg, *Livre de la grâce spéciale*, pt. 4, Éditions Bénédictines de Solesmes (Tours: Mame, 1921), chs. 59 and 56.

[53] Saint Teresa of Avila, *Poésies*, XIX. Saint Catherine of Siena says: "As seized with love, he runs without delay to the ignominious death of the most holy cross." *Le dialogue*, tran. Hurtaud (Paris: Téqui, 1976), pt. 1, 362, and pt. 2, 147.

7:9   *May your breasts be clusters of grapes,*
      your breath sweet-scented as apples,

7:10 *your speaking, superlative wine.*

All the senses of the Bridegroom seem to be held in thrall now, especially those that are the most susceptible to intoxication: taste and smell. But the ear is also involved: "your speaking, superlative wine." In the end, he gives way to the intoxication. "I drink my wine and my milk", he had said at the feast of his love, at the end of the third poem. "May your breasts", he says more daringly now, "be like clusters of grapes [for my thirst]." And do you know that the very breath of your mouth, your very breath, has the obsessive sweetness of the apple scent?

How could the breath of the Bride not always be yielding the perfume of the love fruit, of the cherished apple tree that she had found to be "so sweet to her palate" (2:3)? And how could her words not be intoxicating for her Bridegroom when he had made her drink from the wine of his cellar (2:4), made her taste "love that is sweeter than wine" (1:2–4)? If, in consequence, her breath has the scent of the apple and her words are more delightful than wine, while her eyes are doves (1:15), the reason is in fact that all she has comes from him who gave her the eyes, the scented breath and the very strong wine of "this love he brought into her heart by the Spirit he gave her" (cf. Rm 5:5). William of Saint-Thierry expresses this in a remarkable way: "He taught us to love while he was the first to love us. . . . Yes, this is good: you were the first to love us, O God who are sovereignly good and sovereign good, and your love is the Holy Spirit, inspiring and yearning. . . . He offers himself to all and draws everything to himself."[54]

Thus the wine that intoxicates me goes straight back to you, my beloved:

[54] William of Saint-Thierry, *Traité de la contemplation de Dieu* (Paris: Cerf, 1968), 93ff.

7:10 *Wine flowing straight to my Beloved,*
as it runs on the lips of those who sleep.

Coming from you, my words tend naturally to return to you
in this dialogue in which my words are your words; in which
I tell you and give you what I received from you; in which I
love you with the love with which you love me; in which the
wine in my mouth comes to me from your mouth; in which
the scent of my breath is that of your breath. This then is like
a continuous ebb and flow between us. From my heart to your
heart, from your heart to my heart. And even in the night,
when I sleep, the same wine of love comes and goes, straight
and without any intermediary between us as it does between
those who share the same sleep of love. Between us, at every
time of day and night, are exchanged and mingled my wine
which is your wine, my scent which is your scent, my spirit
which is your Spirit: just as you had promised: "I shall put my
Spirit in you" (Ezk 36:27). For "if the Father is the cupbearer of
this intoxicating life, the Son is the cup and the Spirit is the
wine."[55]

The beloved has nothing of her own anymore. She does not
even belong to herself.

7:11 *I am my Beloved's,*
and his desire is for me.

She belongs to her beloved. She is his, in a way that is impossible for any being to belong to another being; for there is in me
something that is inalienable and that can be surrendered to no
man on earth, no matter how bound he is to me.

But at the same time as she experiences the fact that she belongs totally to her beloved, the Bride discovers with astonishment that he is totally dependent on her. This is well expressed

[55] Mechtilde of Magdeburg, *Livre*; cf. *Dictionnaire de spiritualité*, vol. 10, c.
881.

in her modifying the second part of her sentence. Indeed, instead of saying as before, "I am my Beloved's, and my Beloved is mine", which was the expression of their perfect reciprocity and equality in the love uniting them, she now says: "and his desire is for me." She does not live at all through the fact of her relation with the beloved as bride with Bridegroom, as the Creator had established it in the beginning: "Your yearning—God had told the woman—shall be for your husband, he will lord it over you" (Gn 3:16). For her, the situation is quite the opposite. The Bridegroom has no dominion, no empire over her. The power is not on his side. Now he is the one who desires his Bride. "His desire is for me", she says. The relationship of the couple, such as God had determined it in Genesis—and this is the only place in the Bible where it is explicitly recalled—is therefore turned upside down. The roles are inverted. In the wedding feast of the new covenant, the Bridegroom is dependent, the Bridegroom desires, the Bridegroom is thirsty and implores, "Give me a drink. . . . I am thirsty" (Jn 4:7; 19:28). *"Deus sitit sitiri."*[56] "God is thirsting to be my thirst", says Gregory Nazianzen.

The Bride desires to quench this thirst. But how can she respond to his desire? How can she be with him in this communion that he requests when she must live in the world where their love is incessantly crossed, opposed, threatened? Has not the time come to leave together for the country where he is the King and which will be the definitive and peaceful land of their love?

7:12 *Come, my Beloved,*
    let us go to the fields.
    We will spend the night in the villages,

7:13 *and in the morning we will go to the vineyards.*

"Come, my Beloved"! *Lekha dodi!* sings the old Jewish Sab-

---

[56] Saint Gregory Nazianzen, *Discours sur le baptême,* 40:27; PG 36, 397C.

bath and Passover hymn. It is not difficult to recognize here, under the poetry of images, the language of Exodus—the aspiration to leave the land of servitude and exile and to reach the promised land. The people, at the time of Moses, had received the order to leave, under the protection of Yahweh (Ex 12:42), to leave in haste (Ex 12:39). And they left "at midnight" (Ex 12:29). However, Yahweh had imposed on them a detour and long stages, lest, having started valiantly, they succumb to the temptation of turning back (Ex 13:18). Lastly, "in the morning watch" (Ex 14:24), the final liberation of the people took place during the crossing of the Red Sea. We find again in the verses of the Song the same words and the same images: leaving, night, early morning, passage, flight from the former land, "let us go to the fields", the stages of the road (night in the villages) with a perspective on the new land, the land of promise with abundant fruits, the vineyard of the Lord ("we shall go to the vineyards").

But today the Bride is the one who takes the initiative for the departure. She, for the first time, says, "Come". Many times, so many times already, we have heard this word "Come" from the mouth of the Bridegroom or the chorus echoing him (2:10, 13; 4:8; 7:1). And before it was the Bridegroom who invited his love to enjoy the spring: "Come then, my love, my lovely one, come. . . . Winter is past. . . . The flowers appear on the earth. . . . The blossoming vines give out their fragrance. Come then, my love, my lovely one, come" (2:10–13). But how slow his beloved was, as if numb in her response, like a dove hidden in the cleft of a rock! Now today, she herself is pressing her Bridegroom to leave, to reach solitude with her. (How new is this word *we,* which she utters for the first time, expressing the communion of two destinies: "We will spend", "we will go". How determined she is today!) And she is also the one who invites the Bridegroom to wait peacefully in the villages at the threshold of the city, after the night of the world and the Exodus, the morning of Easter: "We will spend . . . and in the morning we will go".

But even more than recalling the great adventure of her past, is not the Bride of the Song leading now toward another Exodus and another land, which this time are before her? Do we not see appearing in her heart a great desire for the blessed city? Indeed, the night of exile must last a while longer, I know this, my beloved. But let us start on our way and leave! "The night is almost over, it will be daylight soon" (Rm 13:12). Together we will wait in the villages, i.e., near the city, until the night is over, and when morning rises, we will enter Jerusalem, our new city, my vineyard but also your vineyard, which says: "I am the true vine" (Jn 15:1). "In the morning we will go to the vineyards."

Such is the interpretation that Saint Thomas Aquinas gives to this stanza of the Song, the last text of Scripture he comments on.[57] And Saint Francis de Sales tells us that these words of the Bride were also the last ones of him who spoke so much about God all his life and was now in haste to join him in his kingdom: "Joining his hands, raising his eyes to the sky and raising his voice very loudly, he uttered impetuously, very fervently, these words from the Song that had been the last he had explained: 'Come, my beloved, let us go to the fields.' "[58]

For Saint Thomas Aquinas, as for the Bride of the Song, there is the same urgency because the same unbearable waiting is expressed in the striking antitheses within the song of the Bride: night and morning; night in the villages and morning in the vineyards; and this verb "we will spend", which sounds here almost like the name of Easter.[59] The humble Bride of the Song is singing, as it were, the first notes of the Church-Bride's refrain in the first chapter of John's Revelation: *Ma-*

[57] A. Touron, *La vie de saint Thomas d'Aquin* (Paris: chez Gissey, Bordelet, Savoye, Henry, 1737), 291–292.

[58] Saint Francis de Sales, *Traité*, VII:9, 692.

[59] In French *nous passerons* ("we will spend") also means "we will pass", which brings to mind the Passover, the Pasch, in French *Pâques* (Easter). — *Trans.*

ranatha! "Come, Lord Jesus" (Rv 22:20). " 'Come, my Beloved!' is still her cry resounding down the centuries until the
consummation."[60]

However, in spite of her haste, she is already happy to belong fully to him whom she loves. Ah, this time, he will have
to admit "going down to his garden" that he does not have the
slightest perplexity. No more winter to fear, no ephemeral
springs. The beautiful garden has flowers that will not close
anymore. Let the Bridegroom recognize this together with
her. Come,

7:13 *We will see if the vines are budding,*
      if their blossoms are opening,
      if the pomegranate trees are in flower.

Thus does the Bride echo, not without a small ironic smile as
we can imagine, the words with which her beloved had once
confided his concern to her: "I went down to the nut orchard"—he had said—"to see what was sprouting in the valley, to see if the vines were budding and the pomegranate trees
in flower" (6:11). Will you be fully reassured now, my beloved? "I will see", you had said. You will see, "we will see"
together "if the vines [are] budding", truly "what [is] sprouting", in fact if the trees of love, "the pomegranate trees, [are]
in flower" and if the time foreseen by the prophets for your beloved has finally been accomplished: "In the days to come, Jacob will put out shoots, Israel will bud and have blossoms, and
fill the whole world with fruit" (Is 27:6). Yes, my beloved, the
time has come and will not pass when

7:13 *Then I shall give you*
      the gift of my love.

In fact, she has given him this gift many times before. Yet, it is
absolutely new. "I gave him my heart", Marie de l'Incarnation

---

[60] de Lubac, *Méditation*, 323.

writes in the same vein in her Relation of 1633. "But", as Dom Oury points out, "Marie offered her heart to God many times after 1620. However, what is special at the time of this grace is the awareness that Marie has that her relationship with God now has a unique intimacy. An immense joy floods her when she feels that she is irrevocably united to God."[61] It is the same joy that now fills the heart of the Bride of the Song. Now she understands that she is offering herself as an irrevocable gift, an absolute gift, which cannot be taken back or go "through intermittences of the heart". "I shall give you", she stresses, "the gift of my love."

Beyond the season of the flowers. (How the signs have multiplied in this stanza! Each one of the three verses, in the original Hebrew, is loaded with flowers: flowers of the vines, all the flowers of the garden, those of the trees; the vineyards are budding, the flowers in blossom, the pomegranate trees in flower.) After the ephemeral passage of the flowers and the summer, now comes the autumn of ripe fruits, from now on her season of eternity with him:

7:14 *The mandrakes yield their fragrance,*
the rarest fruits are at our doors;

According to André Robert, the mandrakes have two properties: "to incite love (in Hebrew, the word *doda'im*—mandrakes—and the word *dodim*—love—have the same ring) and to give fecundity" (Gn 30:14–16). The gift of the Bride to the Bridegroom—as the chorus of the nations has already hinted (cf. 7:3)—is necessarily called to be fruitful. And here, indeed, the gift she made of herself is succeeded without any break by many symbols of the fecundity of their union, the rarest fruits—"the rarest fruits are at our doors"—all the fruits of the universe and the tastiest ones. But at our doors also, within reach of my hand, I can already pick the better fruits of our new garden of Paradise.

[61] Oury, *Marie de l'Incarnation,* 207ff.

7:14 *the new as well as the old,*
I have stored them for you, my Beloved.

"Stored" also means "set aside" for you alone and "consecrated" entirely for you alone. Through these simple words of the Bride is expressed the desire—unlimited as it were—to surrender to her Bridegroom the totality of her being. Not only her life today, in its riches and fecundity, but her life since the beginning. Yes, even the hours that seem to have been lost forever, even the hours that were gray and mediocre; she must catch everything up today in an act of perfect love. Old and new fruits are part of one sole basket of fruits. The Bride is so sure that all can be taken back, reoriented, reconverted—even what was the least avowable—in the gift she is making now of herself to the Bridegroom!

Saint John of the Cross is able to sense the novelty and tremendous meaning of these words uttered by the Bride: "The Bride says that she has surrendered totally to her Bridegroom, without retaining anything for herself. . . . Her soul, her body, her powers and all her abilities are now used not in the things that worry her, but in those that serve her Bridegroom. . . . She is not seeking her interest or her tastes. . . . I have no other task, she says, than to love. It is as if she said: all the powers of my soul and body that I was using before in useless things have now been put at the service of love. . . . I am doing what I do out of love, and suffering what I suffer out of love. . . . Blessed is the soul that reaches this point when all is now substance of love, pleasure and delight of betrothal; when the Bride can truly speak to the Bridegroom these words of pure love that she utters in the Song: 'I have stored [all the fruits] for you, . . . the new as well as the old'. It is as if she were saying: My beloved, because of you, I want all that is harsh and painful, as I want for you all that is sweet and tasty."[62]

[62] Saint John of the Cross, *Cantique spirituel,* Stanza XX, 622.

May we pause here briefly before we go on? May we consider now in one single glance the entire second part of this fifth poem, included in chapter 7 of the Song? There is no need to stress it forcefully, but can we not be struck by the impressive connection in all the themes developed so far—a link which is that of the paschal mystery itself, as the Gospel, especially that of John, manifests it? First of all, the eucharistic theme, which is suggested in the description of the Bride through the symbols of belly, wheat, wine, unity. Then, the theme of the Passion and Cross with the palm tree that the Bridegroom wants to climb; "his desire is for me", where is foreshadowed all the submission and thirst of Jesus in his Passion. In connection with the themes of Passion and Cross, the theme of the Spirit rushing out of the open side (cf. Jn 19:34) under the symbols of breath, perfume, wind. Then the theme of the Resurrection, with the end of the night, early morning and the concept of passage from night to morning and from the villages to the vineyards. Lastly, the perspective of the Kingdom, with all the flowers and fruits—spring and autumn all at once—in the joy of consummated love.

But the passage to the Kingdom and total communion with the Bridegroom in sheer being—to which the Bride aspires with her great desire and strength—cannot be achieved unless he himself does not only join us but also takes our condition upon himself to usher us, being only one body with us, into the house of his Father.

There is thus a close continuity with the great prophetic drive that inspired her in the words the Bride utters now:

8:1 *Ah, why are you not my brother,*
   nursed at my mother's breast!
   Then if I met you out of doors, I could kiss you
   without people thinking ill of me.

However, our first reaction might be one of surprise. One cannot help being startled: after all the love declarations that she made openly (cf. 5:10–16), the Bride wishes now that the one she loves, rather like a Bridegroom apparently, be her brother so that she could freely kiss him without people thinking ill of her!

Father Buzy writes: "This is because oriental customs do not allow a Bride to give public demonstrations of affection to her Bridegroom: such are more easily tolerated between brother and sister. As a consequence, the Bride comes to the point where she wishes that instead of being her Bridegroom, the beloved be a brother, so as to be able to love him more freely and to offer him, wherever they meet, the gestures of love."[63]

We must admit though that until now the Bride did not give the impression that she was bothered by public opinion! As to preferring being a sister rather than a Bride of the one she loves, such a thought cannot even come to her mind. All her declarations since the first verse of the poem go against it.

Other commentators expressed the hypothesis that the young woman was expressing here an ideal of chastity. She would like to love her Bridegroom as chastely as she would a brother, "the relationship of sister and brother being more pure, more solid, more durable than that of wife and husband".[64] But such an interpretation, besides being quite contestable in itself, is belied once more by the entire Song, which tells of the love of her who is a Bride, in its most beautiful and perfect truth.

In fact, what we see appearing here in the heart of the Bride, as is so deeply understood, among many other commentators on the Song, by Father Joüon, André Robert, Father Feuillet, André Chouraqui, and others, is the desire that the Bridegroom, while being her Bridegroom, also be a brother to her. Already the Bridegroom has called her five times "my sister"

---

[63] Denis Buzy, "Le Cantique des Cantiques", in Louis Pirot and Albert Clamer, *La Sainte Bible,* vol. 6 (Paris: Letouzey, 1943), 198.

[64] F. Delitzch, quoted by André Robert, "Le Cantique des Cantiques", *La Bible de Jérusalem* (Paris: Cerf, 1958), 283.

(4:9, 10, 12; 5:1, 2) But never had the Bride herself dared to give her Bridegroom the name of brother. This is because she is only too conscious of her tremendous inequality and inferiority. He loves her, and this is incredible, but it is an unheard of condescension. Now what she has come to desire today, with an extreme daring that his love cannot resist, is not that her relationship of Bride be changed into that of mere sister, but that her Bridegroom also be a brother with whom she can deal, according to the felicitous expression of Saint Bernard, "if not as equal at least as one of the same species".[65]

Did she not already, at the time of the betrothal (3:4), wish that she could draw him into the room of her mother, to share her life with him? She now has this far more insane dream: that the Bridegroom become similar to her in all things. Not only that she be like him, but that he be like her. Not only that she be reborn "from above" to his life (cf. Jn 3:3), but that he be born to her humanity. That he be by the very fact someone of the same nature, the same race, the same mankind as she is. Someone, as she daringly and wonderfully says, who has "nursed at my mother's breast", who has been fed with the same milk of human tenderness. Someone, in a word, who, while remaining her incomprehensible and inaccessible Lord, shares in all things her condition and destiny, who is her brother.

Undoubtedly, in these verses of the Song, we have the highest and most beautiful expression in the history of Israel of her ardent and ineradicable expectation of the messiah. The whole thrust of the Song leads us in fact to this prophetical summit, where the Bride, giving way to the inspiration of the Spirit, begs Almighty God, already her Bridegroom through grace, to become her brother by nature, in perfect equality and con-

---

[65] Saint Bernard, *Sermons sur le Cantique des Cantiques, Oeuvres mystiques*, Sermon 83 (Paris: Seuil, 1953), 849.

formity with her: God, her Lord by creation and her Bride-groom by the covenant, becoming thus her brother through a community of flesh and blood, which will enable him to tell her in all truth, sending her to all men, "go find the brothers" (Jn 20:17)—to the point that she who had been created at the beginning in the image and likeness of God (Gn 1:26) can see God making himself in her image and likeness.

It is striking that a Jew like Chouraqui, even though he does not of course discern in this passage of the Song any reference to the Word incarnate, in fact has this perspective, albeit imperfectly so. He writes, "Love is a desire of absolute identification. The beloved aspires, even at the summit of the gift that she makes of herself, to a more essential union yet, that would make of her not only the friend, the lover, the bride, but also the sister. She wishes to transcend any duality. . . . At the end of her loving life, the beloved, dazzled by the face of love that she has closely contemplated, is so deeply overwhelmed that she aspires to shed any otherness. . . . Brother and sister, yet united in the eternity of an embrace of love and mystical exchange. . . . The maid of Shulam asks for a total mutation of his being and, in the absolute of love, her absolute union in an identification with her lover."[66] We add: and in the identification of her lover with her, according to the extremely vigorous and compact phrase of Saint Irenaeus: "God made himself the very thing we are, to make of us that which he is."[67]

8:1 *Then if I met you out of doors, I could kiss you without people thinking ill of me.*

In the celebration of her beloved's love, the Bride will not have to fear the insulting mockery of the pagans, the contemptuous questions of those who tell her today: "Where is your God?"

---

[66] Chouraqui, *Le Cantique des Cantiques,* 76.
[67] Saint Irenaeus, *Contre les hérésies,* V (cf. SC 153) (Paris: Cerf, 1959), 15.

"What is he like?" How can one make those worshippers of
idols and painted and engraved images understand the unsur-
passable beauty of him whom nobody in the world can represent? The Bride was reduced, as we heard, to launch into rather
incomprehensible discourses about her absent prince (5:10–
16); but most of the time she was protesting bitterly in her
heart together with the psalmist: "How much longer, God, is
the oppressor to blaspheme, is the enemy to insult your name
forever?" (Ps 74:10). "Why should the pagans say: Where is
their God?" (Ps 79:10).

Now the Bride, having in her Bridegroom a brother in her
image and likeness, will be able in broad daylight proudly to
show him to her detractors. "Where is your God?" they were
asking me. Here he is, among you. Such is my God, such is my
Bridegroom, such also is my brother; Immanuel is his name.

"I could kiss you without people thinking ill of me" since
your face will be exactly like mine. And when I say "to kiss
you", I do not mean something vague and sentimental or a pious formula, but the very strength of your embrace; "and they
become one body", as it is written in Genesis (Gn 2:24); to the
extent that, being reborn of you in our union, I am divinized
by you, while you, being born of me, are humanized by me.

With what pride and also what happiness will the Bride in-
troduce the one she loves into her house, which has become
their house on that day. Not yet, it is true, a house of cedars
and cypresses, as he made her dream during their betrothal;
but, to begin, her very humble dwelling, the bed of green, narcissus and lilies in the valley (cf. 1:16; 2:1). To begin:

8:2 *I should lead you, I should take you*
  into my mother's house . . .

"I should lead you, I should take you", she says with an incredible candor. And, as we can see, the Bridegroom does not raise
any objection. He does not interrupt her. We surmise that he

agrees wholeheartedly. He who had always led her so well until then, taking her "to his rooms" and "to his cellar of wine", how he lets himself be led by her now and makes himself very small to enter her house! Yes, the day will come when she will take him, joyfully and solemnly at the same time, to her "mother's house", in the midst of Israel his people, in the midst of the Church, in the midst of all mankind: when, having become herself the beloved among all the beloveds of the world, he whom she now calls her Bridegroom and her brother while knowing full well that she is only his "handmaid" will be like a little child in her womb. "The Word was made flesh, he lived among us" (Jn 1:14).

8:2 . . . and you would teach me!

After such a prophecy of the Incarnation, the most wonderful of all, we cannot be surprised to see the Bridegroom devoting himself to the activity that will be his essential mission on earth: teaching. "You would teach me." We understand, of course, that those who see in the Song nothing but a poem celebrating human love are keen in wanting to suppress these words.[68] For it is quite inappropriate, they point out, and even ridiculous to hear a woman in the fire of her passion for her lover asking him to give her lessons! Such words are to be found though in the original Hebrew as well as in the Greek text read by Origen. And they fit perfectly.

Indeed, here is the Bridegroom responding to the so frequently repeated pleading of his Bride throughout Scripture: "Yahweh, make your ways known to me; teach me your paths. Direct me in the way of your truth and teach me" (Ps 25:4–5). He becomes the only teacher of his people, in keeping

---

[68] Osty, "Introduction au Cantique des Cantiques", in *La Sainte Bible* (Paris: Edilec, 1981), cf. 8:2.

with what Jeremiah had foretold: "They will not have to teach
one another saying, 'Learn to know Yahweh'. No, they will all
know me!" (Jr 31:34). And did not Moses say in Deuteronomy: "Yahweh your God will raise up for you a prophet like
myself from among yourselves; from among your brothers.
To him, you must listen. I will put my words into his mouth"
(Dt 18:15–18)? "Then, opening his mouth, he taught them"
(Greek text, Mt 5:2). Thus it will be enough one day for Mary
of Bethany to sit at the feet of her master and to "listen to his
word" in order to be fulfilled (Lk 10:39–42); in the same vein,
many centuries later, the only occupation to which Elizabeth
of the Trinity wanted to devote herself was quite simply to listen to the Word of God in herself: "O eternal Word, Word of
my God, I want to spend my life listening to you. I want to
make myself all-teachable, so as to learn everything from
you."[69]

The Bride of the Song does not aspire to anything else. And
if she does not stipulate the form and nature of the teaching she
wishes to receive from her beloved, it is because it could be
only one lesson as she well knows: that of love. "Love is the
abbreviated version of all theology", as Saint Francis de Sales
puts it very plainly.[70] It is also the only teaching that Jesus will
give to his disciples: "Just as I have loved you, you must also
love one another. By this love you have for one another, ev-
eryone will know that you are my disciples" (Jn 13:34–35). Indeed this kind of teaching is not given in schools or in books
but in going deeper and deeper into the heart of the Bridegroom, as Origen perceives it so well: "The Bride-Church is
taught by the Word of God, her Bridegroom, about all that is
contained and hidden in the royal palace and in the room of the
King."[71]

[69] Cf. Études Augustiniennes, vol. 16 (1981), 11–14.
[70] Saint Francis de Sales, Traité, VIII:1, I, 715.
[71] Origen, In Canticum Canticorum, PG 13, 180B.

In this school of the heart, the Virgin Mary was the first pupil and the most alert and receptive. "And finally on Calvary," writes Father de Lubac, "through the three long hours, holding the Church's place at the foot of the cross, she received from her Son the definitive teaching—a teaching not of words but of act, through which all words are illuminated." This is so strongly expressed in this passage of Claudel: "On Calvary our Mother Mary had something better to do than cry; she has to learn her catechism lesson in the name of the whole Church which has just been instituted in her person. . . . There, dazzling and painted in red, is the great page that separates the two Testaments. All that the Virgin learned at the lap of Anne, all the scrolls of Moses and the prophets which are gathered in her memory, all the generations since Adam which she bears in her womb, the promise to Abraham and David, the wisdom of Solomon and Daniel, the incandescent desire of Elias and John the Baptist and all those at prayer in limbo—all that has begun to breathe, to understand, to see and to know in her heart under the life-bringing ray of grace."[72]

This is the teaching of the Bridegroom, which causes the one he loves to surrender the most precious and also the most secret part of herself:

8:2 *I should give you spiced wine to drink,*
   juice of my pomegranates.

She did, however, believe in good faith that she had given her all! But there was a part of her soul, unknown to herself until now, that she was not yet able to offer: the last depth of ourselves, that we usually take so long in discovering and thus to be able to offer. It takes years of ripening and listening in the school of the Bridegroom. "Shoulder my yoke and learn from me", Jesus says (Mt 11:29). What the Bride learns in this school are spaces so far unsuspected in the heart of the Bridegroom;

[72] de Lubac, *The Splendor of the Church*, 344–345.

but also, inside the same experience, her own mystery is revealed, her intimate essence, what she calls her "spiced wine" and her "juice of . . . pomegranates", i.e., the heart of her heart that could only escape her awareness as long as she had not received "the new teaching" (Mk 1:27) and that she will not therefore be able to surrender until then. Revealing to me the unfathomable mystery of his Heart, he reveals to me my own heart in its most unsuspected depths. Then "I should give you spiced wine to drink, juice of my pomegranates."

Having been carried away by the prophetic wind on which she rode for so long, it seems that the Bride is now exhausted and can only let herself go blissfully in the arms of the Bridegroom:

8:3 *His left arm is under my head*
    and his right embraces me, she whispers.

She only feels the strength of this left arm under her head and the infinite tenderness of the right that embraces her. Such a rest is not as it had been before, that of a still languid soul, but one of beatitude. The Bridegroom, for the third time, charges the daughters of Jerusalem not to stir the one he loves, thus responding a last time to the refrain of his Bride by his own refrain:

8:4 *I charge you,*
    daughters of Jerusalem,
    not to stir my love, nor rouse it,
    until it please to awake.

But this refrain is not sung in the same mode and key as before. The music and structure are now completely different. Here we are in a major key! André Chouraqui points out very subtly that "if the hinds and the fawns of the fields are not evoked here and taken to charge, it is because the possession is such, achieved in such certainty, that no adjuration is needed anymore."[73] We will say that the sleep to which the Bride now yields is of another nature than the others. It is as if the fifth poem is bearing witness in its ascent to the rest of perfect quietude of a soul fully abandoned and surrendered.

[73] Chouraqui, *Le Cantique des Cantiques*, 76.

The Golden After-Season

Conclusion

Chapter 8:5-7

The Chorus

Who is this coming up from the desert
leaning on her Beloved?

The Bridegroom

I awakened you under the apple tree,
there where your mother conceived you,
there where she who gave birth to you conceived you.

The Bride

Set me like a seal on your heart,
like a seal on your arm.
For love is strong as Death,
jealousy relentless as Sheol.
The flash of it is a flash of fire,
a flame of Yahweh himself.
Love no flood can quench,
no torrents drown.

The Golden After-Season

The chorus of the nations, at the apex of the Song, which is the fifth poem, introduces the conclusion:

8:5 *Who is this coming up from the desert*
leaning on her Beloved?

For the third time we hear the admiring exclamation of the nations' chorus. The first time was at the overture of the third poem, when the chorus saw on the horizon the column of smoke, perfumes, myrrh and incense mysteriously shrouding the Bridegroom; the second time was in the fifth poem, in response to the beauty of the Bride, rising like a star on the horizon, when the chorus sang in ecstasy: "Who is this arising like the dawn, fair as the moon, resplendent as the sun?" This third time, the chorus wonders and marvels in the face of the growing vision not only of him, not only of her, but of the sacred couple, the reunited Bridegroom and Bride. And if she first draws and keeps the attention—"Who is this [feminine form] coming up from the desert?"—she appears as a Bride softly surrendering to her husband, leaning on him, united and identified with him in the unity of the couple. Thus is she seen: "Who is this coming up from the desert leaning on her Beloved?"

They both come forward, in this last hour of the Song, in the apotheosis of their love, like a Bridegroom and a Bride on their wedding day. Or rather like the Bride and the Bridegroom marching on in the last book of Scripture: "This is the time for the marriage of the Lamb; his Bride is ready" (Rev 19:7). Together, "they go up to Jerusalem." Together they ascend toward the new Jerusalem, which will be the definitive city of their union. One always goes up to Jerusalem in the Bible; one can only go up to the blessed Jerusalem.

The couple arrives from the desert, which is the biblical locus of the betrothal, where the Bridegroom spoke at length to the heart of his beloved, waking her up little by little to the absolute majesty of his love, preparing her for the perfect union with him: "This is why I am going to lure her", he had said to the prophet Hosea, "and lead her out into the wilderness and speak to her heart" (Ho 2:16). The Bridegroom has done nothing else in the Song. One cannot attain the consummated wedding with the Lamb without a long preliminary novitiate, endlessly renewed in the desert with him. In the same spirit, one leaves the desert to reach his Kingdom only by leaning, softly and strongly at the same time, on the arm of the Bridegroom. Should one read "leaning on the arm"? According to Origen, the original Hebrew text does not say—though we read this in several manuscripts—"leaning on her Beloved", but, and the nuance is a moving one, "leaning on the heart of her Beloved".[1] As it is said in Isaiah about the Shepherd of Israel, "gathering his lambs in his arms, against his heart" (Is 40:11), and as it will be said of Saint John at the Last Supper, "He rested on the breast of Jesus."[2]

This time, the Bride is fully in control of herself. Her eyes are opened. And the Bridegroom himself bears witness to this:

8:5 *I awakened you under the apple tree,*
 there where your mother conceived you,
 there where she who gave birth to you conceived you.

Truly it is the voice of the Bridegroom that we hear. Only the Bride sleeps in the Song (2:7; 3:5; 5:2; 8:4), while "the guardian of Israel does not slumber or sleep" (Ps 121:4). The Bridegroom took the initiative, after having respected for a long time the sleep of his beloved, to awaken her when she was rest-

---

[1] Origen, *Homélies sur le Cantique des Cantiques,* Homily 1 (Paris: Cerf, 1966), 89.
[2] John, 13:25 and note in TOB.

ing in total abandonment in the shade of an apple tree (cf. 2:3): "I awakened you under the apple tree". For the time has come to leave the shade, no matter how sweet it is to the pilgrim, in order to share in the glory of the Bridegroom. This is the time of the risen Christ, the last three transfigured months of Francis of Assisi and Thérèse: "the golden after-season".[3]

Passage from shadow to light, from the obscure light of the faith to the illumination of the spirit and heart's eyes. Astonished awakening of the Bride, whose eyes open in wonder on the dawn of the new creation: "I saw a new heaven and a new earth", Saint John says in Revelation (Rv 21:1). "Coming up from the desert", her former dwelling, the Bride discovers the immense garden of God, in which the tree of life, as was the case in the paradise of Genesis, is at the center (Gn 2:9). "I awakened you under the apple tree", he whispers. Her friend does not say "under an apple tree", for the apple tree is unique. Didn't she say herself: "As the apple tree among the other trees, so is my Beloved among the young men" (2:3; French version)? At the end of the Song we see the tree-bearing fruits and flowers, which have the shape of the Bridegroom. Not that tree which, caught by his wild passion for his Bride, he wanted to climb when he exclaimed, "I will climb the palm tree" (7:9), the beautiful palm tree of the Bride that he wanted to embrace until death. The only tree today is the radiant apple tree at the heart of the garden of paradise, the forever-glorious Cross of the Bridegroom's wedding. Saint John of the Cross, commenting on this verse of the Song, places these words in the mouth of Jesus: "It is at the foot of the apple tree that you became my Bride, there I gave you my hand, and you were reestablished at the very spot where your mother had suffered violence."[4]

---

[3] Paul Claudel, *L'annonce faite à Marie* (1st version), Act IV, Scene IV, Bibliothèque de la Pléiade (Paris: Gallimard, 1956); *Théâtre*, vol. 2, 97.

[4] Saint John of the Cross, *Cantique spirituel*, Stanza XXIX, *Oeuvres complètes*, Bibliothèque européenne (Paris: Desclée de Brouwer, 1964), 630.

Indeed on this very earth, in this very garden that had been turned by sin into a desert of thorns and bushes (Gn. 3:8), where my former mother conceived me, Eve, the first mother of my life, whose name means "mother of the living" (Gn 3:20), my Bridegroom gives today—thus fulfilling the wish of his Bride (3:4; 8:2)—a rebirth to a new life. "I awakened you", he says. This is the very word of the Resurrection; this is already the song of the new Easter that Paul will teach to the Ephesians: "Wake up from your sleep, rise from the dead and Christ will shine on you" (Ep 5:14).

This new birth is far more admirable than the one I received from my carnal mother. The theme of carnal mother seems to be heard only in counterpoint, so as to enhance that of the new birth, "the birth from above" (Jn 3:3). But how impressive it is throughout the whole Song, this reminder of the mother who conceived me and gave birth to me (1:6; 3:4; 6:9; 8:1, 5). On the other hand, it is rather peculiar to notice that if the word *mother* is repeated so insistently (six times for the mother of the Bride, and only once for the mother of the Bridegroom—3:11 —which is remarkable), nowhere is there any mention of either one's father. As if there were only one Father, whose mysterious name cannot yet be revealed for "no one knows the Father except the Son and those to whom the Son chooses to make him known" (Mt 11:27).

The Bridegroom introduced the con' usion of the Song; he spoke only in order to assure his Bride of her full awakening, or rather her true and definitive rebirth. Now, she whose ardent words had started the whole poem, in the joy of her transfigured and fulfilled love, concludes it:

8:6 *Set me like a seal on your heart,*
    like a seal on your arm.

We agree with most of the critics: these words cannot be placed in the mouth of the Bridegroom. Indeed, it would be beautiful to hear him say, "Set me like a seal on your heart, like a seal on your arm" also, since his own image is indelibly imprinted on the heart and arm of his love. Thus Saint Paul says of the Holy Spirit that he is the seal, the image of the Bridegroom, that the Father engraves on the heart of the believer (cf. 2 Co 1:22; Ep 1:13 and 4:30). And Saint John in Revelation talks about the seal of the living God imprinted on the forehead of the one hundred forty-four thousand servants of God (Rv 5:2–9). It is in this same and very beautiful line of interpretation that we must understand the prayer of Saint Thérèse that we already quoted: "Adorable face of Jesus, only beauty that ravishes my heart, deign to imprint in me your divine resemblance, so that you may not look at my soul without looking at yourself."[5]

However, the context and parallel scriptural texts do not allow us, as the new edition of the Jerusalem Bible points out, to retain this interpretation. The voice of the Bride is indeed the one that is heard in the last stanza of the Song, as a prelude to the celebration of victorious Love, the triumphant note on which the whole poem is ending, in a way that is at first imploring, in a prayer: "Set me like a seal on your heart."

The Bride is so conscious, even at the highest degree of union, of her inherent weakness; she is so sure of her Bridegroom but so unsure of herself—this is the gist of the fourth poem—that her entire train of thought will never let the love that has triumphed in her become weaker. Not that there is any doubt or worry in her at this triumphant moment. Has she not been confirmed in love and grace by her beloved himself ("I awakened you under the apple tree")? But instead of turning to him, whispering very lovingly as she had done earlier, "I am my Beloved's, and my Beloved is mine", she is now the humble Bride, "leaning on her Beloved" and exclaiming, "Set me like a seal on your heart, like a seal on your arm." Now she

[5] Saint Thérèse of the Child Jesus, *Histoire d'une âme*, Édition du Carmel de Lisieux (Lisieux, 1953), 258.

knows that, no matter how high she has reached, her fidelity comes only from him whom Saint John, in Revelation, calls "faithful" (Rv 19:11).

What does she mean exactly by these words: "Set me like a seal"? She does not think at first and directly, as we might be tempted to believe, about the imprint left on wax by a seal, as on an official document for instance. Rather than the imprint of a seal, she thinks about the seal itself such as the landowners of old used to wear around their necks with a cord or as a ring on a finger. This was their mark, their signature fixed at the end of all their deeds; something committing them and from which they could never part imprudently.

Before the Song, the image of the seal had been used several times in the Bible. When Jerusalem complains about being abandoned, Yahweh replies: "For Zion was saying: Yahweh has abandoned me, the Lord has forgotten me. Does a woman forget her baby at the breast? Or fail to cherish the son of her womb? Yet, even if these forget you, I will never forget you. See, I have branded you on the palm of my hands" (Is 49:14). And more explicitly yet, Yahweh had told Zerubabel, a prefiguration of the messiah to come: "I make you like a signet ring" (Hg 2:23), i.e., all that you will say and accomplish will commit God himself.

But the Bride of the Song is asking for more. In the unlimited daring of her heart, she also claims to be the signet ring, though not with the mark of the Bridegroom, but with her own. She herself will now be the seal of her Bridegroom. And it is easy to see what she expects from this: since she will be the seal of her Bridegroom, she will by this very fact be constantly on his finger or around his neck, on his heart. This then is far more than what exalted her when she was saying, "My Beloved is a sachet of myrrh lying between my breasts" (1:13). Her place will now always be on the very heart of her beloved. And thus he will never be able to cease thinking about her. Not only will she not be absent from his memory, but she will always and everywhere be with him, accompanying him everywhere and at all times. And who could take her place away from her?

And because she will be his seal, all that he will do in the world throughout the creation and history of men she will also do with him. She will participate in all his works. Without her, he will not do anything anymore. They can work only together. They can be committed only together.

Lastly, because she is his seal, they will thus have the same mark, the same identity, the same name. Your name will be my name. As I belong to you, you belong to me. Thus does the Bride want to mark with her own seal the one of whom Saint John says that the Father had marked him with his seal (Jn 6:27)! Double seal indeed since it is divine and human at the same time, inscribed in the humanity of Jesus.

One day, on the staircase of the novitiate of the Carmelite Convent of the Incarnation in Avila, young Teresa, who was then between eighteen and twenty years old, met a boy about ten years old. She was not too surprised at first. In those days, monastic discipline was very lax, and the kin and friends of the nuns moved about freely in the monastery. The time of Teresa the reformer had not yet come! But the child approached her daringly and asked her, "What is your name?" "Teresa of Jesus", she replied, rather surprised. Who was that boy to interrogate her so freely without the usual ceremony? "And you," Teresa went on rather abruptly, "who are you?" "Jesus of Teresa", the child replied, and he vanished. Teresa of Jesus, Jesus of Teresa: same identity, same name, same seal.[6]

"Set me like a seal on your heart," begs the Bride in the Song. She who at the start of the fourth poem showed a love that was still incomplete and heavy with sleep is seen here at the conclusion of the whole drama held only by the heart, the marvelously faithful and sure heart—the heart that in her long praise of love she had never been able to name—of the one in

[6] Joseph Gicquel, *Fioretti de Sainte Thérèse d'Avila* (Paris: Cerf, 1977), 14.

whom she has at last found her true home, her perfect peace. However, if she wants above all to be always present in the heart of her love, she also knows how to avail herself of the strength of his arm. Seal on his heart, she will also be on his arm. Robert de Langeac is therefore very deeply in harmony with the feelings of the Bride when he writes: "As soon as one has won the heart of God, one has all his power. If he wants to place the faithful soul as a seal on his heart, he also puts it in the same way on his arm. It is a constant fact in the life of the saints that the all-powerful strength of God is theirs."[7]

Thus powerfully armed, the Bride is wholly convinced that from now on nothing within or without can take her away from her beloved, nor him from her. "I know who it is that I have put my trust in" (2 Tm 1:12). Without being able to recognize herself in the features of the unhappy people described by Saint Bernard in one of his last sermons on the Song, she would thus have undoubtedly fully agreed with the quite astonishing words that the abbot of Clairvaux addressed to his monks at the thought that one or another among them still did not dare entrust himself blindly to the power of merciful Love. "I have shown to you", Saint Bernard says, "that any soul, even laden with sins, captive of its vices, held by its pleasures, imprisoned in its exile, locked up in its body, nailed to its worries, distracted by its concerns, frozen by its fears, struck by manifold sufferings, going from error to error, eaten up by anxiety, ravaged by suspicion and, lastly, according to the prophet, a stranger in a foreign land . . . , every soul, I say, in spite of its damnation and despair, can still find in itself reasons not only to hope for forgiveness and mercy but even to aspire to the wedding feast of the Word: as long as it does not fear to sign a covenant with God, and to place itself with him under the yoke of love. . . . For the Bridegroom is not only a lover:

---

[7] Robert de Langeac, *"Commentaire spirituel du Cantique des Cantiques"*, *Virgo fidelis* (Paris: Letheilleux, 1931), 277–278.

he is Love. You will say: yes, but is he not also honor? Some affirm this; as to myself, I never read anything of that kind. I have read that God is Love."[8]

Is this text written by Bernard, the abbot of Clairvaux who lived in Burgundy in the twelfth century, or by Thérèse of Lisieux, the little Norman Carmelite of the late nineteenth century? We can say that both are holding hands over the centuries, with the same unshakable faith in merciful Love.

It happens at times that he who has perfectly surrendered and abandoned himself to love then conceives such an assurance that his words, like those of the Bride in the Song, ring with tones that are almost like those of a challenge: "In God I put my trust, fearing nothing" (Ps 56:5–12). And what could one still fear? No obstacle in the world, and no one, himself included, could do anything against the love to which he surrendered.

8:6 *For love is strong as Death,*
     jealousy relentless as Sheol.
     The flash of it is a flash of fire,
     a flame of Yahweh himself.

8:7 *Love no flood can quench,*
     no torrents drown.

After celebrating unity in love, "Set me like a seal on your heart," the Bride sings the duration without obstacle nor end of her love: "Love no flood can quench, no torrents drown." Thus are already announced the two themes that are going to be described in the last discourse of Jesus: "Make your home in me as I make mine in you" (Jn 15:4) and "that joy, no one can take away from you" (Jn 16:22).

---

[8] Saint Bernard, *Sermons sur le Cantique des Cantiques, Oeuvres mystiques,* Sermon 83 (Paris: Seuil, 1953), 846–848.

Neither death, nor Sheol, nor floods nor torrents, the Bride says. She contemplates all that in the world threatens her love, all that cannot be resisted by men, all the powers of disaster and evil, with this distinction between the floods and the torrents: the floods represent above all the great abyss, the sojourn of the monsters, the bestial Leviathan and the "tortuous"[9] Behemoth, in other words, the locus of the infernal powers; while the torrents symbolize above all the anxieties and distresses to which the soul is exposed in this life. And the Bride proclaims in a last superb thrust of passion, which is as serene as it is vehement, that nothing, absolutely nothing, could ever put an end to our love.

She starts with death, the most frightening enemy, not this country from which the dead do not come back and which is called Sheol. Thus she adopts the words of the psalmist that Saint Peter and Saint Paul heard as genuine prophecies of the Resurrection: "You will not abandon my soul to Sheol, nor allow the one you love to see the pit" (Ps 16:10; Ac 2:25–28 and 13:35). "Death is swallowed up in victory" (1 Co 15:55). Of course, death had so far been left unconquered. Even the powerful ones of this world had to bow before it. But the love of the Bridegroom is more powerful than death. From the dry and scattered bones on the plain after the battle, he brings up an army of the living (Ezk 37). Of the sheep that the Father entrusted to him, Jesus affirms that "they shall never die", that no power in the world could tear them away from his hand (Jn 10:28) because love is always the strongest.

The only time when death is mentioned in the dialogue of the two lovers is when it is defeated and vanquished, for having defied love. Saint Augustine exulted at the thought: "Love", he exclaims in the middle of a sermon, "is as strong as death: what an admirable phrase, my brothers! Love is as strong as death. Brothers, who resists death? Listen to me: one resists flames, waves, the sword. One resists tyrants and kings.

---

[9] Job, 40:15–25 and note in TOB.

But when death comes, who resists? Nothing is stronger. Only love can be as strong. One can say that love is strong [*valida*] as death."[10] Did the ancient humanist of Carthage and Milan remember the verse of Virgil? *"Omnia vincit amor, et nos cedamus amor!"* ("Love conquers all. Well, let us also surrender to love!")[11]

And if one wants to talk about the relentless jealousy of Sheol, which never lets go of what it has swallowed—"who can evade the clutches of Sheol", moaned the psalmist (Ps 89:48)—what could one say about the jealousy of the Bridegroom? Yahweh is a jealous God! How many times does Scripture say it again and again: "I am Yahweh your God, a jealous God" (Ex 20:5). However, as Father Tournay points out very wisely, until now, let us say until the Exile, divine jealousy, the intransigence of divine love, was in proportion to the idolatrous faults of his people and thus essentially directed against adulterous Israel. Divine jealousy was against Israel. There is here, in the Song, a complete turnabout.[12]

In fact, the old text quoted earlier in Exodus went on as follows: "I, Yahweh your God, am a jealous God and I punish the father's fault in the sons, the grandsons and the great-grandsons of those who hate me" (Ex 20:5). But the jealousy of the Bridegroom in the more evolved Song—also the only time when this word is uttered in the drama—is revealed as an essentially positive jealousy. It is not directed anymore against the unfaithful people but, on the contrary, is meant to defend, protect and save the Bride. This is an admirable inversion of the concept of jealousy, which will find in Jesus a tender expression: "Jerusalem, Jerusalem, how often have I longed to gather your children as a hen gathers her chicks under her wings!" (Mt 23:37). Jealousy of a mother hen, comments Saint Augustine, watching over her chicks and placing them jeal-

---

[10] Saint Augustine, *Enarrationes in Psalmos*, 121:12; PL 37, 12, c. 1628.

[11] Virgil, *Bucoliques*, X:69.

[12] Cf. Raymond Tournay and Miriam Nicolaÿ, *Le Cantique des Cantiques* (Paris: Cerf, 1967), 153.

ously under her wings when the dogs bark![13] Jealousy of love, defensive and protective of those who entrust themselves to it: "Father," Jesus is able to say on the eve of his death, "I have kept those you gave me and not one was lost" (Jn 17:12). Divine jealousy, throughout the whole Song, is the strength of the Bridegroom put at the service of the Bride.

Then comes the image of the flashes of fire—

8:6 *The flash of it is a flash of fire,*
    a flame of Yahweh himself.

It comes from the same inspiration. It is indeed a cliché to talk about wounding love (it has darts, arrows) and burning love (love is a fire). But what is now in the mind of the Bride when she talks about "flashes of fire" is the living flame of love of her Bridegroom, which destroys and consumes all around itself, all that might wound and reach her. The love of the Bridegroom draws a circle of fire, as it were, around the one he loves, just as Yahweh had promised in the Book of Zechariah: "I will be a wall of fire for her, all around her" (Zc 2:9).

8:6 *a flame of Yahweh himself.*

This name of Yahweh, which is incorporated in the word *alleluia*—literally: praise Yahweh!—is an abbreviation. But

---

[13] Saint Augustine, *In Joannem*, PL 35, XV: 7, c. 1512–1513. The image used by Saint Augustine was taken up by the ever-gentle Francis de Sales in the *Treatise on the Love of God:* "See what love, what care and what jealousy a mother hen has for her chicks (our Lord did not deem such a comparison unworthy of his Gospel). The hen is a hen, i.e., an animal devoid of courage and generosity when she is not a mother; but when she becomes a mother, she has the courage of a lion, her head held up at all times, with haggard eyes, always going back and forth if there is any semblance of danger for her young ones. She would fight any enemy to save her beloved chicks, and she cares for them all the time, clucking and moaning: if any of her chicks dies, what a disaster! What anger! This is the jealousy of fathers and mothers in respect to their children." Saint Francis de Sales, *Treatise on the Love of God, Oeuvres,* Bibliothèque de la Pléiade (Paris: NRF-Gallimard, 1969), X:14, 854.

didn't we jump when we saw the word? It is the first and only time in the whole poem that the name of Yahweh appears. This Song of Songs, in which God is omnipresent, though under the constant cover of the scriptural symbols of Shepherd, King, master, Bridegroom, Temple, vineyard, is spelled out here, at the conclusion, lifting up delicately and, we might be tempted to say, with what literary refinement, the veil that covered him until now to surrender himself at the last stanza with his full and true meaning: Yahweh, the Bridegroom who is madly in love with his people, is the unique theme of the Song.

As if this unique word *Yahweh,* which is in fact the key to the Song and the very name, we might say, of the Bridegroom, should suffice to illumine the entire poem like a beacon! One imagines the inspired scribe who wrote the Song, lightly drawing the two divine letters (*yod* and *He*) at the bottom of his scroll, with a luminous and mischievous smile on his lips. *Inteligenti pauca!* Those who love need so little! And it is to him, the confidant of infinite Love, that the words of Bernanos apply: "It is the mark of a great love to remain secret for a long time."

Is it not also remarkable that fire, which is always associated with love in all the civilizations of the world and which we should have met a hundred times in a song exclusively devoted to love, is found only here? Is it not also remarkable that fire, God's privileged symbol in all the theophanies of Horeb and Carmel and later on Pentecost, appears in fact the first time only in the very last verses of the Song, and precisely in connection with the only mention made of the name of Yahweh?[14]

Flame of Yahweh, fire of the spirit, fire of love, the Bride is sure that nothing could ever stop this conflagration.

---

[14] It is suggestive that in this ultimate stanza of the Song appear for the first time and together three words—Yahweh, fire and heart—in connection with what concludes the Song: love.

8:7 *Love no flood can quench,*
no torrents drown.

Throughout biblical literature, the floods are synonymous with anxiety. It seems that Israel never lost the memory of the initial disaster of the flood! The people who spent so much time in the desert do not like the sea. "The waters of the sea abyss", *Le vocabulaire de théologie biblique* points out quite aptly, "gave it the most eloquent image of mortal danger (cf. Ps 69:3), for their depths are felt to be akin to Sheol."[15]

But what can the floods of disaster do against the Love of the Bridegroom? Saint Francis de Sales shows very well in the *Treatise on the Love of God* that, far from extinguishing love, they can only and paradoxically stoke it. "The waters and tribulations and the floods of persecution", writes Saint Francis, "cannot drown out love. Moreover, not only does it not die, but love grows richer in poverty. It grows in abjection and humility. It rejoices amid tears. It is strengthened when abandoned by justice and deprived of its help, when, if it claims it, nobody gives it. It is re-created amid compassion and empathy, when it is surrounded by miserable and suffering people. It is delighted to give up all kinds of sensual and worldly delights to obtain purity and clarity of heart. It is courageous when it puts an end to wars, quarrels and dissents, and has only contempt for temporal grandeurs and reputations. It is strengthened by all kinds of suffering. And knows that its true life is to die for the Bridegroom."[16]

The flood will not be able to extinguish, to drown out, love. It is the last image of the Song, the image that grows in intensity and ends up imposing itself irresistibly and sovereignly until the last verse becomes a vision of the world burning with the universal fire of love, through the truthful one who said that "he had come to bring fire to the earth" (Lk 12:49).

---

[15] "Sea", *Le vocabulaire de théologie biblique* (Paris: Cerf, 1966), 603–605.
[16] Saint Francis de Sales, *Traité*, XI:19, 935.

Therefore the Bride of God can fear no disaster, no abyss. She knows no other abyss than "the fatherly abyss", to use the phrase of Father de Lubac, the bottomless abyss of merciful Love. As to the rest, winds can howl, torrential rains fall, savage floods attack the house where she lives, as is described in Jesus' parable (Mt 7:24–27); the house has nothing to fear, "it is leaning", founded on the rock of the Bride. No, the flood cannot quench nor the torrents drown out Love. Such is the vehement and peaceful challenge that the Bride throws, as it were, to the whole world at the end of her song.

And it seems that Saint Paul captures the last tones of her voice and that he simply echoes them with his own rhythm and timbre in the hymn to Love closing the eighth chapter of the Epistle to the Romans: "Nothing can come between us and the Love of Christ even if we are troubled or worried or being persecuted or lacking food or clothes or being threatened or even attacked. As Scripture promised, for your sake we are being massacred and reckoned as for the slaughter. . . . These are the trials through which we triumph by the power of him who loved us, for I am certain of this: neither death nor life, nor angel, nor prince, nothing that exists, nothing still to come, any power or height or depth nor any created thing can ever come between us and the love of God made visible in Christ Jesus our Lord" (Rm 8:35–39).

This is the very same thrust, the same passion, the same panting and controlled breath that were once animating the Bride at the end of her poem in the Song. Thus it belonged to her, who had once praised the Bridegroom beyond the power of words (5:10–16), to conclude the whole poem with a hymn to Love itself, revealing the name above every other name: "Yahweh!"[17]

[17] The end of verse 7 and verses 8 to 14 given in the Bible editions cannot be seen as belonging to the original text of the Song. It is evident for the two epigrams (8–12, 13–14). "These two passages", writes the Jerusalem Bible, in agreement with most exegetes, "were attached only secondarily to the Song" and also the last two additions of verse 7, quite beautiful in themselves—

"were a man to offer all the wealth of his house to buy love, contempt is all he would purchase." Love cannot be bought, it is priceless. These two additions, as Émile Osty notes quite rightly—"Introduction au Cantique des Cantiques", *La Bible,* (Paris: Seuil, 1973), 1374–1375—"contrast with what precedes them and are not connected with what follows." "They cannot therefore have the same author as the Song or at the least have been written by him at the same time"—Paul Joüon, *Le Cantique des Cantiques,* (Paris: Beauchesne, 1909), 318–319. One could rather see in these two verses a reflection added later on and as it were in the margin by a commenting scribe or an elder of Israel. But the Bridegroom and his Bride of the Song do not indulge in reflections. They never analyze or moralize. They are too entranced with each other to speak in the tones of the Book of Proverbs. They sing their love, they do not reason it. (Though counted in the Bible among the Wisdom books, the Song of Songs would be much better set among the prophetic books.) We must add that the movement, the very unity of composition and tone of the entire poem, compel us to end on the last poignant cry of the Bride: "Love no flood can quench, no torrents drown."

Love's Long Patience

The music that sang for itself, pure ecstasy and pure intoxication, reveals itself little by little as a drama, the most poignant of all dramas.

More than Tamino and Pamina in the *Magic Flute* of Mozart, the Bride of the Song had to pass through many stages, endure many trials, and mold herself to a slow pedagogy before reaching the definitive wedding of Love.

We see her at the onset of the drama, with a face that the sun has burned, laboring painfully in the desert of her exile, enslaved and watching over the flocks and vineyards of the foreigners—since she had been unfaithful to her own vineyard—miserable mare attached to the chariot of her oppressors. From the depths of her distress, she cries and implores her beloved, whom she knows always loves and admires her, to take her back to him, and we hear the first duet of their reborn love: first poem.

But she is still so weak! The assaults of all powerful Love are not enough to tear her away from her tremendous languor. However, the Bridegroom does so much to wake her up completely! From the heights of the mountains he rushes to her, overcoming all obstacles, showing her the wonderful spring of their betrothal, pressing her to join him without any fear. At one point, he even pretends to leave her so as to increase her desire. But fearful dove in the cleft of the rock, she dares not turn totally toward him; and when she finally surrenders, as if without return, her love remains aware that the foxes are still threatening his blossoming vines: second poem.

At least, he spares nothing to win the full heart of his beautiful betrothed. Rising, this time, from the depths of the desert, where he wished to experience harsh reality himself, humble and

355

magnificent at the same time, he enters, among a joyful people, into his holy city, his beloved wedded city. He reestab-
lishes his reign while renewing his covenant with her whose
beauty, as he himself says, makes him lose his senses. Ah, no
matter how many the bonds that keep her away from him, in
spite of his constant presence with her, he will know, in the
struggle he will have for her sake, how to win her forever! And
in the intoxicating joy of the hard-won victory, he celebrates
with his sister-Bride—well-enclosed garden and sealed fountain whose key is in his hands alone—the wonderful feast of his
wedding, to which he wants all mankind to be invited: third
poem.

The beautiful love story is about to end. Having now
reached the apex of union, the Bride is beyond any harm. She
is invulnerable to her enemies. But not, alas, to the unexpected
vacillations of her own heart. Something, in the deepest recess
of herself—fear of losing forever her autonomy? anxiety of
falling into the great abyss of love?—pushes her without consideration to withdraw within herself, to refuse herself to the
imploring voice calling her. This is the unforeseen fault, the incomprehensible unfaithfulness, the incurable fall. The Bridegroom left without uttering a word. How mad she had been! It
takes her only a moment to understand. Madly, she rushes in
her quest for him, pushing aside all human prudence. But the
city echoes in vain with her cries. What can she do now but
scream everywhere her distress in the most delirious celebration of a face that, even gone, dazzles her? She does not yet
know, poor unfortunate, that the Bridegroom, when he flees,
never goes to the ends of the world but to the depths of the
heart; and that it is in the most silent corner of her life's garden
that she will see the image of him who does not know how to
go away: fourth poem.

However, will the dialogue with him start again as before?
The song of the Bridegroom, even though it can only retain
the same sweetness, will it not forever be heard now in a nos-
talgic minor key? And her love takes up the theme, higher,

more beautiful than before, the one that had been chosen for the wedding day! Never, before the fall of his love, had he exalted her beauty so fantastically, beyond all the stars of the sky. After the joyful songs of the betrothal spring, now follow the warm accords of the amorous summer, the dazzling autumn of the ripe fruits superabounding on the earth, which opens itself before them: fifth poem.

There! No more separations or partings or tears. No more raging floods or furious torrents. The last enemy, death, is vanquished. All the peoples of the universe are gathered together and their faces are the face of the Bride. Two names alone stand out in the beautiful, changeless sky, both engraved on the same Heart, and they are no more than one single Name: the Denouement.

Thus the Five Poems of the Song, and it is that which makes definitive the division adopted by André Robert. They can be seen as five acts of a drama, really the only drama which is being played out in this world: man's adventure, filled with torments and with joys, as he is ceaselessly sought by the passionate love of his God.

Index

ABSENCE OF GOD. *See* Seek-find

APOSTOLATE, 66–68, 72–74, 76–77, 113, 231–233

APPLE TREE, APPLE, 140–145, 264–265, 340–341

ASCETICISM AND MYSTICISM, 62–66, 68–72, 149–150, 189–190, 254, 300–301, 331–332

BANQUET, 144–145, 151–152, 230–233

BAPTISM. *See* Paschal Mystery

BEAUTY: * *of the Bride:* received, 89–91, 93–95, 123–125, 128–132, 208–209, 257–258; made of the entire creation, 136–138, 259, 295–296, 304–305; imperfect, shiftless, and ephemeral, 89–96, 258, 269–270, 288–289; strong and victorious, 211, 286–287; magnified, 126–132, 177, 208–214, 219–227; unique, 295–296
* *of the Bridegroom:* absolutely unique, 128–129, 130–132, 257–263; immutable and absolute, 264–270

BIRTH (new). *See* Paschal Mystery

BLACK, 89–96, 209–210

BRIDE, BRIDEGROOM. *See* Church, Consecration, Mary

CEDARS, 135–137

CELEBRATION. *See* Praise

CHRIST, 63–64, 115, 203–207, 213, 218, 224, 244, 306–307, 326–333. *See* Incarnation

CHURCH: pilgrim, 68–71, 320–321, *See* Desert, Exile; beautiful and black, coming from paganism, 93–97; ingathering and fulfillment of mankind, 67–68, 214, 231–233, 276, 286, 291–292, 296, 302–304, 308–310, *See* Unity; body in building, 305; in teaching, 330–332; sign of God and of evangelization, 68, 271–272; fecundity, 135–136, 306–309; beautiful and frightening the enemy, 287, 295–296; *See* Israel

Scriptural Quotations